and
His
Love
Shone
Down

and HIS LOVE SHONE DOWN

ELISABETH BARRET
VICTORIA BOVARD

LYNSA PUBLISHING

Printing History
First printing 1997

ISBN: 0-9654962-0-1

Printed in the United States of America

To God , who inspired us to change our way of thinking!

To our children, who needed to have a reason to believe in us!

To our parents, who wanted to love us for ourselves!

CHAPTER ONE

The perpetual roar of the lawn mower outside is all too quick of a reminder of the meaningless task of everyday life. I wished, I was the pilot going freely to and fro, but now that was impossible. My life was behind locked doors. The barred windows gave distorted images of a world slowly ebbing into fall. My heart sank at thoughts and schemes I had once been apart, but now just a memory fading quickly as I sat on my bed and wept.

"I want a divorce!" echoed from my mouth as I confronted Eric head on. His eyes slowly looked away avoiding my words. "I mean it, Eric. I want a divorce, and I don't want our parents to become involved in this matter until we have decided on the terms." He didn't even flinch at my words. He just continued to maneuver the car seat he was reupholstering around to obtain a stronger grip on the material he was pulling off. Quietly he said he didn't have time to talk. But I forced the issue, and to my shock, he quickly spun around and forcefully grabbed my arm twisting it behind me and thrusting me out the door of our upholstery shop. "We'll talk tonight!" he shouted.

Tears stung my cheeks as once again Eric showed his ability to control me with his brute strength. Why did I think he would behave like a Christian with fair and reasonable rights for both of us? Not just for himself!

Eric's dad was a minister who had given his whole life to the church, even to the extent of sacrificing his family. Traditionally, Eric followed in his footsteps; mimicking his every move, especially in camp and youth programs. At first, I greatly respected him for his commitment, but soon I realized that he didn't care about

1

how his service effected our family.

In our home, Eric followed what he thought the Bible taught by using scriptures, like the man having dominion over his wife, and "spare the rod, spoil the child." As a result of this, the children and I were afraid to cross him! He expected obedience now and if our three children did not mind immediately, they were sent to our bedroom for three hard spankings or bobbed on the head with his fist. Whatever I said to defend them led to a tongue lashing, and sometimes being physically attacked in a clenching bear hug that sent all my bones cracking at one time.

He weighed over 250 pounds and was extremely strong and even in my most fighting back times, I knew if I didn't let him win that I would regret it later. For He always played to win and losing was simply unacceptable.

But of course, we always tithed to church ten percent or at least that's what he wanted everyone to think. He always pretended we didn't have much money and made my life miserable over too high of heating bills and stabbing remarks that "we were eating too well." Many times I seethed after writing a check for a month's payment on our Mercedes, when all I had was one nice outfit, two pair of jeans, two shirts, and a pair of tennis shoes that had to last me for an entire year. It just wasn't fair! No matter how much I begged for equal rights, my hopes were shattered time and again; for once again he needed a new tool for upholstery or carpentry jobs that he chose for remodeling on our home.

Christmas was one of my favorite times of the year not only because of the birth of our Lord, but because I loved giving presents. But once again Eric waged his rule and one toy and one set of clothing was given to each child, but he expected his list from clothes to expensive toys to costly tools to be fulfilled. In return, my wish list was never even acknowledged. I received household items like a mixer or a cookbook.

Grudgingly, I walked up the hill to Tori's. She was my only true friend and I could always count on her for

wisdom and insight into my next form of action. I knew
she wasn't going to like Eric's answer, but somehow,
tonight I would have a better attack plan and a deal that
Eric couldn't refuse.

Tori's blond hair encircled her thin face and when
she saw me at her door her face lit up like the morning
sun casting a cheery light of warmth and love. She sensed
my failure, but she was stubborn and when I needed
strength, she supplied. I admired her so much. She
always seemed to know what she wanted in life and if
there was a way, she would have it. Her enthusiasm soon
erased my fears and once again we went over divorce terms
to hash over with Eric tonight.

Tori had just completed a move for the second time
in two months since her divorce to a two bedroom
apartment so that she and Brad could have separate
bedrooms and begin to lead as normal a life as possible.
Unfortunately Alan her ex-husband refused to let go.
During the divorce and custody hearing, Alan was found
guilty of child abuse and a restraining order protected
Tori and Brad from him ever coming close to where they
lived, but this did not detour him from continually
breaking this order. On a nightly basis he woke Tori and
Brad, pounding at their windows and hollering out
everything they had done that day. This sent waves of fear
through Tori, encircling her very being with such dread
that her head responded in constant migraine headaches.

In desperate phone calls to the police they tried
unsuccessfully to catch Alan in the act of harassing Tori.
Even with the additional protection of two plain clothes
policeman sitting outside her apartment on a nightly
basis; he still managed to elude their grasp. The police
department was at a lost of how to solve the problems and
their frustration at not catching him led to them backing
off of the surveillance and leaving Tori to solve the
problems through the courts alone.

Tori was terrified of Alan and very protective of
Brad! During their marriage, he had waged a war of hatred
against Tori's and Brad's bodies, slapping them around

3

and kicking them with his boots and doing any and every perverted thing that came into his mind. In addition, pornographic magazines swelled his mind with vivid imagery of acts of masochism. This led him to using his new found knowledge as a weapon to stimulate his adrenalin and flood his body with the excitement he needed to brutally rape Tori and force her to endure terrifying and agonizing torture. I guess that's why our bond became so great, because we both understood what it was like to be trapped in marriages that were not for love, but for the sake of marriage and what it meant to follow in the path of human tradition.

Evening came rapidly. I paced throughout my house of the past twelve years, holding back tears that threatened to escape. To my utter despair, Eric had convinced my mother to help him pressure me into giving him a divorce on his terms. Confidently, Eric pushed his terms for our divorce into my hands and a pen to sign at the dotted line as my mother supporting him looked on.

I couldn't believe my eyes! He wanted everything. He expected sole custody of the children with visitation rights being given only upon his consent; if and when he deemed me worthy! He had to be kidding! I refused to sign! I felt so helpless and inexperienced in these matters yet no woman in her right mind, would willingly hand over all this control of her children. I loved them dearly and I was a good mother. Blocking the door way, he tried to force the issue, but again I wouldn't give in. Running into the other room I slammed the door and I reached for the phone and quickly dialed Tori and I whispered into the receiver what was taking place. Her voice was calm, but her words were urgent that I not sign anything and to get out of that house; we would settle this in court! But before I could hang up Eric came barreling through the door and to my shock, mom looked on as he yanked the phone off the wall. I was trembling and frightened. What did he and mom think they could do, force me to sign it?

Unbelieving tears flowed from my eyes. Angry tears of disappointment in my mother and fear that I had

4

alienated myself from my parents as well. I didn't know what to do. How was I going to get away from them and Eric's cruel demands? Finally, I convinced them that I would sign if they just gave me some time alone so I could look over the agreement again. After a few more minutes of tongue lashings, they gave in. Once safely alone, I listened as mother and Eric talked in the shop. Ever so quietly I exited out of the back door running as quickly as I could for the car. Holding my breath, I fumbled with the keys to the ignition. Eric's angry face glared at me from the shop door, furious that I had fooled him. Before I knew what was happening he was out the door. Fear consumed my entire body as he lunged for the car door handle. Quickly, I locked the doors, revved the engine and screech the wheels as I backed out of the driveway.

Just two months before knowing that our marriage was over Eric had gone to our bank and taken my name off the check book. Literally he had me under his thumb, I couldn't buy anything; not even groceries! Only upon me begging, was I allowed a dime. I had nothing to my name, even if on paper I owned half of everything, it didn't mean anything in cash. In my entire life with him I was never allowed to have a charge card and desperately, pleading that God would help me, I sent off for one. Each day, I anxiously waited on the mail, fearing that Eric would get it first and find out what I was doing.

Envelope in hand, I tore open the letter, a large credit limit was established. My heart was overjoyed. Now, I had the money to fight and to obtain a lawyer. With Tori's help, we quickly established income and assets and found a lawyer through a referral service. I was very pleased with the fast pace that everything was accomplished. Terms for the divorce were different this time. I refused to be pushed around by Eric and I was going not only for full custody of the children, but my rightful half of our property.

My lawyer promised to have the papers prepared by the next day. Breathing a sigh of relief, I entered my home only to be met by Eric at the door with the news that

5

he was seeking council. A panicky feeling spread through my entire body, consuming me with fear that he could get custody of our children through filing first.

The next morning, I hurried into my lawyers office and was greeted with a bright and cheery smile. The documents were ready and waiting for my approval. The only thing left, was for him to have a judge's final signature placed on the papers to show that they were approved. My load lightened and slowly he went over all the details explaining terms of the temporary divorce motion. After my name was signed, he phoned the court house to see if a judge was available who could put the motion into effect. The lines were busy. I waited outside for a few minutes, but still he had no luck. He sent me home with the assurance that before the day was over he would have the signature. My tension rose, but I knew there was nothing I could do except wait. Returning to my newly acquired apartment, I watched my clock and phoned Tori. Together we prayed for strength and speed for finding a judge.

The stress of seeking a divorce and being thrust into a legal world I didn't understand was making my stomach upset and taking becoming inches off my 5'6" frame. My short dark brown hair encircled my face and my blue green eyes showed signs of stress, but quiet determination.

"Why didn't my lawyer call?" The words stuck in my throat. Tori gave me a hug and encouraged me that everything would work out in God's timing. So much had changed since Tori's and my friendship began. She was high society and debutante material, while I was an average small town Bible preaching Baptist. Her faith in God was firmly established, but not as freely spoken as I had been raised to be. Just months before I was encouraging her to pray out loud and give all of her problems to God. Now our roles were reversed and she was giving me the support in my faith, I so badly needed.

Music was where we found our calling together and God's grace shone in both of our abilities and immersed our talents into one. Tori, from the earliest age of four showed great abilities in piano and excelled in the music field. Not only was she quite versed in piano, but she also had a lot of vocal background. Any song I chose she easily played at sight and for a choir director, who had written plays and directed musicals, I wasn't easy to please. I loved complicated music and elaborate presentations and anyone who dared to work with me, knew I expected perfection. But I met my match with Tori. Together we intimidated each other, but even this worked out for the best as we encouraged each other to excel at our fullest ability.

The clock clicked slowly, finally Tori gave in and called for me. My lawyer had decided to head for the courthouse himself. He had heard, that all phones were not working and he was going to take his chances on finding a judge. My body broke out in a cold sweat. It was already coming to the end of the day and I would have to travel over twenty miles to his office and then make the return trip to the courthouse in my home town to file, this consumed over an hour's worth of travel! Holding my breath, I whispered a prayer as I jumped into my car and drove to his office.

It was nearing closing time, but still no papers. I knew I could just make it if he would return from the courthouse now. "Where was he? Why didn't he come?" so much depended on me filing first. Silently more pleads were sent to heaven! My whole body was trembling. Thirty minutes passed, then forty-five, an hour, now there was no way I would make it! I felt defeated. All I could do was pray that Eric hadn't made it either. The phone rang with Tori calling to say that it was already past closing time, but as far as the courthouse knew no other papers had been filed. I praised God! Silently my lawyer motioned me into his office. Again he explained all the conditions, while I pretended that I understood every legal term that was clarified. With a farewell handshake and the papers securely in my hands, I headed for home.

8:15 a.m. the next morning I waited on a bench near

7

the door of the clerk of the courthouse where the papers were filed for divorce proceedings. Several people greeted me as I quietly waited for the office to open. Perspiration broke out on my palms and forehead as I thought of everything that could possibly go wrong. Visions of Eric breaking in front of me and beating me to file first, played in my mind. Finally, to my great relief the doors opened and leaving the papers they informed me that he would be served by the sheriff's office tonight. Days later I was informed that Eric's lawyer arrived just minutes after I left.

Just going through a divorce Tori had developed a good sense of the legal system, which gave me some what of an advantage over Eric. She explained in detail what my lawyer had done and how my filing first would effect Eric. I was given custodial parent and thus I had control over when the children would visit their dad. In addition Eric would be responsible for paying child support. And with the quick thinking of my attorney, I also obtained temporary possession of our Mercedes, while Eric retained the house.

The next step was to break the news of the impending divorce to our parents. I hoped that together we could work out a fair settlement and custody arrangement in a Christian environment. After calling and inviting our families to my new apartment, I asked the Sheriff if he would serve Eric at my home at 8:00p.m. He readily agreed. I suppose most people would not want to be present for this, but I was determined that this way I could control the outcome of the reaction of the papers would have on both families and I could justify my actions for doing this.

The apartment I had rented was scantily furnished. Through my credit card, I purchased a bed, love seat, and table from the used furniture store in town. And with a great deal of pleading I managed to get on chair and a dresser from Eric. It certainly didn't look like much of a home, but at least it was mine.

It wasn't long before evening arrived and my long

awaited guests appeared. Mom entered my home first with tears in her eyes and a refusal from my dad to attend. Soon Eric and his parents followed. Everyone eyed me suspiciously. Eric quickly looked over my small two bedroom apartment with the shared laundry room with a glint of contempt in his eyes. As my mother and his parents looked on as he opened cabinet doors, drawers, and even the refrigerator. I asked him to stop, but he refused. I pleaded with my mother to tell him to stop, but she just stood there. A smile played on Eric's lips as he saw my discomfort and slowly he went back into my small living room and sat down. By now my heart was pounding, fearing that I was losing the edge that I thought I would have and that Eric now would take charge.

Before I could take my next breath, Eric turned on his best charm and took complete control of the room. I couldn't believe it, even talking over our divorce brought out his best behavior. Why couldn't he act as nice to our children and me as he always displayed for others? He was the perfect gentleman, sympathetic with my mother's tears, helping his own mother into her chair and shaking his father's hand like a diplomat. His words were always eloquent and when he addressed me his whole face changed into the expression of a whipped puppy. Of course, I was at fault for the whole mess and he was the innocent party. Everyone suckered into his hand leaving me to be Satan in disguise. Yet I knew that they were being deceived by his behavior, for God saw into the house that this man dominated and God knew the truth about his lies. Quietly His word came to my thoughts, 2 Corinthians 11:13-15: "Those men are not true apostles-they are false apostles, who lie about their work and disguise themselves to look like real apostles of Christ. Well, no wonder! Even Satan can disguise himself to look like an angel of light! So it is no great thing if his servants disguise themselves to look like servants of righteousness. In the end they will get exactly what their actions deserve."

All talk about fairness was quickly tossed to the wind. Eric argues marriage counselors, and that he loved

me, and he didn't want a divorce. All three parents loved
every word, but I still remained firm refusing to be
trapped again. Still the Christian values that were
pressed into their minds would not let them come to terms
with divorce and all my efforts of division of property and
custody arrangements were quickly played down for terms
of reconciliation. How I hated Eric and all his fancy
words, he had won their affection and total support.

Suddenly, a knock sounded at my door and my heart
sank with impending disaster. The sheriff entered serving
Eric his papers. My mother fled to the bathroom in tears
and Eric's dad became heated, preaching that God created
marriage and for me to break it was a sin. Eloquently,
Eric noting my discomfort, warmed to the Sheriff, shaking
his hand and asking all the right questions, and
responding with overwhelming friendliness. As the
minutes elapsed, I half listened as Eric thanked the
Sheriff for coming out on a night like this when there was
probably more important things for him to do instead.
Waving goodbye, Eric once again came into my apartment
and took advantage of his victory among our parents.
Gloating, he listened as his father's voice rose with points
of arguments as if on the pulpit in front of crowds instead
of my humble living room. For four hours, I had pleaded
for Eric and I to come to a civil divorce, but now I watched
the people I loved, flee from my house as if they never
knew me. My heart was crushed and tears flowed freely
down my cheeks. What a royal mess my life had become!

Eric had fought me so hard over the children before
the divorce action, that it was quiet a relief to finally have
them around me without fear that they would be punished.
As much as I loved my children, it was hard to protect
them from their dad's tongue over what he thought of me
and even being happy with the visitation arrangements was
not always enough to ease their fears.

Eric's parent and my parents had made up their
minds that I was Satan-possessed and an unfit mother. My
actions on serving Eric proved that and the burden that
their mother was a sinner and unforgivable burned into

their minds. They questioned my every move and were very untrusting. So I sent my mind on proving to them that I loved them and cared how they were feeling. We watched T.V. programs that they liked, cooked food that was their favorite and did things they wanted to do. During my entire marriage, I was so busy competing with Eric's demands that now I found that I had so much more time to spend with my kids.

While I was growing up, I had silently vowed that my children's lives would be filled with adventures and they would know without any doubt that i cared about what they wanted. Now I put my words into action and they spent warm summer days at the pool. We read books at the library, had picnics at the park and spent time just being together as a family. I also took a great deal of time explaining that they needed both parents and I intended for them to live as normal a life as possible with fair visitation for their dad.

Tori's lawyer had explained to her when she filed for divorce that she should take everything that she wanted from their joint property. So together, her parents, and I packed up everything that she chose, while giving Alan an equal share of their joint belongings. Since Eric continued to refuse to do this, I felt I was justified to use the key that I still had to our house and to take it myself.

The house sat stately on the corner of Morest and 21st. it was over 100 years old and Eric and I together had remodeled most of the house. Our upholstery shop was in the back third of the house and opened up into the newly constructed garage. It was Sunday morning, the only time I could count on Eric not being at home for he always attended church. And today proved to be no different. Tori and I quietly walked up the sidewalk to the front door, watching a neighbor's house across the street, who went to the same church as Eric. I tried the door.

Eric had secured the front screen with a pair of vise grips. I tried the windows to the boys room, but he had screwed every window down that didn't have a latch. i couldn't believe my eyes! Thankfully, I had worked with tools everyday since I married him and I knew if I looked hard enough, I could figure out a way to enter. Looking at my watch, I signed knowing that Tori's dad was scheduled to come by soon and help us with the boxes that we were supposed to pack and any furniture that I wanted to take as well. This was taking longer than I expected and I silently pleaded with God that he would show me the way. The gardening shed caught my eye and suddenly an idea formed in my mind filling me with excitement. Opening the doors, I surveyed the contents and found the best levy I could use to take the hinges off the kitchen door screen. Eric had only used a small rope tied to the handle on the screen to the kitchen doorknob to secure that door. I picked up an ax and very carefully slipped out the pins while Tori held the door. It was so easy and in less than a minute Tori was on the phone telling her dad we were just beginning and to give us an additional 5 minutes. We had less than an hour to take anything that I thought was my fair share of our belongings. Tori headed for the children's clothing and toys while leaving a few behind for the children when they stayed with Eric. We took none of the furniture in the children's bedrooms, dining room, or even any shop tools. I took only what I had to have to have a functioning household. Even in the kitchen I was careful to leave an equal amount for Eric so as to give a balance for both household needs.

By the time we had packed up my choices and delivered them to my small apartment, I was satisfied with what we had accomplished in such a short time. Quietly, Tori and her father left to eat lunch at her parents and I nervously waited to find out how Eric would react. In truth, what seemed like just a few survival belongings to me was like declaring war to Eric. And even though I comforted myself with the knowledge that I had a right to some of our property, I still felt uneasy as to what he would do.

After another hour had passed, Tori called excited

on her end of the phone and commanded that I get to her apartment immediately. Entering her home, she quickly recounted a story of going past Eric's house on her way back from her parents. Her face lit up as her voice described the images of 3 police cars parked in the driveway. Eric had apparently reported that he had been robbed and he was listing everything I took as stolen.

Astonishment flooded my senses as I carefully dialed his house not knowing what to expect on the other end. Upon hearing Eric's familiar hello, I flatly asked him, just what he was trying to prove when he knew that I had taken those things? Eric's voice resounded with confidence as he angrily snarled that I was a criminal, and I had trespassed on private property. He further stated that the police were there to see to it that I returned everything I had stolen.

I could feel the color drain from my face and my legs felt as if they had turned to jello. "What will they do to me?", kept running through my mind. A police officer took the phone and demanded to talk to me immediately. In the background as Tori listened to the conversation, she kept giving me reassurance that I was in the right, and to stay calm. But the policeman on the phone was saying I had made a big mistake and that he wanted to know where everything was, who had helped me, and where was I now?

In my entire 30 years I hadn't even had a speeding ticket and now I was trembling all over because I had taken my own belongings and furniture from my own house. The police officer started rattling off that if you no longer sleep in a home and you occupy another premises as your residence, that it was unlawful and considered breaking and entering.

Quietly, I gave him the address to Tori's home and soon he was pounding at the door to her apartment. As he resumed the conversation, the officer watched my every move, warning me that if anyone had helped me that they would be charged with felony theft. Tori, who had been listening intently to his every word, quickly chirped in that I had done it all by myself and since I was still living

13

in the home then I hadn't broken the law. A smile crossed the officer's face and the atmosphere somewhat relaxed.

Tori had dealt with this officer before over restraining violations that Alan, her ex-husband had broken, and now Tori's legal mind went into action and instead of the officer interrogation us, she completely interrogated him. I was relieved when she asked the questions for I felt everything was going over my head and the technicalities were more than I imagined.

By the time the police officer left, he relayed everything Eric had said, and he brushed the incident off as a civil dispute with no laws broken. A sigh of relief flooded from Tori's mouth. This time Eric's plans had been foiled, but what about the next?

CHAPTER TWO

The world looked so peaceful outside my jailhouse windows. Children gleefully played on the sidewalks and front steps of the courthouse sending waves of depression and loneliness through me for my own flesh and blood! What were my children doing? Were they laughing too? I imagined them playing joyfully together enjoying the warm sunshine and scattering leaves as they ran and played. Lord, I wish they could just come and visit me and I could hug and kiss them and tell them how much I love them.

Each night, after tucking in our kids, Tori and I started walking together. As each night passed and our walking continued, we used it as a way to escape our down-hill marriages. There must be some truth in the night air that persuades people to let go and reveal their inner core of hurt. But as Tori and I let go, our bond strengthened steadily every day making us accountable to each other. I probed and questioned and prompted Tori about everything to many points of embarrassment and she did the same to me. At first we teased about our marriages, and then cried, until finally the unveiling of the truth was a our only goal.

Eric was a consuming person who wanted everyone in his family under his absolute control. I was allowed few friends and never a close friend and if a person was getting too close to me, or taking too much of my time, he quickly ended it by making them uncomfortable when they visited. Laughingly he would tell me to work or he would make direct comments like, "didn't I have other things to do?" It wasn't long before another friend fled and went for someone who wasn't under the watchful eye of her husband. Many times, I would talk to Eric about this, but he was oblivious of his actions, he justified his behavior with the statement that he had a right to expect me to work. "We were a business and we had to put our customers first!" I found myself working at night if I had an obligation during the day, but then Eric would punish me by not working either so we were twice as much behind. I could never win!

On top of this, I was never allowed any idle time to do things just for myself. If I wasn't working, I had laundry and housework too. The food was also my job and making sure the children cleaned their rooms as well. I was over-burdened and many times I lashed out at Eric telling him that I wished I was him and all I had to do was work in the shop. Angrily, I would flee the shop, slamming the door. Eric usually ignored these outbursts and waited for me to calm down and begrudgingly, I would come back to work fearing if I didn't, he would stop working too.

Now Alan had a whole different tactic with Tori, she had lots of friends and as long as he wasn't around she had the freedom to do as she pleased. For Tori was the major wage earner in her family and as long as she worked as a piano and vocal teacher, he could afford his own pleasures in his boots and misc. collections. Alan worked for Tori's dad and the construction business was at an all time low, forcing her parents into bankruptcy and shortly they were forced into it too. So in view of this, Alan many times would put in two weeks of work and he wouldn't get paid.

As the financial pressures at home mounted, Alan would take his frustrations out on Tori, slamming her around the house, inflicting pain and bruises anywhere it wouldn't show to people who were around her. Three year old Brad suffered too and the more Tori would shield him, the worse punishment Alan would inflict on her and then Brad. Alan was so abusive to Brad that he would make a game of seeing how much pain Brad could take by pushing small nails into his skin, kicking him across the room with his boot or tying hysterical Tori in a room so the could knock Brad around until he was satisfied that his son knew he was master. Alan's moods were so unpredictable, that rarely was Tori able to calm him down and talk him out of his actions. As a result, Tori found herself in a living nightmare and the two times she sought out people to help her, Alan denied everything that she said happened and in turn it back fired and she was beaten worse.

Each agonizing detail came slowly to the surface filling me with grief and pain for Tori's problems and mine. The more we shared, the fonder we grew of each others company and it came as no surprise that the music we both loved became a haven to release our fears and lighten our hearts. Each night our walks would lead us to church to work on taped songs or practice for duets sung in church. Many times our tears over helplessness would get in the way and quietly we would embrace in prayer. Pouring out the truth calmed our fears and verbal praying directed our needs to the most high God who knows what goes on behind closed doors. We read the Bible, prayed, and I wrote down our problems looking for a glimmer of light that would bring peace to our lives.

Months before divorce had entered Tori's or my mind, we were praying for healing over Tori's heart. She had just gone through another abortion, due to Alan raping her savagely without using protection. Part of Alan's vicious control over Tori was purposely getting her pregnant. He knew that her heart condition would prevent her from having another baby and in his medieval way he showed her how weak she was to him and how easy it would be for him to hurt her.

Coupled with all the above and her recent bankruptcy, her heart had enlarged and her doctor informed her that she would be facing open heart surgery if she didn't calm down. Stress complicated her heart condition and since there was no way to get rid of her problems very easily, I was determined that the Lord Almighty would heal her. So in complete trust and faith and following the word for word teachings in James the 5th chapter we beseeched the Almighty God for healing!

Together, after our children were once again safely tucked into their beds, we went on our usual walk to the church, but this time we were going to pray for our miracle. Having been raised as a Baptist, I believed that once you were baptized you automatically received the Holy Spirit. But to my amazement upon praying for healing, suddenly an intense feeling came over Tori and I causing me to tremble uncontrollably and igniting my hands with fire. An inner peace settled upon us and an unexplainable power sent joy ebbing into both our bodies. Acts 2:2-4: "Suddenly there was a noise from the sky which sounded like a strong wind blowing, and it filled the whole house where they were sitting. Then they saw what looked like tongues of fire which spread out and touched each person there. They were all filled with the Holy Spirit and began to talk in other languages, as the Spirit enable them to speak."

Moving my hand over her heart, Tori immediately sensed a warmth and to our amazement her heart condition went into remission for the next few months. In Acts 2:17-21; " This is what I will do in the last days, God says: I will pour out my Spirit on everyone. Your sons and daughters will proclaim my message; your young men will see visions, and your old men will have dreams. Yes, even on my servants, both men and women, I will pour out my Spirit in those days, and they will proclaim my message. I will perform miracles in the sky above and wonders on the earth below. There will be blood, fire, and thick smoke; the sun will be darkened, and the moon will turn red as blood, before the great and glorious Day of the Lord comes. And then, whoever calls out to the Lord for help will be saved."

Immediately following our baptism in the Holy Spirit we grew closer than we had ever been before. It was almost like the Spirit that came upon us in a still small voice was giving us permission to love each other with a flame of passion that we had never felt before in this narrow world that man had made.

I opened the door and entered Tori's home. I marveled at the true warmth I found in the beautiful decorative surroundings. Her grand piano brought lightness to my heart as familiar sounds sparked from its keys. How at home I felt here as peace so sweet touched my lips and ignited my voice and Tori's in song.

Many times I had told Tori I loved her as my very best friend in the whole world and she had responded the same. But our closeness had grown for more than that, awakening feelings inside that I didn't understand. I would touch her cheek with mine in a friendly greeting and a strange warmth would glow and turn into fire. This worried me so much that in my own home I would beg the Lord to lead me in scripture and cleanse my soul from the power of Satan. Now I was not sheltered from stories of man loving man, and woman loving woman, but I had never thought or understood why anyone could rightfully allow themselves in a wrong relationship. I only loved Tori as a friend and the feelings, whatever they were, were not true!

The lectures that proceeded from my mother's mouth after seeing Tori and I sitting close together in my home put me in a state of panic. I radically denied each accusation and after talking with my sister about what mom said, I felt much better. "It's O.K. to love your friend and I don't see anything wrong with you or Tori," Mary assured me. She referred me to a close friend who received the Holy spirit with her best friend. Her story was so close to mine and Tori's and the intenseness was the same. My church friends assured me that we were just close friends brought together under terrific pressures from home. They marveled at our baptism in the Holy Spirit and they encouraged us over our complete dedication at serving the Lord. They further delighted in our singing during church and encouraged us to keep it going. I listened glad for their remarks, but in prayer I feared the worst possible thing was happening to me. I begged God to help me, lead me, show me that my feelings were holy and pure.

19

For I found myself craving Tori's closeness; wanting to be with her every hour of the day. If Eric tried to fight me about this or asked me to stay home with him, I would run away to Tori even faster. I felt such an intense spiritual bond with Tori and when I was near her my Spirit found immediate peace and security.

I read about Sodom and Gomorrah, how God destroyed the homosexual perverts and I read passages that Paul wrote condemning homosexuals to hell. But all this did was break my heart. I was completely confused and tears flowed from my eyes repeatedly. I begged God to release this hold that was so strong binding Tori and I together. I questioned every feeling I had for her to myself and later directly to her.

Tori's hair shone like the sun, her slender body was perfectly shaped and accented her womanly statue. Her face sparkled with two large blue eyes that could see into the depths of my heart and her mouth and nose were so lovely to gaze upon. How I envied Alan, that he could kiss her lips while I wondered longingly what it would be like. I felt my eyes wonder and want more and my feelings and dreams saw only deep passions encircling Tori completely and never letting go. I resisted all these thoughts, punishing myself by not seeing her, playing sick or futilely saying, "I was trying to work things out with Eric."

I couldn't understand why God was allowing this to happen. Tori and I had prayed so long together, for each others problems and strength in our marriages, that I just couldn't believe that so much good could turn out to be so bad! I even at first questioned Eric about Tori and I, and he didn't see any problems. But as our marriage kept crumbling he established this stronghold and used it behind my back to make him look like the gentleman and me the serpent.

Thanksgiving day was the first complete day, Tori and I had been apart since her abortion and bankruptcy. All day the festivities seemed endless. I constantly looked at my watch, hoping the day would end and Tori would be back from her grandparents home. We walked every night and this day would be no exception. I needed to pray with Tori and that was the reason my insides felt like knots tied over and under in a large lump in my stomach. That was why I was feeling so anxious for the day to pass.

Quietly, I pushed Eric to leave our family thanksgiving gathering and finally he consented. Once at home, I paced. I called Tori's home but there was no answer. I waited a few minutes and dialed again and her voice broke the silence on the other side. I felt elated and craved her in person. We decided to meet at church and run through some tapes for the Sunday special music. This time I let Eric put the children to bed and I left early to wait for her arrival.

Tori had come early too and my joy at seeing her brightened the dark sky. We held each other in prayer, but this time it was different. No songs were sung, just heard in the background as we hungrily sought each others cheek until our lips met for the first time. I couldn't get enough of her soft eager lips or hug her close enough. After realizing what I'd done I burst into tears and walked away ashamed. But Tori found me and took me in her arms again, kissing me over and over. A flood of love bubbled up and embedded itself permanently in my heart! I loved her more than I imagined anyone could love! This wasn't at all like the love I thought I had with Eric, when we first became serious about our relationship. This love was a consuming fire burning brightly in my heart, mind, and soul.

What fear I woke with the next morning! My mind recalled over and over again every kiss and feeling I had felt and I wanted more. When Tori called the next morning, I ran to her house and she assured me over and over again that everything was fine and we had done nothing wrong. Again our lips met and I dared not turn away for I eagerly craved them.

As the weeks passed, Tori and I grew closer until the day when both of our bodies became one. I had begged

21

Tori pleading if we went too far, she had to stop us, but she was as weak as me. We needed each other and until our hunger was complete neither of us were satisfied, but the war that broke out inside me was more than I could bear. Eric ran a substitute mail route and the children were at school. I was desperately depressed that I had allowed myself to commit such a terrible sin.

I cried to Tori on the phone that I was sorry and she pleaded with me saying it was O.K. but all her words made no difference. I swallowed all the medicine in the house that I could find and looked for a razor to cut my wrists. The phone kept ringing over and over again, but I refused to answer. The medicine was making me sleepy and the only razor I could find was a disposable. I smashed it on the table breaking the blades loose. Tori was outside my house pounding on the doors, ringing the shop doorbell and screaming my name. I made a small cut on one wrist but Tori's frantic pounding woke me to my senses and I let her in.

In a daze I refused to let her touch me, and I asked her to leave me alone. Helplessly, I stated I didn't want to ever see her again. She refused to leave until I promised I would be O.K. I don't know what happened next, but my desire to destroy my life ended. Tori talked so fast and hard that I was ashamed. She prayed for me! I felt better and my hope returned. When she left I threw away the razor and never touched it again. Romans 12:2, "Do not conform yourselves to the standards of this world, but let God transform you inwardly by a complete change of your mind. Then you will be able to know the will of God- what is good and is pleasing to him and is perfect."

My children slept so soundly in their beds that my heart melted and swelled with pride and love. Divorce is such a hard term to understand and yet there was no turning back even for their sake.

Eric and I went to ministers to discuss our problems, but even when he was confronted with why I was unhappy in our marriage, he just wouldn't change. Our own pastor listened as I talked about problems and difficulties we had and he wrote 7 pages of notes. He promised when he talked to Eric that he would not let him see the pages, but would just talk over new ways to bring love back into our marriage. So anticipating everything he said to me, we sat down with Eric, and after 2 hours of endless talking and Eric telling our minister that he thought he married the perfect wife, our Pastor handed him all the pages. I guess that was one way of showing Eric that I didn't think he was perfect! After another 3 or 4 sessions the pastor threw up his hands stating that Eric was no more than a Pharisee and completely unbendable. Well, I already knew that! Yet still another minister said that we had fallen out of love and that we needed to go back to the basics so we could start showing love again.

We went home, I knew now that if Eric was going to show love for me he would understand that music was my ministry, just like his was church camp, and since I didn't hold him back, I expected him to support me. "Forget it," was his reply. Why was everyone building me up with false hope just to have Eric pull out the rug from under my feet? That was the end of our marriage counseling, at least for me. Behind my back, Eric kept up the counseling, but this time I wasn't the perfect wife. Our problems in his opinion, was that I had changed. Well, I had heard enough, it wasn't because I had changed, but that I had wised up to him, at least that's what I wanted to believe for I still was struggling with my feelings of tremendous love for Tori.

Tori's marriage was rapidly coming to an end and I was worried, because she was losing weight and her energy was at an all time low. She was also having problems with high fevers. Since winter, we had started writing about the abortion she had just gone through and little by little, Tori opened up confessing that her parents had forced her into marrying Alan. Only after she had been 'date raped' by him! She was only sixteen at the time and going to a beer party with her parents full knowledge, she drank in excess. On the way home from the party she passed out in the car and Alan took advantage of the situation. The next

23

morning to her terror she realized what he had done and to further the problem she became pregnant. Once she confessed to her parents that she was late on her period, they immediately forced them to become engaged and later the pregnancy was aborted. Unfortunately the damage had been done and her parents felt that she had no choice but to marry Alan in order to justify having had sex together before God. Two years later they were married and the reality of living in a marriage 'with no love', began and the feelings of being trapped surfaced with Alan beating Tori to satisfy his own unhappiness with his life.

Lying on the bed in the starch white hospital room with an I.V. in her arm, Tori looked like she had given up and her face was pale and feverish. My heart was in my hands as I prayed for her strength to return with a quick recovery. She had a severe vaginal infection caused from Alan in a fit of anger shoving his shotgun up inside her during sex. She smiled when I entered the room. She was so weak and frail. I wished, I could change places with her or at least give her my strength, I felt so helpless. "Alan is the reason for this, isn't he?" I demanded. She wouldn't deny it. I wanted to cry. So many times I had threatened Tori that if Alan didn't leave her alone I would hit him over the head with a baseball bat. Why didn't she leave him? But I knew she was in as much denial as I was over our relationship.

Two weeks later, Tori, Brad and I fled in the middle of the night, after Alan came home drunk and started to beat Tori and rape her in front of their now 4 year old son. From the excessive drinking he became sick and retreated to throw up in the bathroom giving Tori just enough time to escape! She finally had come to her senses over the danger she and Brad were in and had enough of Alan's abuse! Her divorce began and she moved into her first apartment. And quickly a temporary restraining order was put into action to provide protection for Tori and Brad from Alan's continued abuse.

Alan was admitted, through his own consent, two days later into the State Hospital for observation because he threatened to kill himself in front of Tori's dad Bill and a police officer who was there to give him the restraining order protecting Tori and Brad from being harassed or abused by him. He thought that through sympathy he could regain Tori's forgiveness and win her back, but Tori refused to buy into his lies this time. The divorce processing continued!

Up until this time, I was very careful not be seen by Alan because of the repercussion of him abusing her after seeing me with her. Now we had more freedom and after I put my children in bed for the night under the care of Eric sometimes I would go to her apartment until 1:00 or 2:00 a.m to give my support to her, because Tori was extremely frightened to be left alone long. Many times during her marriage, Alan threatened to kill her and she was sure he would follow through. And to further her fears, Alan released himself from the State Hospital within a week of his admittance. Now things were different and he no longer was looking for Tori's support as much as he was looking for a foot hold to make her let him back in her life.

CHAPTER THREE

The dirty white walls of my cell reflected years of use. The room was oblong, six feet wide, 15 feet long, with a shower and a stool. There was a metal bunk bed welded to the wall, three windows with bars, and metal screening to protect the glass from being broken. Gray-blue paint covered the paint chipped floor and the sun cast a shadow of bars making an eery effect of confinement. My imagination spiraled as thoughts of escape flooded my mind. This was my eighteenth day in jail. There were no other women since Tori bailed out and my room was so quiet that I wanted to scream. One of the jail rules was one phone call a week and solitary confinement for punishment purposes, but after intense pleading and practically falling on my knees in humility, I convinced the Sheriff that I was a model prisoner and to at least bend the rules and allow me one phone call a day. This seemed more than reasonable to me, for I didn't foresee another lady prisoner. This was a small town!

My mother took my impending divorce very hard and for years she had used me as her ideal daughter married to a good Baptist man. she felt comfortable with Eric. She knew we had problems, but never to this point! She felt it her duty to point the blame. All the weeks I spent at Tori's and the fact that now I had even refused to go to church, made me look like the culprit. It was her job to straighten me out, but I refused to heed. Then she dropped the bombshell.

When I was five, mom had a really bad ear infection where both of her eardrums burst leaving her totally deaf. Dad was overseas in the Navy and he was flown back on a helicopter to be with mom. All the neighbors rallied to mom's support helping her every way they could. A week later she regained her hearing.

She was embarrassed, because of all the attention and the great expense the Navy had gone to, to bring dad home from overseas. By then everyone she knew, her parents, in-laws, brother and friends were aware of her misfortune and were offering sympathy. She was unnerved as to what to say. Before her hearing loss, her friends were constantly putting her n the middle of neighborhood arguments or family disputes. Anything wrong she was made aware of for mediator purposes. My sister was a baby and my brother and I hadn't started school yet. She was all alone to care and provide for our needs, and she was overworked and overwhelmed. Taking what seemed to be the easiest route, she went with the flow. Secretly promising herself that after everything calmed down she could regain her hearing. So drawing upon her high school experience in plays and drama she began to act out her deafness. Soon her neighbors weren't knocking because she couldn't hear them and the phone wasn't ringing because no one would answer. Unfortunately, once people think you are deaf and put their trust in you that you are a honest, upright, God fearing woman, it's hard to tell them the truth without them judging you with distaste. So the longer she put off the truth, the more she knew people wouldn't understand why she did what she did.

My mother was a very religious person and daily she constantly watched programs of faith and sermons on T.V. She attended church and Sunday School. She taught us to love God and saw all four of us through Baptism. She loved her children and wanted the best for us, but if we weren't living up to her expectations as far as she thought God was concerned, then it was her duty to do something about it. So taking the guilt of my failed marriage and my unseemly relationship with Tori upon her shoulders, she confessed before Eric and myself that for 24 years she had pretended deafness. Surely God in all his Glory and forgiveness would grant her prayer for my marriage to

27

heal and for Tori's and my relationship to end!

Immediately Eric announced it to his father, who told the deacons, who told their wives, who told the entire town and before the week was over the entire church was shocked! People's tongues were judging and picking her apart for everything she ever did in the church. People literally stopped on the streets when she passed to gap at a person who fooled not only them, but her own family for 24 years. My brothers and sister gave little understanding of her lies and her own parents would hardly talk to her. When the tidal wave slowed down all the reaction of mom's sacrifice from her confession of her worse sin for my sake, turned into 'one liar breeds another.' No one believed anything I said. Eric in their eyes had done no wrong and I was just following in the footsteps of my mother.

Eric took the helm and started writing letters to every man, woman, and child I had ever had contact with. Stories grew with how I had fallen in love with another woman and my changing had crumbled our marriage. He expressed concern over me filing and getting temporary custody of our children when I didn't want or desire them. He asked for sympathy for my parents and prayers and financial aid for himself, because the divorce was crushing him financially. And to make his point of view more convincing, he praised God through the entire letter and thanked him for counting him worthy to go through such harsh testing. The letter ran like syrup!

My mother was crushed from the unforgiveness of others about her deafness and supported Eric. My sister wouldn't talk to me and my brothers pretended like I didn't exist. I had no friends except Tori. No one remembered my singing or any programs or responsibilities I had fulfilled. Eric had marked me a homosexual; the kiss of death!

Soon I discovered that everyone including my mother,wrote letters to the Court Service Officer supporting Eric. When my lawyer found out, he dropped my case. I had never felt so alone in my entire life. But

Tori refused to let me give up; she loved me and helped me find another lawyer.

Tori had problems of her own. Her parents heard the stories and refused to believe and put pressure on her to date. One of the lawyers from the law office she used in her divorce, kept asking her out and finally to calm her parents she pretended to go off with him on a weekend in July. Her parents excepted this for he was very rich and he would be a good catch for their daughter. I could hardly believe the news that we were going away for the weekend. Our finances weren't good, but I had enough on my charge card that we could stay at a cheap motel.

When Tori first divorced, Alan in a fit of revenge, went to each of the 33 students that she taught piano and vocal music to, and said she was a homosexual and how could they allow her to teach their children? Before school ended that spring she lost all but 3 students from what he said, and many close friends. This put additional pressure on the problem of income for not just herself, but I knew there was no way that she could help me. Leaving Eric lost my friends too, but also my livelihood as well, for since the beginning of our marriage I had done upholstery along with him. Paying another retainer fee to a new lawyer took the last dollar bill I had. Even after Tori and I combined our SRS checks for 2 separate households, we had just enough left to pay our phone bills. We had nothing left for extras in our homes, or for clothes for the children, or even gas for a car. Seizing the opportunities during our weekend away, we opened up several charge accounts on my good credit rating. A month later a Visa card came in the mail helping us meet our bills. And not long after this creditors were sending me pre-approved money in the mail. With my continued fight for custody and divorce proceedings accelerating, all of this money were badly needed.

Then unexpectedly disaster fell when one of Tori's fingers was slammed in my car door and cut severely just above the joint. She had to have several stitches and was unable to play the piano or organ. We were both

29

devastated. From the time we both started singing together with Tori accompanying, we had dreamed of a music ministry. Now our hopes seemed ended.

In prayer we searched for God's immediate help. God opened a door that we never expected. I had personal liability insurance on my car. It paid all of Tori's doctor bills and the intense physical therapy for her finger and it paid workman's compensation for lose of wages. After proving Tori's income from her past income taxes she was able to collect over $800 a month in benefits. Her finger improved nicely and we easily met all of our bills. For all of Alan & Eric's accusations, God delivered us with just enough to meet my credit payments.

Since Tori's boyfriends was 'rich' and also as a front for her parents, Mark began to provide her with extravagant gifts of jewelry and clothes. This kept Tori's parents content enough to allow her to go on more weekends. But they pressed to see Mark and Tori would calm them down and feed them whatever they wanted to hear, which put a lot of pressure on her, more than I understood as my divorce proceedings dragged on month after month. But of course when there wasn't a real Mark, there was no choice, but to fabricate more stories and soon I realized that Tori was very capable at doing this if it kept them away and allowed her to continue on with our relationship. Since her early childhood days, Tori was forced to lie in order to have freedom from her parents. I could not begin to understand the control they had on her until I was involved with Tori for years and all too soon I understood the reason behind these lies.

After losing my first lawyer and my so-called friends, the problems of court mounted with me having no choice but to outright lie that Tori and I were friends only! I loved Tori. She made my burdens light and filled all my needs, but the people around us hated us because of what we were. We read books, we watched movies, and read magazines and all literally had the same answers. If I fought as a homosexual, I would lose. So we covered up! Next I sought counseling for myself and my children and I reported Eric to the SRS for physical, emotional, and child abuse.

The SRS investigation did not prove Eric guilty, but it sure cast a lot of doubt as to what kind of parent he was. It was recommended that he seek parenting classes.

I took an MMPI test under my therapist's directions and was found with no homosexual tendencies and a perfectly normal person. Also a parenting exam was taken and I scored the highest test she had ever given, showing that I was an excellent parent.

Next, I regularly wrote letters to the CSO countering anything that Eric said about my virtue. I didn't have any recommendations from friends, but many past friends wrote letters of concern and memories of things I did for them. I used these letters for character references. They were all good letters. Even though some of them wrote letters against me it made their court letters supporting Eric, look wishy washy. Eric had liberal visitation for I shared the kids equally with him. I had them from early morning to evening and he had them at night. This arrangement hurt, but my apartment was small and the children liked sleeping in their childhood rooms. When school started, I would pick them up each morning and take them to school and then pick them up after school as well. Truly at this point of my life, I didn't know how to juggle the pressures put upon me from my now new secret lifestyle and how to handle the care of my children with the divorce quickly approaching. So with this in mind, I did what I thought was best for the children and even though I didn't like how Eric disciplined our children, I still wanted my children to have their father. And with the SRS investigation he was on his best behavior with them with their constant visits.

In my entire life I had never drank, smoked or used bad language. I was not a follower, I was a leader and seldom did I give into peer pressure of any kind. But after leaving the Baptist church, I started going to the Lutheran church and in communion you drank real wine, social drinking was acceptable and Tori and her parents did this. So I tasted wine and remembering in the Bible that Jesus performed the miracle of changing water into wine, I learned to like it.

Tori and I probably drank a glass of wine a month, but Eric made me into a drunk. My mother was horrified at this drinking and Alex my youngest son, loved to get me in trouble with his grandmother. Immediately before entering their home, I would scold Alex and threaten him to be quiet. But he loved grandma's response and since Eric was confusing them daily as to what kind of mother I was, he would bring it up. Alex really wanted to believe in me, but Eric was so vindictive over our divorce that the children were constantly put in the middle and told that I was a bad influence. Drinking was a sin and divorce was even worse. Eric even condemned me for taking the children to the Lutheran church and not going to the Baptist with him. This made church a real problem.

The children were constantly put in the limelight at the Southern Baptist Church. Everyone wanted to know how they were and how sad it was that they lived with their sinful mom. All church activities brought pressures that I was a sinner not only because of the divorce, but also my relationship with Tori. All the members pretended indifference to me, but regularly patrolled Tori's and my home. The Southern Baptist Church were people directed by every word that proceeded out of Ordained Deacon, Eric's mouth and every vicious tale fed fire to their gossip.

Being cast in such doubt in front of church people who were to show God's love and kindness was very alarming to the children. They loved me as their mother, friend, and comforter, and for their own Godly wisdom. And now these people were judging me. Many times I would explain to the children that even Jesus our Lord and Savior said in John 12:47b, "I came, not to judge the world, but to save it." These people were surpassing the law of God and making themselves God by condemning me. Paul even states in 1 Cor. 4:3, "Now, I am not at all concerned about being judged by you or by any human standard; I don't even pass judgment on myself." Both passages of scripture directly point out that if you judge, then you are not walking in the light of Jesus. Further the Bible states that the greatest thing in 1 Cor. 13 is love. I loved Tori and the Southern Baptist Church was condemning me by judging my behavior as wrong, because I loved. Yet in 2 Tim. 3:1-5, "Remember that there will be difficult times in the last days. People will be selfish, greedy, boastful, and conceited; they will be insulting, disobedient to their parents, ungrateful, and irreligious; they will be unkind, merciless, slanderers, violent, and fierce; they will hate the good; they will be treacherous, reckless, and swollen with pride; they will love pleasure rather than God; they will hold to the outward form of our religion, but reject it's real power. Keep away from such people."

The Southern Baptist Church was so wrapped up in the outward form of religion that they thought that God approved of them handing out punishment on me by stripping me of church and family. They had the resemblance of a church, but lacked the power of love that strove for peace and unity and not judgment. Jesus said be careful what speck you take out of your brother's eye, for a log is in your own! God commands us to stay away from wrong teaching and for me to allow my children to attend a church that taught hate, I would be guilty of teaching them to sin.

Crystal was 6 and never baptized and her desire to follow God's commands brought more problems. I could not allow my daughter to be baptized in the Southern Baptist church when I didn't feel they were following God. So after talking to the Lutheran pastor over the problems, eliminating the homosexual part, he agreed to baptize her. Crystal was thrilled and excited, but I very carefully did not tell her dad!

Eric was so fully convinced that being a Baptist was the only way to heaven that from the first time I took the children to the Lutheran church, he only condemned it from the worship service to the way they baptized. Whenever the children were in his presence, he furthered his case with statements, stating that they were wrong on their beliefs, eliminating all consideration that God gave different churches to meet different peoples needs. I, on the other hand, loved the foundation of the Lutheran church that stated it was a church ever moving to meet the changing needs of all people. Filling people's changing needs were essential in today's world with very poor to very rich who need the wisdom and guidance of God. How can the church of God grow if we don't feed the people what they need? God told Peter three time to feed his sheep. To feed is to give substance, a living, walking, and talking word. For Eric, to condemn a church and a people, he knew nothing about, was plain sin! Crystal was baptized naming Tori and her parents as Godparents and truly it was one of the most beautiful ceremonies I had ever witnessed.

A week before court was scheduled, Eric and I had another combat. He wrote up another divorce agreement on property settlement. The car I was driving was due for insurance payments and Eric said if I didn't sign he would call the police and have my car towed away for driving without insurance. He further stated I could go to jail. Knowing I didn't have any money, his threats scared me a lot! So after talking it over with Tori, I felt that I had no choice but to sign. I needed transportation. He paid the insurance and signed over the car and our small tent camper as part of our agreement in turn I was forced to sign over my interests in the house.

Finally the night before court dawned and mom with tears in her voice called stating that they had received another letter from Eric calling me a homosexual and a drunk. The letter further asked for everyone to pray so Eric would get the children and for my lost soul. My parents were clearly shocked that Eric would send such a slanderous letter out to all of their friends without considering their feeling over the situation. Trying to calm Mom down and reassure her that Eric was lying, I stated that I wanted to use the letter as proof of Eric's vindictiveness against me in court the following day.

Dad was clearly upset by what the letter said for

the first time since I was a small child being disciplined
for wrong behavior, he resisted giving me the letter
stating that if he ever found out that I truly was a
homosexual, he would personally kill me. I begged for the
letter, pleading with mom and after minutes of continued
threats from Dad; mom gave it to me. She had a change of
heart just from the sheer embarrassment of what Eric had
done to them through the letter. Not only did she side
with me over this letter, but she also renounced the letter
she wrote from the previous letter Eric had sent to
everyone asking for their financial support for him to
have custody of the children.

My legs were like rubber from the devastating
effect Dad's words had on me. I wept all the way home in
my car. My parents actually would be happier if I were
dead than to love Tori. Why did it seem, like my whole
world was falling apart before my eyes, when I was just
the same person I had always been? Why was I so
despised,when less than 6 months ago, I was admired and
loved?

CHAPTER FOUR

Friday, the 13th of November began with a chill of anticipation that God would conquer the evil this day held with his wonderful bright shining love. I knew I was ready, but I couldn't help but look upon the courthouse which loomed in stately fashion before my eyes and feel my stomach become jittery and my body tense. Tori's image came to my mind as I recalled her nervously taking charge of my kids while I would be gone, and firmly stating in a sure voice that God would be victor and to remember to allow him to work through me. Even with this final statement of assurance, I still was afraid knowing that Eric had a whole church on his side and I would be on my own in Divorce Court!

Searching the corridors for signs of my lawyer, only produced Eric, his parents, and a few members from the Southern Baptist Church. Quickly I retreated to the CSO's office making sure my mother's letter had been taken out of the file and for a breath of fresh air away from the enemy. There was a small scene while Helen, the CSO, resisted my efforts, but then verified my request by calling my mother. Papers shuffled until every copy of her letter was deleted from all files. A shutter of air escaped my lungs. I prayed silently that I was ready. My lawyer entered, busily plowing through the files and verbalizing last minute instructions on my testimony. He complimented me on my dress and whisked both of us through the door and into the large courtroom.

As a true gentleman, he helped me into my seat as

whispers from the Southern Baptist Church pierced the stillness. I refused to look at them, but I smiled at my therapist, Sherry and Ruth from the SRS. We were ready! I was called to the stand first.

As each question was answered I slowly relaxed. He attacked Tori's and my relationship which I quickly denied, Eric's and my finances, children, everything that ever happened, punishments to abuse were questioned and answered. Two hours and 15 minutes later, I exited the stand while Eric testified for 20 minutes. We recessed for lunch.

Ruth took the stand first this time, producing a file on her investigation. All questions asked about the children's abuse contradicted Eric's testimony on discipline and methods of punishment. Then Sherry testified supporting that neither I nor Tori had any homosexual tendencies since she had given both of us our MMPI tests as our therapist. She confirmed my high parenting score and her own recommendation that I should receive residential custody.

Last, Eric's attorney called Mike, the Southern Baptist minister to the stand. His testimony was brief only casting doubts on Tori's and my relationship. We sat close in church, held hands in prayer, spent lots of time together and looked at each other reflecting love. The Judge recessed to make a decision.

The atmosphere turned tense, everyone shuffled in their seats. Eric's dad kept giving me unhappy looks and his mother refused to look up from her feet. The courtroom was given a short recess and I quickly stood up to leave the courtroom and call Tori. After the testimony from my former pastor, I was feeling very nervous and I wanted encouragement and confirmation that Tori was praying with all her might. Not only this, but I was concerned over how the children were handling the pressure of who would be their residential parent.

With the sound of Tori's voice on the other end of the phone, I immediately sensed stress in her voice and soon the calmness that I wanted from her turned into added pressures that my children were out of control and taking it out on Tori. Before court recessed for lunch earlier, Richard my oldest son, had accidentally broken a window in the garage opposite our house. Alex was getting pushy and Crystal just wanted to be held. Generally Crystal and Brad played well together, but this time all they did was fight. Tori had her hands full, so she quickly made a game of raking leaves with promises of reward, to only have them fight over which rake they were going to use. Instead of getting the strength I needed so badly from Tori, I needed to assure her I was praying for her too. To my relief, my lawyer came 15 minutes later stating that the Judge was ready to hand down his decision. Tori immediately hung up promising to pray and I quickly entered the courtroom.

Custody of all three children and $600 in child support was awarded to the mother. The property settlement that Eric forced me to sign was thrown out, because Eric admitted to threatening me in his court testimony so I would sign the agreement. All property in my possession was mine including 1/2 of the house to be paid to me within 5 years. Eric had to pay half of the debt from the credit card money I used to leave the house and obtain a divorce and I was to pay the first $50 on the children's medical with Eric paying the rest. I had won!

The Judge exited while my attorney explained, stating that I had done very well. Eric was shocked, his mother was in tears, and his father was shaking mad. He walked over to my lawyer and told him, "You should of dropped her like her first attorney," my attorney politely responded saying that if he had any questions, to take it up with his son's attorney. But Martin wasn't finished. After we left the courtroom he attacked me again. "You got just what you wanted!" He shook his fists and raised his arms in the imitation of praising Satan. Eric noticing his father's uncontrollable anger, quickly pulled him away before he was near enough to touch me or before he could say anymore in front of his church friends.

My lawyer quickly took me aside noticing my shock

over his behavior. Quickly we left the courtroom and Eric's support group behind and I left to rescue Tori from my kids and relay the news of victory to her and my parents.

We had a celebration supper at Tori's parents that night. With a pretend, stable boyfriend and fast talking from Tori, her parents warmed to my support. They were sympathetic over my parents desertion and furious over Alan's and Eric's accusation. They deeply loved their daughter and were very protective of her welfare. In they eyes, Tori could do no wrong or make them any prouder. Tori, Brad and her parents were openly affectionate and good naturedly teased each other, making a relaxed atmosphere. My children loved their company and warmed to their unjudgemental affection by calling Tori's parents, Pa & Gram, just like Brad.

Crystal especially liked Pa. Running to the door, she would promptly crawl on his lap and cuddle, capturing his heart forever. Gram was so loving and kind, hovering over all the kids making sure of what they wanted to eat or what they wanted to play. Their every wish was granted and every demand she fulfilled. Pa took them on wheelbarrow rides in the backyard and sled rides down fifth street road after snowfalls. The children soon caught on that they were pushovers and begged to see them often. Every meal prepared by Gram was always loaded with kid food. My children learned to eat spaghetti with butter, cheetos, and popsicles for supper. They could eat balanced at home, but with Gram everyday was a tea party. All of our birthdays were celebrated at Pa & Gram's, Thanksgiving, and even Christmas. And they made careful plans to attend all the children's special programs at school. They cared about us and were not afraid to show it.

Now the Southern Baptist security patrols of Tori's and my house tightened up after the first court hearing. We were stared at in public and Tori was denied service from Southern Baptist members working at the two biggest stores in town. She took this lightly, but I did not. My

Mercedes was being vandalized and I promptly rented a garage. We were talked about, pointed at, and together we very politely turn the other cheek.

We made my apartment sleepable for the children, buying a day bed for Crystal's room and borrowing bunk beds from my parents. We busied ourselves by making crafts for the new antique store that Tori's parents opened up, even more intensely because the holidays were here and we tried to settle in until my next court hearing. To my surprise, there was scheduled another court date to review the results of the Judge's decision three months later on January 6th. Nothing could be filed or even written pertaining to the court decision until this final date. My lawyer said that this was not a normal procedure and I needed to be very cautious and appear to be the perfect mother. More letters from the southern Baptist Church arrived daily compromising my mothering abilities and blaming Tori. My parents again weren't talking to me because of the rumors. Eric was on a rampage stating that our visitation arrangement of him keeping the kids on some nights was because I didn't want them. I was frustrated and mad at Eric's lies. I threw out the first visitation arrangement and started keeping the children all the time except when Eric requested them.

Up until this time I had spent the nights that I didn't have the kids with Tori. With me taking the children every night, I would be forced to not be with her. She in turn was terrified with being alone at night and she moved for the third time, 2 doors down from her parents. She was afraid of Alan and keeping in constant contact with the police accentuated her fears, because Alan continued to come back to Winfield for the purpose of watching her. After their divorce had been granted and sole custody of Brad was given to Tori, he left town and moved 100 miles away to take a carpentry job with a big construction company. No attempts were made after their divorce to contact Tori or even write a letter to Brad. Only once did he talk to Tori's parents and that was to talk only about Tori. He never asked about Brad openly to anyone except Eric.

Soon I discovered that my children were used as spies for Eric to tell Alan what Tori was doing. They were drilled into believing that Tori lied about Alan's abuse to her and Brad. Eric further proclaimed that she broke up our marriage. Emphatically he stated that she was a homosexual pervert and satan possessed. This upset them a great deal confusing them as to which parent told the truth. Richard and Crystal handled everything pretty well, but Alex didn't.

Alex's grades dropped. He became very violent at school pushing desks across the room and picking fights with other students. He walked out of class and would not obey his teacher. If he wasn't violent, he sat and stared into space. His teacher remarked that he wasn't provoked and after a short time he would calm down.

Tori knew I had problems with Alex from years before I was divorced. He needed more of my time, he needed my help in school and he demanded attention even if it resulted in punishment. She pushed me into having Alex completely evaluated by Sherry. She responded by giving him a four hour examination. It was found that Alex had possible brain damage that could only have been from head injuries. She advised that I go to my Pediatrician for further testing.

I was a devastated by her news. I had no idea that Eric's abuse caused brain damage. All my fears came tumbling in front of my eyes and I felt weak all over. Tori and her parents took over persuading me to go forward. My numbness wore off only to replace it with anger. Tori and I discussed what to do and I called Alex's doctor. I explained everything and an appointment was made not only with him, but with a Neurologist.

Alex's behavior became critical. He took all of his pent up anxieties and ran at Richard. Richard was Eric's favorite son. He was given his dad's total attention since the day that Alex was born. Eric talked to Richard like he was an adult and praised him for all his accomplishments in school. Alex received no attention from Eric except for spanking him for wrong behavior. So for his fury to unveil on Richard seemed only right to him. He fought with him, provoked him, or broke into fights over simple matters.

If Richard or Crystal didn't close the door to their bedroom, he would hurt them. If he wanted to watch a different TV program than them, even if it was in the middle of a show, he would turn it and dare them to not like it. If they yelled, he would attack. He would play with Crystal and pull her hair, pinch her or hit her, saying he was just playing. He refused to be disciplined and the one spanking I gave him in desperation to get some control with him was treated with indifference.

Sherry, our therapist, encouraged me to use time out where Alex would have to sit in the bathroom for 5 minutes for disobeying rules, but he refused to go. I was forced to pick him up and he would push away from me falling down and saying I hurt him. He cried, whined, and kicked. He became so violent that from the moment he came home from school until he went to bed, I would have to literally hold him down from hurting us or himself. I was exhausted from trying to meet his needs and the frustration of having no support from anyone except Tori. Even my faith that God would help me through was greatly questioned, but yet the still small voice inside me urged me forward to keep trying and to not give up the fight.

Alex's teacher wrote a letter emphasizing his lack of control in the classroom and the continued unprovoked outbursts with his classmates. From what I said and the letter from the teacher, Dr. Jones wrote a letter stating that observation of Alex's behavior under a trained specialist was necessary. He recommended inpatient evaluation. I was stunned, yet I felt I couldn't ignore what Alex was going through and so I continued down the road of doctors to get him the support he needed to get well.

A neurologist appointment was schedule and a test was run. A brain scan test in the hospital found nothing, but that was to be expected. The verbal neurological test indicated that he was possibly having brain seizures that caused the sudden abusive behaviors which would account for his apparent listlessness in class. He recommended further testing and inpatient evaluation for observation by trained professionals.

Tori and I made endless phone calls to children's hospitals with the doctor's recommendations and talking to psychologists about Alex's behavior. Finally, a Children's Hospital was found in a nearby city and going on another weekend together we visited the hospital and looked over the facilities and talked to the staff. They explained the procedure telling us that Alex would go to school and be observed 24 hours. If there were any seizures they would see them. A complete medical and neurological checkup and a psychologist would see him daily. But the price was astronomical! They said it would be insured through major medical minus the deductible. The deductible could be stretched out over 2 years in payments.

Eric did not believe in doctors. I spent many years hearing long detailed accounts of how all state hospitals were filled with demon possessed people. Medical doctors were a waste of money and medicine just made you an addict. When he was young, his parents never took them to the doctor and they survived. He then would recount all of the times his mother got sick as though it was a terrible weakness and lack of faith on her part.

I was determined if Eric could pay over $300 a month for a car, he could pay that much for his son to get well because of what he did to him! So gathering up all the facts and information a new day dawned to another beginning at Court. I represented the letters and information about the Children's Hospital to my lawyer and together we entered the courtroom.

My lawyer was agitated over the letters telling me that we would get help for Alex another time. He wasn't sure what the Judge would do with my accumulated information. This could make me look like Alex wasn't doing well with me. I didn't understand what he was saying. I thought everyone would be interested in helping a child who was having such abusive behavior in school and with his brother and sister. Yet reality dawned and once again Tori and my relationship was the real issue at least where the court was concerned.

The judge entered stating that in this session he wanted each parent to tell him how the children were doing in their homes. Eric took the stand first this time and quickly our visitation arrangements were opened for criticism. He stated that the children practically lived with him and that he never had any problems. Cautiously, I took the stand. I denied Eric's accusations and beamed over how well they were doing in school.

But when it came to Alex, I confessed that he was having real problems. I had to tell the truth about Alex for his behavior was making our home a war zone. I was afraid if he didn't get help soon that he would hurt Richard or Crystal permanently. And his own safety greatly concerned me as well. My lawyer worriedly presented the letters to the court and called Sherry to the stand. She confirmed the possible brain damage and supported the doctor's recommendations. The Judge recessed to look over the reports.

As the Judge left the bench his gait walking to his office was a little swayed as he fumbled for the doorknob to the outer judges chamber off the courtroom. It was common knowledge to the entire courthouse that this Judge had a drinking problem, unbeknownst to the people who came into his courtroom to have him settle their disputes according to the law. Quietly both attorneys followed entering his office that was located a short distance from the courtroom.

After a short time had passed, my attorney came back shaking his head and we all rose as the Judge came in and sat down. Without the least bit of hesitation, the Judge looked directly at me with indifference in his face and pronounced a judgment that sent all of my fears tumbling into my body with a force of unbelief. He turned Alex's custody over to his dad, reduced the child support, and made me responsible for all medical bills. He stated that if he had to choose between putting Alex in an institution and having him live with his dad, he would rather he lived with his dad. The Judge had not listened to the testimony given by Alex's therapist or the letters from the other doctors and he had totally misunderstood about the length of stay for Alex's observation in the children's facility, which would have been at the very most, 3 weeks. He further stated that all the children were to attend church with their dad. So much controversy erupted over Eric focusing all attention on the church that the Judge was moved to act on the amount of mail he was receiving on a daily basis from the people at the church, than on the best interest of Alex. He further openly rejected with harsh criticism, my decision to take them to the Lutheran church and scolded me over my actions to allow Crystal to fulfill her desire to be baptized. The Judge was forced to make some sort of peace. But his words stunned and further they were illegal. My lawyer pointed out that he was acting in an area that could not be broached by the courts. But the Judge held firm, adding that the children were not allowed to go to church with their mother or any of her church activities. Forcefully my lawyer said we would appeal.

Forty minutes after entering the court, it was over. I fought back tears not believing that the Judge actually gave Eric permission to take Alex and abuse him. Later my attorney informed me that the Judge was tipsy from too much to drink before the hearing and if he had been sober he would never have made such an illegal and immoral decision as he had done today.

Getting into the car my tears flowed steadily. After court, Tori and I had made plans to talk immediately afterwards, but I was so hurt from what happened at court that I just didn't want to face her. I didn't understand. I knew God had put us together, yet was it going to be at the cost of my children? I couldn't believe a God of love would give a child to an abusive father. Yet the more I questioned God over the results of court, the more I became confused over the verdict. God was my best friend and I knew He would never betray me, yet why? Why?

45

Tears stung to my cheeks as I ascended the staircase to my second floor apartment. I had to face my son. I loved Alex. How could I let him go to Eric? I tried wiping my tears away, but I couldn't stop.

My youngest brother was visiting from California. He was my children's favorite uncle and he easily agreed to babysit for me. Aaron was nine when Eric and I were married and he warmed to each of our children, completely endearing their very hearts. He met me at the door and I choked out that I lost Alex in the custody hearing. Aaron was at a loss of what to say to me and he was very uncomfortable with my sudden burst of emotions so with an awkward hug of encouragement, he quickly left. Alex came out of the bedroom with Richard & Crystal. I burst into tears again. I hugged him close and together he and I packed up his things before his Dad came to pick him up. While I held Alex in my arms, I brushed away his tears and I solemnly called Tori and to my relief she came just before Eric strolled to the door in a victory stance.

I loved Tori so much I would die for her and now one son, I lost because I loved her. 1 Cor. 13;13, "Meanwhile these three remain: faith, hope, and love; and the greatest of these is love." If faith is not as great as love then loving Tori was God's will for me. This is the reason that satan attacks love, he wants us to reject love in it's truest form that begins with loving another human being so much as to become one with them. God's love surpasses all understanding. In plain terms if we love we do not sin. Love is the greatest thing we can do!

I did not give up Alex for Tori. People clinging to the outward shell of God's word and not listening to the spiritual core of the Bible, which is love, took Alex away from me. The Bible, like no other book in the entire universe is not black and white. It goes beyond human wisdom and surpasses all understanding because it's spiritual. The Spirit of God does not conform to man's images because it's foundation is a word that people feel and describe in so many different ways, it is not concrete it is a thing called Love! God sent his son because of love.

If the Judge had acted in the best interest of Alex by loving him, he would have paid attention to the doctor's advice and he would have acted upon it swiftly, but instead he chose to act upon societies hatred of homosexuals.

They say that 10% of the human race is homosexual. Why are there so many if God did not make them too? Galatians 5;18, "If the Spirit leads you, then you are not subject to the Law." From the time Tori and I were baptized in the Holy Spirit and after I almost took my life from out relationship, I found a new teaching of love implanting itself in me. I no longer looked at the world as I did when I was married to Eric, but now my eyes were opening and I was looking at it as it really was. A world where people reigned! As my eyes opened to the corrupt things going on in the world and the spiritual blindness of those who called themselves Christian, but lacked the Spirit of God, I wondered how I could have ever thought that God had abandoned me. For it was not God, it was the people, who thought they were doing God's will by holding on to the laws in the Bible, instead of the new law of love given by Jesus! How blind, Eric and his friends had become, when they could not see that a little child needed help, but instead they had turned court into a mockery of injustice by condemning homosexuals instead of taking care of nine year old Alex's needs.

Tori took me in her arms weeping with me over people who cared so little for a child that they condemned what they didn't understand! Court again was scheduled in three months with another review of custody.

The time without Alex took alot of pressure off me. Immediately I started working in upholstery again. In our divorce settlement I was given one of our upholster sewing machines and some tools. Working took my mind off all my problems and helped ease the stress. Which in turn helped me to get my life back together and of course earn the money we needed to pay Tori's and my bills.

I still kept up a close weekly contact with Alex's teacher and some visitation was scheduled with him

47

through Eric. Helen kept in constant contact with Eric to make sure Alex was attending therapy and wasn't being abused. Alex's behavior problems lessened in school, but did not dissolve for Eric still held fast to his feelings that Alex's problems were the result of my so called lifestyle. Only through Richard and Crystal's visits with their dad, did I find out that Alex was doing as bad as ever.

CHAPTER FIVE

Evening time in jail cast shadows around the room. The activities of the courthouse came to an end and people relaxed relieved that the day was over. The quiet of the outdoors gave an appearance of harmony and a gentle breeze softly blew down the autumn leaves forming piles nestled at the foot of the trees as if to signify that it was time to rest, while adding to the serenity that only nature could portray. But rest does not always come as easily for people cut off from the truth because of a so called wrong kind of love. For deception feeds intrigue and constant questions only lead to even more lies.

Mark became a real focal point of conversation with Tori's parents. Her parents had never seen him and their curiosity was causing severe stress to Tori's heart condition. Everyday her mother constantly called checking up on what Mark was doing and wasn't it time they got married? She loved her parents and it was important to keep the front up over Mark in order to help me fight and get custody of my kids so we could all move away. If Tori's parents found out about us, they would have sided with Alan and fought for Brad's custody. So the cover up was essential.

Tori's parents were content as long as Mark continued to give expensive gifts to Brad & Tori. So for Christmas Tori received a stove, washer, dryer, and a small inexpensive car. Not to mention jewelry and a fur coat. In an effort to further the cover up, Tori had dreamed up an elaborate story with Mark going to Canada on a big criminal case. Because of this, the only time that Tori could see him was when he flew into the nearest city that was two and a half hours away. Tori informed her parents that Mark had to be to court to check in and pick up prisoners from the State Reformatory for witness purposes in his court case. Using this cover it was only natural that there was no time right now for them to see him. Her parents easily believed this story as long as Tori was receiving her gifts from Mark.

This front cost lots of money and every penny from insurance, working and anything else went to feed it. In December, my car was bumped and the insurance money went for payments. We were collecting on SRS, food stamps, and medical so all green money could be used to keep up the front on Mark and also pay my continued court expenses.

In November, I went off SRS because of the child support increase, I was told that I would still be covered under the medical and receive some food stamps. But in effect, I didn't have any more medical coverage and the food stamps were reduced making my income less than before I went off. Before all was said and done, it was smarter to stay on SRS than to go off of it and as long as they didn't know I had any extra money, I might get ahead enough to get by.

Keeping the children at night put pressures on Tori too. She couldn't handle staying alone at night and as a result she had nightmares about Alan stealing Brad or killing her. So occasionally after the children were sound asleep, I would ride my bike to Tori's for a while and then go back home. I hated doing this, but Crystal and Richard would tell their dad if we slept at Tori's; Matthew 10:36 "A man's worst enemies will be the members of his own family." All too soon, I discover the truth in this statement.

Already talk and intense patrolling by the S.B.C. was getting to Helen, the C.S.O. I sent weekly to monthly reports to Helen contradicting anything that was said. This front to cool talk was not fair on us or our families. I don't know why they just couldn't leave us alone and let us be happy. When all of us were together we were a family, content and caring for each other. But again people were fed more and more hate, by what Eric said about us and some out of curiosity just couldn't keep from watching our every move.

In March, Eric's mother and my dad had birthdays. As always I called to make visitation arrangements between Eric and I. He took Richard and Crystal on Tuesday and I had Alex on Wednesday. After their return from their Grandmother's birthday, I waited for the children to fall asleep before I took off to be with Tori for a little while. Everything was peaceful when I returned an hour later.

Wednesday, dad's birthday went fine, but Thursday I received a call from Helen. Apparently, Eric called her at around midnight, saying I was leaving the kids during the night. I was afraid to tell her the truth that I had really been at Tori's and since many times in the past, I had gone to the garage that was separate from the house to finish up a job, I quickly stated that I was home, but I was out in the garage upholstering. I didn't think anything more about it until Richard was getting ready for bed. I questioned him about what Helen said and Richard's face turned white and a funny smile crossed his lips like he had a secret.

Many times since the divorce, I left Richard in charge to watch his sister. He was almost twelve and I saw nothing wrong with him babysitting, especially since when I was his age, I watched my cousins all summer. Furthermore he was a very responsible child and even his teachers at school said they wished they had more students like him.

Slowly the story unfolded with Rich confessing that his dad showed him how to pretend that he was asleep. Unknowingly, I had fallen hook, line, and sinker into their trap and quickly upon my exit he called his dad. His dad and Mike, The Southern Baptist minister, came over and called the police. The police refused to do anything more than write a report stating that the children were left alone at home. Richard thought that the incident was nothing more than a joke on me. In his child mind he saw nothing wrong with me leaving him alone to babysit, but I was devastated over the cruel judgment that could come from Eric further maneuvering the court system with this incident to his favor.

Shaking, I called Tori. She was shocked and insisted that I get a babysitter and come over now. I was frightened and I didn't want to leave them again, but Tori knew that we needed a plan on how to handle the strategy with the court system and so she quickly called a babysitter for me. Throwing on my coat, I warned Richard if he touched the phone while I was picking up the babysitter, he would be grounded a long time.

Within 10 minutes, I dropped Theresa off at my house and left to go to Tori's. Arriving at Tori's, she quickly took me into her arms, assuring me that everything was going to be OK and not to worry that God would help us see our way through this new problem. Talking it over, we came up with a simple plan of attack. Shortly I left somewhat assured that I could counter what Eric had done.

The night was cool and turning the corner to my apartment, I was taken by surprise. Eric was on the sidewalk in front of my home and a SBC man was coming down the stairs from my door. I pulled up my car beside Eric's in the parking lot leaving my car lights on. I was half out of my car when to my complete surprise, Eric ran at me flinging his 250 pounds, full force against my body, pinning one leg between the door and my car. I screamed in pain, begging Eric to let me go because he was hurting me. His face radiated with hatred and he verbally screamed out profanities while accusing me of leaving the kids alone at night. With each word, he let pressure off the door only enough to again ram his full weight against the car door for effect. He continued to repeat his attack against me three more times, while the other men watched his actions in stunned silence. Yet neither of them moved to come to my aid. In the backseat of the car was Mike, the SBC minister. He was seated in full view of what Eric was doing. I screamed that Theresa was babysitting and for the first time, Eric released his weight from the car and

52

grabbed ahold of my coat. Sharp pain radiated from my leg and in an effort to calm the pain, I reached my hands down to give support to my leg. I again looked pleadingly in the direction of Mike for help, but instead his expression of shock turned to hatred and he jumped out of the car and headed for me along with the other man. Surrounded by the men, Eric still filled with fury, commanded Robert to check my apartment to see if I was telling the truth. Robert began to turn around to do what he asked and just at that moment for a brief second Eric loosened his grip. Taking advantage of this, I broke past all three men, hobbling with all my strength for my apartment.

Momentarily, I had caught them all off guard. They hesitated, then quickly ascended the stairs in hot pursuit. Miraculously, I had held on to my keys during the attack and fumbling through them, I found the right one to the door lock and quickly slipped inside and shoved the door closed behind me. Taking a shaky breath, I leaned against the door in an effort to hold it just in case it wasn't secure. Satisfied I ran for the phone bumping smack into Theresa. Seeing my apparent distress, her face turned white. She extended her arm to offer support when she notice that I was hurt. Luckily, she held the remote control phone in her hand for she had heard the noise out front and she was getting ready to call and inform me that someone was outside just like I had asked her to do if someone came to the apartment. Her words ended, only to be muffled by the intense pounding and yelling from Eric and the other men on the other side of the door. I was in no shape to look through the phone directory to find the number to the police station so I called Tori and immediately she called the police for me while pleading with us to stay away from the door. Within five minutes three policemen arrived. By then Eric and his friends had fled.

The police were concerned over my condition and they advised me that I should go to the hospital and have my leg examined. I was in shock over Eric's violent behavior towards me and the uncaring actions of his church friends and it took a few minutes for me to pull myself together and decide what to do next. I was very grateful when the phone rang and Tori's voice came through the phone commanding me to let her talk to the officer, who had just finished taking down a short statement from me on what had happened.

Theresa, on the other hand was giving a brief account of what had happened to the other policeman. After she finished the officer volunteered to take her home and explain to her parents about the situation. I thanked him and they left.

A few days later, more of the story unfolded when Tori called to thank Theresa for babysitting and her father answered the phone. He expressed concern over what had happened and wanted to know if anything had been done to Eric. After Tori relayed the story, he informed her that he had taken it upon himself to barge in on Eric that very night. He went on to describe Eric sitting in a chair trembling with the color drained from his face and Robert and Mike encircling him while rapidly talking. Upon entering the house and in a mad fury of emotions over their behavior, he warned all of them to never harass his daughter while she was babysitting for me again or he would personally kill them. Within minutes the police arrived and as he prepared to leave, he overheard them warn Eric and his friends to stay away from my house. They stressed that they had made a terrible mistake and that I was going to press criminal charges for assault and battery. They further stipulated that I was currently at the hospital, because of injuries he had inflicted to my leg. They also commanded them that they were to come down to the station and give a full account of their story. All three men were visibly shook and Eric promised to stay away. Noting that the police seemed to have control over the situation, Theresa's father left satisfied that everything was going to be handled. Tori thanked him for the information and for his support.

Getting back to that night, by the time that Tori

hung up the phone, she had agreed to have the police drive me to her house so she could take care of my kids, while I went to the hospital for ex-rays on my leg. Alarm registered on her face as she looked at my leg from the front seat of the police car. Determined, I told her I would be OK and not to worry, I would call her from the hospital as soon as I knew something.

Thankfully my leg wasn't broken, but I had a severe contusion traumatizing the muscle and several veins. This appeared on the lower back of my left calf as a protrusion the size of a softball which was deeply discolored by several broken blood vessels surrounding the area. The doctor was alarmed at the size of the injury and he called a lady from the Crisis Center in to talk to me about abuse. She advised me to get out of town and have a restraining order put on Eric immediately. They were both very firm that Eric was out of control and that I needed to take precautions. I thanked them for their concern and assured them that I would think about what they said.

Before our talk had concluded, the police entered to pick up a report on my condition from the doctor that would be filed with the documents over the assault. satisfied with the doctor's account of my condition, they came to where I was sitting with my leg up on the examination table and assured me that they had informed Eric that they would be watching my house closely to prevent him from ever coming near me again. After another interview over what had happened the doctor released me from the hospital after wrapping my leg and giving me extensive instructions to not put any weight on my leg for fear that a clot from the injury could occur. As a result of all the above, I was on crutches for 6 weeks and in physical therapy for the next five months before my leg had healed enough for me to return to work.

Immediately the D.A.'s office filed charges against Eric and then he advised me if I wanted to take action against Mike that I would have to write to ministers in power above him in his church region explaining Mikes part in what happened to me. So together, Tori and I infuriated over Mikes part in the assault on me, wrote and also sent out letters to parents of children who attended the Awana program voicing our concern over who was teaching our young at the church. All three men were directors of leaders in this program that was geared at children from 3 years through high school to equip them as Christians in memorizing Bible scriptures. Tori and I were satisfied that we had done the right thing by letting the parents know who was directly in the forefront of this program so they could reconsider, who they wanted to be role models for their children. By now, however, Eric and his friends had collaborated their stories, stating that I had forced the car door in Eric and he batted it at me to keep from being hit. The doctor said that was impossible, but the men had the whole church convinced that I was to blame. I was surprised at their complete blindness to the evidence of my injuries. How could they allow Eric and his friends to draw them this kind of conclusion to this event?

Romans 9:30-33, "So we say that the Gentiles, who were not trying to put themselves right with God, were put right with him through faith; while God's people, who were seeking a law that would put them right with God, did not find it. And why not? Because they did not depend on faith, but on what they did. And so they stumbled over the 'stumbling stone' that them scripture speaks of: 'Look, I place in Zion a stone that will make people stumble, a rock that will make them fall. But whoever believes in him will not be disappointed." My eyes were opening more and more to God's answers to my questions as to why I was continually hitting my head into this so called S.B.C.. For to my utter astonishment, they were not following God. Satan had changed this church by taking out the truth of love, and replacing it with the original laws of Moses. When Jesus came and cleansed us from sin, these laws were replaced with the new law of Christ, which consisted of the forgiveness of sin by just believing in His name or rather by grace. Because of their noncompliance to these

scriptures, they were stumbling over the truth.   When God
originally stated in Leviticus 18:22, "No man is to have
sexual relations with another man;   God hates that."   He
did this with the sole purpose of directing them into
following a 'Law' that would keep them ritually clean
before Him.   When Christ came, he did away with this law,
because now we are clean or simply our sins are forgiven
by believing in Christ and following the law of love.   If we
love, we do not sin.

2 Corinthians 3:14-17, "Their minds, indeed, were
closed;   and to this very day their minds are covered with
the same veil as they read the books of the old covenant.
The veil is removed only when a person is joined to Christ.
Even today, whenever they read the Law of Moses, the veil
still covers their minds.   But it can be removed, as the
scripture says about Moses.   'His veil was removed when
he turned to the Lord.'   Now, 'the Lord' in this passage is
the Spirit;   and where the Spirit of the Lord is present,
there is freedom."   Being baptized in the Holy Spirit
changed my life and opened my eyes to the depth of God's
wisdom.   I was seeing how the Southern Baptist Church was
trying to work their way to God's approval, instead of
obeying the simple way of love that Jesus's death
provided.   From the teaching of the Spirit along with Bible
study, I enjoyed the freedom of being who I am and
knowing that it was God's will for my life.   I repeat, I am a
homosexual and because of my baptism in the Holy Spirit,
I am united with Christ and therefore justified before God.
Love supercedes law!

Romans 13:9-10, "The commandments, 'Do not
commit adultery;   do not steal;   do not desire what belongs
to someone else'-all these, and any others besides, are
summed up in the one command, 'Love your neighbor as
you love yourself.'   If you love someone, you will never do
him wrong;   to love, then, is to obey the whole Law."   John
13:34 & 35, "And now I give you a new commandment:
love one another.   As I have loved you, so you must love
one another.   If you have love for one another, then
everyone will know that you are my disciples."   The SBC

members were not following God at all, because they were placing their faith in Eric's story, instead of applying the teachings of the Bible that directs us to love.

A court date was set for a restraining order against Eric shortly after the incident. The day before the hearing, Tori was subpoenaed by Eric's lawyer. Upon entering the courtroom Tori and I were met by the Southern Baptist Church. This time the SBC came in full force. Tori was lightheaded and she was having pains in her chest and I was concerned for her welfare over the stress of my court. I was alarmed at the intensity of the crowd, and the adamant denial of Eric's lawyer, that he was not to blame, and that I had brought it all on myself. From Eric's stubborn refusal of guilt, I was afraid that he was going to turn the courtroom into a trial over whether being a homosexual was right or wrong, instead of giving me the protection of the restraining order. Furthermore I was afraid of what could happen to Tori's custody of Brad if they should succeed.

The SBC members were becoming louder and louder, to the point of openingly laughing at my crutches, while all the time eying me suspiciously and poking fun at the nerve of Tori and I to accuse Eric of any wrong doing. Eric's dad went even further by trying to pull in bystanders, who were surprised at the large, intense crowd, attending court, so he could openly berate every move I made. It was apparent that the motives behind Eric and his friends were to make Tori and I confess that we were lovers and to once again deny me justice in the courts. Matthew 10:21-22, "Men will hand over their own brothers to be put to death, and fathers will do the same to their children; children will turn against their parents and have them put to death. Everyone will hate you because of me. But whoever holds out to the end will be saved."

I looked at my lawyer and expressed my concern over the goal of the crowd and told him I was dropping the restraining order. Knowing that the restraining order was just a piece of paper that normally had very little effect on keeping the attacker away, and looking at the faces of the mob he promptly agreed, but not until he resigned as my lawyer. He said we were all nothing but religion fanatics! The SBC left the courtroom with the sense of victory, seeded with new observations of more vicious rumors. Gossip over my withdrawal hit the town like wildfire and once again Tori and I were left out in the cold, while hatred raged around us brewing into a thunderous storm.

Custody court was postponed until June while I once again, employed a new attorney, who filed a lawsuit of criminal neglect against Eric. I was afraid, if I didn't put up some resistance to Eric, that he and his friends would attack Tori and I anytime they wanted to vent their anger over who we were. So in an effort to have some control, my attorney suggested that my only recourse to keep Eric under control, was to file charges by asking $20,000 in lieu of damages and loss of work from the injuries of my leg. Unfortunately, in retaliation, the SBC then tried to press charges on the letter, we had written to demand an investigation over Mike's involvement, but the DA refused stating that we had every right to give our point of view. He further informed them that they didn't have any evidence proving that Tori and I were responsible for writing the letters to the Awana parents for we had very carefully not signed our names. But because of the intense pressure of the Church members, he also refused to press charges against Eric. Because once again the church had bombarded his office with letters of protest and he felt by siding with their wishes that this would best handle the situation, thus calming them down so they would leave his office lone. He also was an elected official and his position could be in jeopardy with this being an election year and the last thing he needed was to make the people who voted for him unhappy!

As time passed, Tori's parents started giving her a really hard time about Mark being responsible to care for all of her needs and Brad's. Because of this and for safety purposes, Tori and I felt that we needed to keep my apartment, but we needed a house large enough that all of us could spend the night. We couldn't find any larger houses in Winfield and so we looked at double-wide mobile homes to buy.

To my surprise, I found out that my leg injury could be covered through my car insurance agency. They quickly accessed my loss of work wages, and I began receiving $1,000 a month. I sold my car, bought a used car and we had a down payment for our new double wide. Now this front was impressive to Tori's parents, but it was a terrible curiosity to the SBC. Patrols of our new home were accelerated. Alarmed over the new traffic and impending court, I warned the children not to tell where they spent the night to their dad. Everything was set. My children and I moved in for the night.

Summer began. And soon I was notified that court would be postponed to August because my attorney was sick, so we settled in cautiously. Richard played little league and Alex came to watch with Eric some of the games that he played. Naturally Alex used his time to come and be with me and it wasn't long before in excitement he quietly whispered the news that Richard and Crystal said they were sleeping at Tori's at night. In shock and fear as to what Eric would do to me in court over this news, I pulled Richard out of the game and we immediately left for Tori's. He confessed that he and Crystal had told my mother when they stayed with her a weekend ago. Tori was crying and shaking that Alan would use this to go after custody for Brad. All our hopes were shattered as we realized that we could never lead a normal family life! At least not in Winfield.

Shortly after this confrontation, Helen called asking questions, and I was forced to lie and say occasionally the kids stayed, but not me! I had been dating a man and Tori babysat for me. I also explained that Richard would say anything his dad wanted him to say and naturally Eric would take any staying with Tori overboard. She agreed and let it drop at least from our conversations, but from behind my back she was informing the judge and any other court official that would listen to

60

her stories from Eric. I even heard rumors that she was having an affair with the judge who presided or my case.

In an effort to gain confidence in the court again, Tori made an announcement stating that she was getting married. This time we really had our hands full, for not only were we keeping a front up for Tori's parents, but the court as well. I hated all the lies, but I felt we had no choice if I was going to be able to hold on to the custody of my children.

A month before Tori and I did this, Tori's parents suspected that Mark was part of the Mafia family. Taking this lead, Tori's stories got better and her parents believed every word. Especially when new extravagant gifts arrived daily that confirmed to them that she was in a long lasting relationship and that she and Brad would be well taken care of in the future. This also explained why they never could see Mark, for they expected him to be very discreet for the protection of his family. And this answered their question over why Tori never had any pictures of him.

Immediately Tori got busy finding newspapers that only advertised to gay people. She placed an ad, asking for a man who would be willing to put on a front to protect child custody. "Call collect!" was highlighted.

Since the ad was placed in Bay City we made 2 trips there to try to make arrangements. Tori got a new ring and then I got serious and became engaged to Rick. I hated all of the pretense, but I knew that we had no choice, if I was going to be able to hold onto my children and for Tori to continue to keep Brad. We were hoping to have a double wedding with a gay minister who would actually be marrying us and the men together at the same time. Unfortunately, gay people are not allowed to marry in the United States so any service that we might have been able to arrange would have been nothing more than a ceremony of love with no binding law affirming commitment. In other words we do not have the right to file a joint income tax statement or more importantly be recognized as a family. 1 Timothy 4:3-5, "Such people teach that it is wrong to marry and to eat certain foods. But God created those foods to be eaten, after a prayer of thanks, by those who are believers and have come to know the truth. Everything that God has created is good; nothing is to be rejected, but everything is to be received with a prayer of thanks, because the word of God and the prayer make it acceptable to God." Deep within my Spirit, I felt the gentle prodding of God's truth working within my being. Scripture's were igniting into bright lights of knowledge that opened a whole new avenue of support for Tori and I to be whom God had made us to be. God was proving to me through the Bible, that we were created by Him and that we were good and therefore acceptable to Him. Yet over the years of time and through the misinterpreting of God's word, people had created walls that refused to let people through, because they did not understand the simple truth that love was the foundation of the whole Bible. It is not surprising that when love is denied, that people are kept from forming the unions that God had originally planned by the very practice of not allowing homosexuals to marry. For if food is acceptable before God after a prayer of thanks, then of course, people are freed from the bondage put on them by people's blindness and are set free to marry.

In June, Tori was subpoenaed to court for the restraining order, and so we assumed that she would be again for my next custody hearing. We were afraid that if Tori went to court they could bring up the house, finances, and of course try to trip us up on our living arrangements. Not to mention, the threat of being found out about our false engagements. So after coming back Sunday night from Lawrence and finding a note on our door affirming that the Sheriff had something for Tori. Tori gathered up Brad and took off for St. Louis understanding that she would have to hide out until after my hearing on Friday. She easily persuaded her folks to inform the police that she was on vacation and that they didn't expect to hear from her until next weekend. They happily agreed, for Mark was showering them with gifts and had even helped finance Bill's new pickup. From all of Tori's elaborate stories of Mark's position, they understood that the family didn't want Tori in court. She had to protect the name of her fiance!

Two weeks earlier, I tried to get Alex tested for learning disabilities. I had talked to Helen about Alex getting letters backwards and she suggested I have this done. After I made the appointment, I called Helen to make arrangements with Eric. I said I'd pay for the appointment, but Eric refused to let Alex go. I asked twice, but both times he aid no. Once again, Eric's total disrespect for doctors and his refusal to see any problems with Alex, interfered with getting him the help he needed to grow into a happy, healthy child. Just the same the psychologist felt that this was such an important test that she wrote a letter of reprimand against Eric for his lack of interest in his son.

The same Sunday night that Tori received the note from the Sheriff, we quickly made intense calls to the Children's Hospital and a doctor agreed to see Alex on Monday, but I had no choice, but to do it behind Eric's back. Tori left at 5:00a.m. the next morning to avoid the Sheriff. And at 10:00 Richard, Alex, Crystal and I headed to Paola for the doctor's appointment for Alex. The appointment was a success with the Doctor not only talking to Alex about his problems, but also taking time to talk to Rich and Crystal. He confirmed Alex's diagnosis and expressed concern that Alex was deeply depressed and needed help, now! He then promised to send a letter to my attorney verifying again that Alex needed in depth evaluation, before my hearing on Friday.

Upon returning after the evaluation in Paola, Eric was upset and he called Helen once again to complain. He then picked up Alex from my home and Richard, Crystal and I headed out of town to rondevous with Tori and Brad. We planned a small family vacation to help pass the time until court and of course to evade any questions about Tori's whereabouts from the police and their subpoena for her.

On the home front, Bill and Doris were being visited by the police. And not only were they questioned about Tori's whereabouts, but mine also. So her parents started calling my house fearful that Tori was lying to them about Mark and that I was with her instead. Trying to head off the questions and provide a front for Tori, I contacted them and verified that we were staying at Rick's, my new fiance, while he was working at moving his office to a new job. They were easily convinced and after Tori talked to her mom, she was satisfied that her parents had believed every word of our conversation.

By mid-week, the police had showed up at Bill and Doris's everyday, trying to put pressure on them about getting the subpoena to Tori. So after learning about what was happening and to avert further problems, Tori called and stated that Mark was sending them on a paid vacation to St. Louis to check out the church for their wedding and for Gram to look for a dress for the occasion.

Earlier, Tori and I had to go on a spending spree, buying a new larger car, grand piano, and some new furniture for a front of wedding gifts. This front was tremendously important. If her parents suspected our relationship, they would have waged war for Brad's custody and with the fight I was in, we didn't need these added pressures.

All too soon, Friday arrived and I made arrangements to meet my lawyer in Hutchinson and talk over the new information for court, pertaining to the letters from the doctors. He was very positive as we entered court together. We both felt that we were as ready as we could be.

Of course the SBC was there in force. Eric's dad was there as usual. And I was alone once again with no one to stand up for my support. Yet, I knew that God was with me, for my Spirit gave calm assurance that the Father was by my side.

Bud, Alex's new therapist took the stand first, relaying how well Eric and Alex were doing together. He was impressed on how good a father Eric was and he agreed that splitting the kids was good for Alex. He also confirmed that the custody arrangement should be left the same at least for now.

My goal was to get therapy for Alex. Alex's problems continued to be severe. He had grown depressed and I was really concerned about his safety. So bearing this in mind, my attorney asked questions to Bud over any tests that he had run to verify any learning disabilities or behavior problems, Eric was having with Alex. Bud admitted that Eric had some difficulties with Alex, but nothing that warranted any further testing. He exclaimed that the tests were expensive and Eric said that he didn't have the money to do any special tests.

Months before court, I had made several contacts with Bud, which only resulted in him pointing a finger at me and Tori, and not solving Alex's problems at all. He refused to listen to me over what had happened to Alex from his father and he ignored the results of the different tests that Alex had undergone earlier. He made comments about Alex that were uncharacteristic of him, stating that he was a quiet person. When he said this, I knew he didn't know my son at all. Alex was always the first one to tell what he did with a friend or what happened in school. He was a very open child, affectionate and kind, except for the problems that he was going through, it didn't have anything to do with his regular personality. I could tell that Bud was so wrapped up with Eric's firm convictions over my relationship with Tori that he wasn't effectively helping Alex. I hoped that through my attorney's questions that the judge would see this too.

Eric was next, and basically it was the same old thing about me being the problem and Alex a victim from my lifestyle. By the time my lawyer brought out Eric's refusal to allow me to pay for further testing, the court's focus was on Tori and my relationship and not on his neglect to help Alex. Still my attorney made headway, by punching holes in Eric's testimony and tripping him up on how Alex was behaving at home.

Silence hit the courtroom when I took the stand.

My lawyer proceeded to ask questions. I reflected on past incidents, where Alex disregarded his own safety and threw himself head first down a ten foot hill. He was constantly causing problems at the pool and he totally destroyed a neighbors fence. The stories flowed endlessly. The doctor's reports were presented and were read for the court, highlighting the need for treatment concerning Alex. At the conclusion of my testimony, my attorney looked intensely into my face and asked, "At this time do you feel that it is best to keep things as they are with Alex living with his father and Rich and Crystal living with you?" I choked back the tears. I loved Alex, but until he received the needed treatment, he was a threat to Richard and Crystal. Fear of having a repeat of holding Alex down so he wouldn't hurt any of us burned in my memories.

As I descended the stand, Eric's dad loudly called me a liar and questioned Eric and his attorney on how I could lie so well in the court? I stared right through him. The Judge, just ignored his outburst and said he wanted to think about his decision and that he would have it ready by Tuesday and would mail it to both attorneys.

I returned to Tori, all the time remembering my attorney's words that everything went well, except for the letter from my mother. She stated that I threatened to burn my children's toys if they talked about Tori. Otherwise nothing else was said against me. Later Mom said that she wrote no such letter, and that Eric's attorney had lied. So many things had happened that by now I didn't know what to believe, except that I knew that God was with me, even if it seemed that no one else in this world was.

CHAPTER SIX

The light shone brightly in my jail cell, never dimming always present. Only shutting my eyes tightly, or pulling the blanket over my eyes was there welcomed reprieve from the bars that were in my room. The light afforded me comfort too, many a time tossing and turning in my sleep, I would awaken and dream that the Father of heavenly lights was shining his lights of love, giving me hope and security that my rescue was close at hand.

Once in our home again, Tori urged me to call the courthouse for the results of the hearing. Going to my apartment, I called the courthouse, the verdict was in, but they would not release the information to me by phone. I called my lawyer, so he could get the information and Tori and I waited for his return call. During the January hearing, the Judge ruled that the children were to attend church with their dad and not with me. At court new questions were asked, over why I refused to follow through on the court order demanding that the children attend the Southern Baptist Church?

When Eric and I first started our custody war, it was evident that he would stop at nothing to muddy my name. I appealed to him focusing on how his words would hurt our children, but he didn't care! Rich started having problems with being bullied by the son of the Awana Director, who also was Eric's best friend. One day at school together with some classmates, they surrounded him, calling Tori and I names, and kicking and hitting him in his groin. Everything got so out of hand to the point, that I pleaded with Eric to talk to the boy's dad. He refused, stating that I was custodial parent and I was responsible to handle it. I was mad, but after conversations with the principal in which he threatened to expel the boy, the problems somewhat subsided, but still the boy taunted him. Richard was a very friendly child and wouldn't hurt a fly, yet Eric's vindictiveness was not only hurting me, but also our children. No matter how much I confronted him with this, he would ignore my remarks by stating that they were self-inflicted from my sinful life.

Crystal was having problems too. I had to force her out of the house to Awanas, Sunday School and Church. She cried, refused to get dressed and pleaded asking me not to make her go. Crystal was my pride and joy. When she was born I was elated. After having two fine sons, I wanted a girl. But like all mother and daughter relationships, mine wasn't perfect. When Crystal became unreasonable, I simply couldn't find out what was wrong.

Tori could talk to her. She loved my children and they in turn loved and trusted her. Finally after some prompting and affection from Tori, Crystal said that she hated church, because the people asked mean questions about me. She also remarked that Daddy was so busy doing things in church that he never let her sit by him, she always had to sit with another child and his family.

I took these stories to my lawyer and he talked to the Judge. The Judge did not change the order, but my lawyer told me to act on my own convictions. I pulled them out of the church refusing to allow them to go. Eric and the church once again went crazy writing letters to the CSO and I was called again by Helen to explain my motives.

The pastor of my church wrote a letter supporting me and I wrote a detailed account of my reasons and the persecution Richard and Crystal were undergoing in the church. I rightfully stated that the church was biased to Eric and was inflicting cruel emotional harm to the children. The issue was dropped at least until court and once in court, I stated these same reasons.

My tension was mounting. I began trembling, as once again I dialed my lawyers phone number. They put me on hold and shortly my lawyer's voice filled the silence. I braced myself. The Judge said, because of the

68

constant conflicts apparent between Eric and me, that the children needed to be together and he gave SOLE, not joint custody to Eric. The rest of his words seemed muffled as panic and dread filled my body. He stated that the mother's emotional problems inhibited her in her relationship with Alex. Alex thus did not have to see his mom if he didn't want to. Visitation was scheduled for one weekend a month and every other holiday. My lawyer explained, that I needed to make the easiest possible transition for the children's emotional well being. I choked back the tears, while numbness ebbed over my entire being as his final words trailed with the stipulation that I had a little more than 2 weeks with them before their custody was handed over to Eric. Why would he give me two weeks more with my children, if he thought I was unstable?

Eric had his revenge! He had taken the children I loved and devoted my entire life to, all because of he and his friends slanderous remarks. Proverbs 11:9a, "You can be ruined by the talk of godless people."

Tori took me in her arms and insisted that I fight! She whispered that God's glory would be seen in this and that we weren't giving the children back. We would run before giving them into the hands of a man who defiled the laws of God and built hatred and ignored love. She further stated that the judge was paid off and pressured by people's bigotry. We had to fight or we would disobey God's word if we allowed a man to have his slanderous and evil ways pressed upon small children's minds. Her words gave me strength, and a fire burned in both of us to fight a bad judge using the laws for his own political gain. In complete unison of Spirit we felt that we had no choice but to take my kids and run.

The next day, I called my attorney requesting an appeal! We had time before we would leave, but we needed direction as to where to go and what to do and assurance that the legal matters were being fought. My lawyer went through a lengthy explanation over the court of appeals and concluded that until the memorandum was put into an order and decreed, he couldn't start the appeal.

This I later discovered was an outright lie. The document was legal and the appeal could be directly made on it, but he too was shocked over the severity of the court order and he didn't want anything more to do with my case. He didn't care about the injustice of the decree, he just didn't want to deal with a client who could possibly be a homosexual. Furthermore, he stated that once the document was put into an order, the appeal would take up to two years, before a new decision could be made. Each word stung and gave new affirmation that Tori and I were doing the right thing by fleeing with the children.

Tori and I at different times had been in contact with a minister of a gay church. Every conversation had resulted with him several times pushing for us to take our children and run. But we insisted that we had to fight it legally. He explained about his own divorce involving children and how he kept them from being taken away, because he knew about the underground. By using his underground connections, he threatened his wife if she ever tried to keep the kids away from him he would take them and run.

This might have been good for him, but I knew nothing about the underground and although his words gave me hope, he couldn't give me any answers of where I might find this help. He was openly gay, but most gays aren't open and the longer my custody fight for my children continued, the more I understood why they were closeted.

Our heads spun as we worked on details to move. To take our double wide would cost around $10,000. We couldn't believe it! To move our furniture and rent an apartment in a big city would cost around $3,000 depending on whether we had someone move it or moving it ourselves. I knew in the back of my mind that it would be dangerous to move it anyway, especially when the trail would be so easy to follow. So Tori and I just didn't talk about what we were giving up by leaving our beautiful home behind. For we were driven with only one purpose, which was to keep my children from being turned over completely to their dad.

Tori's parents were shocked over the result of my hearing, and they were easily convinced that Mark was right, when he said that he felt I had no choice, but to run with the kids. Tori continued by stating that Mark was furious at what they had done, and he wanted Tori to move to Virginia, because he didn't trust the court system in our county as far as Brad's custody was concerned. Her parents agreed that this was a good idea and made plans to follow Tori in a month.

Phone calls were made arranging a moving van, house, and information on job availabilities. Tori and her parents started busily packing and preparing for the new and exciting move. All the while we were very careful not to let on to my children that they were coming with us too, so I made up the story that I was going to move to Lawrence to be near my fiance who was a scout for O.U.

There were problems that had to be solved before all of our plans could be completed, and one of them was the fact that in July, Tori took on a foreign exchange student from Italy saying that he was Mark's nephew to her parents and he needed to leave Italy for safety purposes. Her parents readily agreed that Tori should take on this responsibility, and Max came to live with Tori. He was more than just another front for Tori's parents that Mark truly was alive, but he represented stability that we were a family. We so craved to be allowed to be like everyone else. So in an effort to have our move run smoothly, we contacted the foreign exchange student advisor and were given approval to take him with us.

In July before Max came, Tori and I took our children to the circus. We went in separate cars, because Tori's parents came along too and so she arrived back at the double wide shortly before I did. To her alarm the front door was open to the house and she caught a glimpse of someone flying out the back door. A month before, Tori and I had bought a gun for our protection. When I reached the scene, Tori was standing with the gun, shaking in her hand, while she surveyed the house for any other signs of life. Her face was white and she was trembling with shock that someone would find it so necessary to search our home. Quickly, I conducted my own investigation of the house, holding on to Richard's bat. I couldn't find anything missing at first, but later we discovered that the Foreign Exchange file on Max was gone. It wasn't hard to know who was behind this, it had to be Eric and his friends! Soon after Max's arrival, Tori took Max to the grocery store and was met by a lady from the S.B.C. Immediately she questioned Tori over why she had a foreign exchange student? Ignoring her, Tori instantly knew that who ever invaded her house and stole the file, had to be connected with the S.B.C. for up until now our children believed that Max was family.

My court was the 12th of Aug. and the children were to be handed over to their dad the 27th. I made additional calls to my attorney and every time I called, he was away from his desk. I asked the secretary if he had sent any appeals to the court system and she answered that she didn't think so. I left messages for him to call any of 3 different phone numbers, but I received no response. So feeling completely abandoned by my lawyer, not to mention the legal system in general, the next day I took it upon myself to have my file copied and all court proceedings as well. Soon I learned that it would cost an estimate of $1,800 for all court proceedings and none could be copied for up to a month. I pressed, saying I would pay, knowing that I needed these documents to substantiate my reasons for appealing to whoever, I could convince to take up my cause from here.

Tori and I were desperate for money and I went to my grandmother hoping that she would lend me some, so I could pay for the copying of the court records for the appeals court. She refused. Even my parents refused to pay me the money they owed me for the satellite dish they had purchased from Eric and I when we were married.

I had a small piece of land connected to my parents

property. I tried to sell it for what it was worth, but I couldn't get any takers. So I put it in the paper for $1000 or best offer. Instantly, I had a taker two nights before we were supposed to leave. But the next day they refused to take it on the divorce decree alone, so with yet another problem to solve I contacted the courthouse in an effort to get a clear title. They said that I would have to come in and they would see what they could do. Reluctantly, I said that I would come in first thing in the morning.

That same day, I tentatively sold the land, another problem developed. The SBC got whiff of Tori moving. In an effort to cover our tracks, we secretly contacted another moving truck company so we could move to Portland, Oregon, instead of Virginia where we originally planned to go. But the only way to move was to do it ourselves and Tori's dad had to go to a big city, 2 1/2 hours away to pick up the truck. Fortunately, he was so convinced about Mark that anything that we wanted to do was just fine with him.

All week long we were packing all our precious belongings into boxes excited that the day was finally upon us to depart to the promised land. The very first thing in the morning Bill was there with the moving van. He and Max began the tedious task of loading. Meanwhile, unbeknown to the packers, my children and I headed to the courthouse to get a clear title on the land and a copy of my file. It wasn't long before a wall once again blocked my passage and I was informed that it would be Friday before my file could be copied and it would cost $88. Sighing with quiet rejection, I exited the County Clerk's office and ran head first into Helen.

She motioned me to her office and while the kids sat outside she handed me a paper stating that if she felt I was going to run, she could take the kids, now! Apparently, my mother suspicious after she had received phone calls from my brothers, that I would do something rash and run, late last night had called and informed her of this fact. Not only was she called by my mother, but it seemed that she was being bombarded with phone calls from Eric and the SBC, that a moving van was at Tori's very early this morning and she wanted to know, Now! What was going on?

Almost swallowing my tongue and feeling suddenly like my legs were turning to rubber, I assured her that I was appealing. Right now, I was at the courthouse for the very reason of getting my filed copied. Hoping that I looked convincing, I quietly replied that I had no intention of running and she would have to ask Tori where she was going . I was not her keeper contrary to what Eric might have told her. Eying me suspiciously, she allowed me to leave only after taking the children aside for a can of coke and leisurely asking them if they were ready to go to their father's. They nodded their heads and off we went.

Immediately, I left eager to finalize the selling of the land and leave Winfield forever. Still it was going to be difficult for the courthouse explained that in order to get a clear title, Eric was going to have to personally sign his name on the dotted line. I called my buyer's lawyer from the courthouse informing him of this fact and to my surprise he had already personally asked Eric to sign over what was rightfully mine the day before and of course Eric refused. Not only had he appealed to Eric about the signing, but he had called the courthouse and was informed that they had no power to make Eric do this and that this was a matter that had to be handled by our attorneys. Dejectedly, I quietly hung up the phone, knowing that this could take months, before it could be resolved.

Looking at my children, I gained new strength to proceed as planned and for the first time in the privacy of our car, I confessed my plans to take them with me. They responded with open enthusiasm. Gaining encouragement from their faces, I ignored the second barrier of my early morning and proceeded to drive to a city in the opposite direction from our intended rendezvous, to pick up our new car, that I had purchased earlier in the month.

Meanwhile, Tori was having problems of her own.

The head of the foreign exchange student program had showed up on her doorstep that afternoon with over 24 letters contesting her as a sponsor. She immediately took charge of Max, stating that if Tori had taken him over the state line, she would have been charged with kidnapping. Everyone started crying, Max who had been like a member of our family for over a month was suddenly ripped away and Brad was crushed and confused that he was losing his big brother. Tori's eyes stung with tears after his departure. We had learned to love him and he loved us in return, but again hate over Tori and I conquered, and a third barrier wall emerged sharply, trying to stop our flight.

Arrangements had been made for Tori and I to rendezvous in Hays. Her dad was going to be driving the moving van with her following in his pickup. From there Tori's bodyguard would then take over and drive the truck to Oregon. The mafia image she instilled in her parents was so important to make our escape easier that soon Dimitri was invented as a bodyguard for Tori, because Mark was very high up, next in line to the Godfather, and it was necessary that she be protected for his safety. To complete the mafia picture, Tori also stated that if she didn't talk directly with Mark, then she would receive messages from Dimitri concerning what Mark wanted her to do. This furthered our front and complied with the family secrecy.

By the middle of the afternoon Helen was starting to panic, because I was nowhere to be found in town and with two policemen she knocked on Doris's door demanding to know where I was. In her hand she waved the document that she had showed me that very morning in Doris's face. Doris bristled, flatly stating she didn't know and gave her a piece of her mind about the SBC spying on them and her daughter and that she wanted it stopped. During the entire moving process, members of the SBC paraded by the mobile home. Some even parked their cars across a ravine to watch Bill's comings and goings with binoculars. Helen quickly backed off

75

realizing that Doris wasn't going to tell her, even if she knew.

Lather that same night, meeting at the mall of our chosen destination, Tori arrived, white faced and crying. Her words were mumbled at first so my children couldn't understand what she was saying, but slowly the story unfolded. Panicked by what had taken place, just before she left, she begged me to go back to Winfield, before they carried out their threat and took Brad. I couldn't help but wonder, how the police could take Brad without proof that Tori and I were together with my kids? But Tori was in such a state of fear, I knew I had to calm her down, somehow, in order to be able to keep going forward. Mustering all my faith, I reaffirmed to Tori that God would help us! I knew I was visibly shaken too, but I just couldn't stop now, I had to be determined! The judge's ruling was terribly unfair! I had to continue on!

Together we decided to lay low until late night and so we rented a room with two double beds. Tori quickly contacted her parents and they quieted her fears by stating that they were taking Brad out of town, at least until everything calmed down. Tori felt much better with this news and once again became supportive to my cause.

Just like the police never followed Tori out of town, they didn't follow her parents. Although for the first 20 miles, Eric followed them, but then as quickly as he had begun, he ended his journey. Upon hearing this, we immediately felt confident enough for us to proceed as planned.

At 2:00 a.m. we hopped into our vehicles and started our pilgrimage. The children exhausted, soon fell asleep and after several hours of driving we hit Portland, with a truck full of furniture and nowhere to live.

Quickly finding the nearest restaurant we pulled over to go through a paper. All day we looked for an apartment, house, anything. We came back defeated, paid for a night's sleep at an economical motel and again called for additional housing. We had until Sunday to return the truck and move into a house and since we left on Friday,

76

we only had one more day left.

As the new day dawned, I was more optimistic that today would be the day that a home would be located. It wasn't long before Tori located a third floor apartment via the morning paper. Shortly after talking to the landlord we got into our car and headed in it's direction. They were asking $900 a month and both, Tori and I swallowed hard, but we felt we had no choice, time was running out on the use of the moving van.

In the car, I lectured everyone that God would lead us, and when we looked at it we were to be open-minded. The apartment was in a slum area! I was mad, I had had it with people, who told us what a lovely home they had and how it was in such a perfect location. All day yesterday, we had looked at one house after another and none of them began to come close to fulfilling our needs. I was sick and tired of wasting our time! Since the time we had been looking, Tori had made all the phone calls up until now and this time I went through the paper and I talked to the landlord. I explained to him what I'd seen, and that I wanted to know the truth. I was so persistent with my demands for the facts that immediately he stated that he thought it was a nice house. He quickly described a 3,000 square feet, four bedroom home, with a pool, and a sun room with a sauna. I was not impressed. This was $100 more than the slum apartment, and I wasn't trusting anyone. Together, Tori and I decided to have a look, just the same.

Rounding the curve we pulled up into a plush neighborhood. Here was this gorgeous house, with a huge pool and exquisite inside and out. Fireplaces in the living room and family room, and the biggest master bedroom I had ever seen. It was perfect! We rented it on the spot with no credit check and by evening our furniture was moved, thanks to some really nice neighbors.

I had never been 'wanted' before and it was scary. Not only was I endanger of being arrested, but Tori could be arrested too. Realizing our predicament, we decided to stock pile. So we wrote checks on the North side of town a good 30 miles away from our newly rented home for everything we thought we needed. Portland had over 2 million people and we felt safe with this decision. Our rent, phone, and everything was under a false name and we immediately called each other by these names too. The children had a good time picking their names, oblivious to the repercussions that could occur from our flight. I'm not sure that I understood what could happen either, but just the same, this had to be done so Richard and Crystal Bovard became Tori's new children, Tori became Victoria Bovard and I took Elizabeth Barrett. Brad came at the end of the week with Pa and Gram and after they left to return to Winfield, we joined the family.

After Tori's parents returned home, the children and I left our small rented motel room and joined them at our new home. Brad ran into my arms, enthusiastic over our appearance and glad that all of the stories he had heard about where we were; was not true.

I had come to love Brad, just like he was my own son. In the past, when I first walked out on Eric, Brad helped fill the void on not having my own kids to care for on a daily basis. A special bond formed between us, and soon I took over as his other parent. At times, I felt as if I loved him more than my own flesh and blood, because he didn't have a father telling him bad things about me and because of this he trusted me completely. Sometimes he would slip and call me mom. When the court decision came giving Eric sole custody, Brad was informed by his grandparents that Elizabeth and the kids were going far away and they would never see us again. Brad cried hysterically, begging Tori later that even if you take Richard and Crystal, please don't take my Elizabeth. That same night, he refused to go asleep, the tears kept flowing down his cheeks and he begged me not to leave him. I whispered in his ear that I was going to tell him a secret that he couldn't share with anyone. I promised him that I would never leave him and we would all run together. He gave me a big hug and kiss and went to sleep.

During all of my court proceedings and the

continued front for Tori's parents, Brad kept all secrets of Richard's, Crystal's and my existence from his grandparents. No matter how much he was prodded from Gram, he pretended to never see us at all, except on special occasions. This was necessary because of all the talk in town. Tori explained to him that if he told, he would never be able to see me. Brad loved me and even his small 5 year old mind confirmed, I was just as much his mother as Tori. He would never let anyone take me away and he proved this time and time again!

Tori enrolled Brad in kindergarten, and she enrolled Crystal in another school. We decided to teach Richard at home. We were in contact with a psychologist and hired a new lawyer to fight the court decision so we could gain custody of Alex. He assured us that we wouldn't get anymore than a slap on the hand if we were caught. He suggested that we change the children's hair color and appearance and get them all in school. He also stipulated that we should go to church and behave as normally as possible, but keep a low profile. Tori and I quickly did as he instructed and we quickly found jobs and tried to locate a piano so Tori could give lessons.

In Winfield, the town was in a panic and all of the pressures from outrunning was totally directed at Tori's parents. The police were coming 10 times a day to harass them and make threats that Tori would have a bond on her head if she didn't call and tell them where she was. The threats scared them to death and Doris made several phone calls directly to Tori's house. I was mortified, I knew phone calls could be traced and I warned Tori. Then Tori's parents started taking extra precautions, calling from pay phones, taking back routes to Oregon, and not telling a single soul where Tori could be found. They pretended that they had not heard from Tori, except for the fact that she said she was somewhere in Roanoke.

The SBC followed them around in shifts. Bill was watched for hours as he finished carpentry jobs. Literally the talk of my running with the kids hit town like a tidal wave and from this it was assumed that Bill was harboring us. With this in mind the town's people took it upon themselves to hand out punishment by firing him from every carpentry job he had, or refusing to pay him for jobs he had already done. The air was so thick with gossip around them that it made it hard for them to breathe or even exist. Winfield was making it quite clear that they weren't wanted in their community, anymore!

Tori and I were having a hard time too. Richard couldn't be trusted! He watched signs, he remembered addresses, he even told me which way to turn. Nothing evaded his attention. He listened to every word we said and gave his opinion. It was like having a do it yourself spy. Richard had the power to underhandedly call his dad and this terrified us. Rich had always been Eric's favorite. Even though Richard had no wish to live with his dad, he also knew that Eric wasn't a real threat to him. If we were found, so what! He'd work in the upholstery shop, it was good for him! I could just hear the words drilled into him by his dad. Constant reminders of what his dad did to him, just brought passive responses. Maybe Richard was being realistic to protect himself, but his words made my legs rubbery.

Another problem we faced was our car's tag. Everything was in my name; insurance, registration, and payment books. When Tori and I left we never thought about payments, just fleeing. Our mail if redirected to us could lead the police, but if we didn't pay our bills, what were the creditors going to do? Our attorney said to pay them, and I wondered seriously if he'd ever been on the run! We already paid him almost all our money in a retainer fee and he thought we had money for bills? Next was our social security numbers, every job available wanted these and drivers licenses as well. Fortunately, God led us to a job that we were able to work as self-employed and thankfully our numbers were not required.

Our phone number had to be changed, because of contacts with Bill and Doris directly. Explaining and making up lies to everyone is very stressful and even if an operator is understanding, you're constantly wondering if they'll discover that your giving them false information. No matter how careful you are, there was always something to worry about.

We also had the added expense of getting all new clothes for all of us in order to not be recognized and the burden of dying our hair to complete our disguise. Crystal and Brad loved it, but Richard was growing bored daily. Our trusted lawyer kept telling us to relax as we frantically dialed his phone number for the tenth time that day.

In moving, we had left our grand piano behind and my upholstery sewing matching. How we regretted this! Tori and her parents were unable to move the piano because of its weight and a $35,000 piano takes a lot of special care. So we called our creditor explaining our predicament and to our surprise the police, Eric, and piano movers were in our house repossessing it that very moment.

Eric stopped at nothing to seek revenge against me for fleeing. He was alerting our creditors along with the county attorney, informing them we had run with their stuff and that we had no intentions of ever paying. Thus an investigation into our finances was raising a war of questions.

Our creditors were stopping at nothing to repossess everything we had, even though we had faithfully been making payments. The double wide was being repossessed by the end of the month. When Doris and Bill went over to get the rest of Tori's things to be moved later, they discovered that the few things in the house that were left, had been dumped and torn through with a court order tossed on the floor showing authority.

Since our lawyer told us to make the creditors happy, we began making phone calls, telling as much as the truth that we could and stalling for time. Most of our money up to now was spent and unfortunately, money or repossessing was the only thing they wanted. With this in mind, we felt we had no choice, but to put Richard in school so we could dig in without him listening, watching, and taking notes on everything we did. I warned him extensively about the harm he could do to me if he told anyone the truth. And I felt hesitant to let him be with other people, but I thought that for now, he could be trusted.

As a parent, teaching my children was very important, truth was essential. When Eric preached about sin and lies, he in effect wanted the children to talk about everything I was doing so he could put more pressure of doubt into their minds about Tori and my relationship. He also used what they said to influence the CSO and SBC. Every truth he ever exposed was for his own gain. Putting our children in the place of being a judge was wrong. They emotionally and physically couldn't handle it. Confronting Richard with this, I explained that Eric used him to hurt me. I told him a simple truth, "If anyone teaches you to hate, and not love, then they're not following God." Richard liked this answer and I could almost see the heavy pack on his shoulders dissolving. Eric had used all the truths to breed pure, adulterated hate. God says to love our enemies and to do good to those that hate you. Holding, these words close to my heart, I realized just how blind Eric was to God's teaching. He wasn't only spreading hate in himself and our children, but he was teaching a whole church and my parents how to hate too. Romans 11:8-10, "As the scripture says, 'God made their minds and hearts dull; to this very day they cannot see or hear." And David says "May they be caught and trapped at their feasts; may they fall, may they be punished! May their eyes be blinded so that they cannot see; and make them bend under their troubles at all times." When a person does not truly know God, they can not see how their very actions can testify against them. Eric was not only violent against me, but he had waged an all out war for custody of our children that was meant for my destruction. He was so vengeful in fact, that he was even willing to sacrifice his children's well being, just for the sake of winning. God specifically tells us to love others as we love ourselves. When we don't follow His commands, our minds become blind to the truth. James 3:14-18, "But if in your heart you are jealous, bitter, and selfish, don't sin against the truth by boasting of your wisdom. Such wisdom does not come down from heaven; it belongs to the world, it is unspiritual and demonic. Where there is jealousy and selfishness, there is also disorder and every kind of evil. But the wisdom from above is pure first of all; it is also peaceful, gentle, and friendly; it is full of compassion and produces a harvest of good deeds; it is free from prejudice and hypocrisy. And goodness is the harvest that is produced from the seeds the peacemakers plant in peace." You can not call yourself a Christian and turn around and be bitter and hateful against homosexuals!

We needed money so we could live and with this in mind, we started making phone calls explaining everything and pleading for help from any gay organization we could find through the yellow pages and help lines. Many rallied with sympathy to our support, but no funds existed to aid in our dilemma. Most of the gay community was so closeted from their own persecutions, that they were not unified to help anyone in a desperate situation, because there was no one to communicate to them the problem.

When everything seemed hopeless it became even worse, our landlord showed up unexpectedly. Tori's parents left their dog temporarily in our care, but the agreement with our landlord was no pets. She questioned the presence of the dog and why we changed the locks on our door and why we changed our phone number? Tori wasn't there and I assured her that I couldn't answer the questions, because I didn't live in the house, but she pressed. She looked at Brad and mentioned how tall he was and how Crystal was so small. By the time she left, I knew that our conversation had not gone well and I prayed that Tori would return soon. Within 30 minutes, Tori returned and quickly called her back to explain, but by now the landlady wouldn't listen. She stated that there wasn't to be any pets and we had 10 days to get out. We were shocked. Our whole world was falling down around us. We weren't prepared for this!

Tori called her parents and they were mortified. They were moving the next day and along with the pressures of the police and SBC everything looked impossible. Now with this added problem, how were we going to do it? We had been holding enough money back, just to cover next month's rent.

Scanning the newspapers, all the while praying, we found a house. It would have to do. It wasn't as nice as this one, but it was OK and less rent, which was a plus! Our motto was when all else fails, Pray! Pray! And Pray some more! God strengthened us and the next two days we spent packing and moving. I was constantly asking Tori how she felt, I was so afraid of what all the stress and lifting was causing on her heart. And indeed it was, but she refused to show anything more than strength.

How much I loved Tori. If I was unsure, she would gently prod me along hugging me and encouraging me that God would be victor. And in her weakness, I became her strength. We balanced perfectly together. I could not imagine why anyone could ever find anything wrong with our relationship? It was just like a normal married couple, except for all of the intense persecutions that we were suffering.

Several times in the midst of our mounting problems, I had called back to the CSO, hoping that something could be worked out if I should willingly take my children back to Eric. I hated hiding, and if they would give me more liberal visitation it would have been better than this constant fear. But everyone was totally unbending, they even refused to give stipulated visitation on the one weekend a month that was written in the memorandum. On top of this they refused to tell me how much trouble I was in by not following the decree. Either it was totally their way or they wouldn't budge. Feeling in a corner, I felt I had no choice, but to follow my lawyer's instructions and wait for the next court.

Along with these mounting pressures, Tori still

had to keep up the front of Mark and she was responsible to find a home for her parents to move into. We had no choice, but to use my credit rating in order to secure a rental home for them and praise the Lord, everything went smoothly. Of course this was two weeks earlier, before we were told to move from our landlady. And playing it safe, we chose a location that was several miles away from where we were living, just in case anything should happen. Yet I knew, that we were playing Russian Roulette by using my credit, and I informed Tori about my feelings. Unfortunately, she was so stressed over our money running out and the problem that her parents might try to move in with her, that she wasn't thinking straight any longer. So once again the day of our moving, Tori pleaded with me to allow her to use my credit to secure a piano so she could teach. Her fear had consumed her to the breaking point and with a great deal of hesitancy on my part, I allowed her to try, but I stressed that she should proceed with caution. Fear surrounded me and I could hardly take a breath, when she relayed the story of them stalling her on the phone and asking her again to verify our address. We immediately became suspicious, but with all of the moving that needed to be done, we put it on the back burner hoping that God would cover our terrible mistake.

After most of the moving was finished, there were a few things left at the old house that needed to be picked up and Bill volunteered to help Tori with these after supper. Richard had a program at school and Crystal and I were going to the mall so Pa and Gram wouldn't see us. I called from a pay phone to see how things were going and Tori said they were just starting and I should be able to come home in less than an hour.

Crystal and I picked up some pop and lunch boxes for her and Richard at school. An hour passed and I couldn't get Tori at either phones. Then another hour passed and I was worried. We drove our car to the new house cautiously, but no one was there. I was surprised, so we drove to the old house and went just far enough to see lights. I was afraid that we would be seen by Pa and Gram, so carefully I drove around a different way. To my terror there were 4 police cars in front of the house and Tori was standing in front of the house in handcuffs in an apparent heated discussion with a cop. I cried to God, expressing my unbelief that this was really happening! I was shaking convulsively and quickly turning my car around, I prayed that God would help me decide what to do, but before I could think about my next move, a police car spotted my retreat and I knew I had to yield to his lights and siren. He motioned for me to follow him as another car pulled up behind me to keep me from escaping his command. Tears flowed from my eyes as I feared that not only had I been discovered by the police, but that I had blown Tori's and my front, wide open regarding her parents. God help me, I begged over and over again as our small caravan pulled up in front of the house, where Tori and her parents waited. Bill was sitting in his pickup with Brad, talking with a police officer and Doris was talking to Tori. Before I was commanded to get out of my car, Tori was placed in the back of a police car that was pulled up in the driveway of our former house. Moments later, and to my utter shock, Doris was handcuffed and placed in the back seat with her.

Rising from inside my car, I grabbed Crystal into my arms and hugged her tight. A police officer immediately pried her way from me and placed her in a police car with another officer. By now, I had regained some of my composure and to my surprise, I was basically left outside my car, while one of the over ten officers present, barked commands for Tori's dad to be handcuffed and placed in one of the other cars. Socked over this turn of events, I asked one of the officers beside me what was going on and I was informed that they had just confirmed a warrant from Winfield for the arrest of Bill and Doris, too. My face grew pale as I tried to explain to them they had nothing to do with this and that they were making a mistake, but they wouldn't listen. I immediately tried to walk over to Tori's car to find out how she was handling

this news and to question her on what we were to do? But
an officer restrained me and at once they frisked my body
and recited word for word everything we had been doing in
Portland and the fact that Richard was being picked up
from school that very moment. I questioned him on what
would happen to my children and he blurted out that my
children and Brad were being taken to Social Services.
Immediately following these words and before this
information had fully sunk into my being, I was
instructed to get into another car separate from Tori's and
Bill's for we were going to jail!

CHAPTER SEVEN

The cold concrete of the massive building dominated my view. A chill waved over my consciousness as my worst nightmare erupted into reality. At once the officer driving my car called into his radio requesting the doors opened and immediately they responded and our cars drove into an underground garage. Opening the door to each of our cars, we were directed together into the main entrance of the facility. The doors were quickly locked behind us as if there was a chance that at any moment one of us would run for freedom, like a convicted murderer. The police were indifferent to my thoughts and continued to prod us towards a group of windows. With our handcuffs still securely on our wrists, they commanded us to empty our pockets and to hand over all of our jewelry, money and purses. Everything was inspected and logged and a paper was thrust into each of our face's for verification by signature of what they had taken.

A few minutes after our incarceration began, a man obviously high on drugs was dragged in by another police officer. He had been arrested with a bag of marijuana in his possession. My muscles tensed as the two officers in charge of him roughly threw him into what was called a holding cell. I felt as if I was watching a drama on TV, not quite believing what I was seeing. The man responded to their gruffness with a defying shout calling them 'a pig' and other vulgar profanities. The two officers responded with a command for him to be quiet, but he refused. Without hesitation one officer grabbed his hair and handcuffs and jerked at them while the other officer put his knee into the man's back pushing him forcefully to the floor. The man screamed out in pain and pleaded for them to stop. To my further shock they did this several more times and abruptly dropped him on the floor like a discarded wad of paper. He didn't talk after that.

I took a deep breath as my senses became keenly aware of the reality of my present situation and to my shock completing the booking they read off our crimes. Quietly, I prayed for God's protection and strength as my ears grew hot in disbelief from the hard cold reality that we were being arrested on fugitive warrants out of Utah with NO BONDS! I couldn't believe what they were saying! There was no possibility of us getting out of jail until Winfield came and picked us up. without any further instructions, we were each taken separately, deeper into the massive building into yet another larger holding area. Several officers were busily working at their desks and in the center of the room was a photograph camera and screen. To the right side of the room there were more concrete cells with small windows in the doors.

Within a short period of time, they removed my handcuffs, I rubbed my wrists softly, while trying to regain back their circulation and ease the discomfort inflicted from the swelling, because of the tightness of my cuffs. As I looked around the room my eyes immediately focused on Tori, she was talking to an officer more towards the middle of the room and Doris and Bill were quietly standing beside her. I was commanded to take off my shoes and socks and stand against a wall, while they inspected them carefully. Satisfied, I was given permission to put them back on.

The gravity of our situation sent fear parading into my consciousness that Mark's front would come crashing all around Tori and I. Now Brad's custody along with my children's would be in jeopardy! Waves of terror raced through my already trembling body as I quietly and humbly surveyed my companions. Doris looked white and very out of place as she was instructed to go into a cell. Bill looked twice his age and helpless as he humbly submitted to an officer's instruction for him to go into another cell that was down at the opposite end of the row of cells. Tori looked frightened, but she seemed

89

determined to find out what steps she needed to take to get us out of here as quickly as possible. She was already braving the way with a barrage of questions, which the police at times would answer.

Next I was fingerprinted and then placed in another cell. To my surprise on one of the walls a phone was hung. Looking at the phone, I tried to think of a number, but my mind only drew a blank. I couldn't even think of my attorney's name. I was concerned and worried over Richard & Crystal. My imagination over the fears that must have gone through Richard's head after he was picked up by the police made me wish that I was there telling him everything was going to be OK. And what about my precious Crystal? Where were they in Social Services? The only answers the police would give was that their dad was on his way. That scared me even more. What was going to happen to Brad? Please God don't let Alan get him, I prayed. Why were the Bovard's here? They're innocent! I didn't understand what was happening.

I swallowed hard and the only phone number that came to mind was my parents number, so I dialed collect. Mom responded coolly to my call informing me that she knew I'd been caught. Apparently they were at a church party and Eric called to tell the news and cheering roared through the entire room. Her words stung, sending my heart plummeting to my toes. The tone of her voice changed abruptly from her remembrance of the embarrassment I had caused her at the meeting and she hung up the phone with a slam!

Once again the police came and took yet another set of fingerprints and this time I was put in the same cell with Doris. She was on the phone with her parents. For some reason she managed to get through the first holding cell without anyone noticing her small address book and a single comb. She pressed her hand against the receiver on the phone to smile and say that she, Bill and Tori were keeping in contact via her parent's phone number. Immediately she continued her phone call giving great details on the phone to her parents of how they had protected everyone from the fact that Tori had been going with a man from the Mafia. She explained that Tori had tried to break her engagement and Mark said if she did, he would make sure she never talked. She was so serious as she spoke each word, that I turned my face to hide my relief that once again Tori had covered our tracks with her parents. With a short goodbye, Doris hung up the phone.

Doris's face registered exhaustion as she turned her attention to me and stated that Tori had a lawyer and was trying to get Brad out of Social Services. Quietly I sat down beside her as she explained that Mark had set us up. Before she could say anything further, Tori came into our cell holding a kleenex in her hand, while trying to wipe off the ink from her fingers. The guard motioned for Doris to come out to be fingerprinted again.

Once alone Tori reached over and gave my hand a squeeze and explained what had happened. Evidently our former landlords had become suspicious and called the police to check us out. Soon the story unfolded of the kidnapping and the police immediately responded by checking out the house we had rented for three short weeks. Finding us already gone they were informed by the neighborhood that a moving truck had just moved our furniture. Contacting the moving company they found out our destination and checked out the location of our new home. By then we had gone and Tori showed up with her parents and Brad to the old home to finish getting a few odds and ends that the movers had not taken. Once the neighbors discovered her presence they called the police. Before Tori and her parents knew what was happening, the house was surrounded.

The police took Tori aside and demanded that she tell where I was and my children. In fear she denied knowing, but after more than an hour of threats over what they would do to Brad and her parents, she told them that Rich was in school and that's how Rich was picked up.

Sitting where I could look into Tori's face, I could see the sadness fill her eyes at the thought that she had betrayed me. I reaffirmed that she had no choice and that it was OK. Quietly, she cleared her throat and wiped back the tears that were fighting to make their way onto her cheeks. With a quick breath, she began filling me in on what she had been doing to protect Brad from Alan and to get us out of jail. An officer had explained to her that it was best to use the phone while she was in here, because once all of us were put into jail, we would share the phone with 15 other women. He was also quite helpful by getting her a phone book and explaining that we would be in these holding cells for around six hours. Once obtaining the phone book, she found a lawyer and her grandparents using their credit card secured his services with a $500 retainer. All in all her grandparent's fell hook, line and sinker into the story of the mafia. And with her parents further support, they rallied to their rescue. Everyone was very fearful that Brad's father would be informed by Eric and that he would use this to try to get Brad, so they knew that speed was of the essence to protect their grandchild. Tori took a deep breath, just as Doris was once again ushered back into the cell. Quickly Doris prompted her to pick up the phone and reaffirm the retainer with the attorney and work out the long details of her grandparents coming to Portland to rescue them from jail and Brad from Social Services.

I quietly surveyed the room. It was six feet by eight feet with a small sink and toilet in one corner and with a cement slab along the six foot side of the room for us to sit on. The pay phone was bolted in one of the corners from where we sat. Doris positioned herself between us and together she and Tori huddled together, while first talking to their new found attorney and then to Doris's parents. My thoughts turned to visions, parading before my eyes of Brad with his teddy bear clinched tightly to his breast and sweet little Crystal in the back of a police car. Tears clouded my vision and I turned my face away from Tori and her mom so they wouldn't notice. Again the policeman returned and each of us in turn were fingerprinted a third time and then photographed.

I was last to be taken and looking out the tiny

window, I saw Bill going to another cell and then coming out wearing orange jail clothes. Next I caught a glimpse of Doris. She looked so small and completely foreign to her surroundings in her orange clothes. It wasn't long before Tori paraded out wearing the same fashions. She looked humble, but I could see a small glint of a stubborn streak in her eyes.

My turn came and I was ushered into a cell that had a shower, a stool, and a large window open to a room full of orange jail clothes and shoes. I was told to take off my clothes and hand them to the guard. Once naked she instructed me to bend over, cough, spread my legs, lift my breasts, raise each arm and each foot. She gave me a towel and told me to take a shower and put the orange clothes on. I was humiliated and thoughts that I was just a mother, kept going through my head as tears flowed down my cheeks in the shower. Stubbornly, but submissively I went back to join Doris and Tori. The room was quiet when I entered with each of us separating into our own world's, while thoughts of what we had so far endured, were embedding scars into our minds.

By now it was two o'clock in the morning and we were exhausted. The guard ushered us into yet another area of the jail where we were then taken by 2's into yet another cement holding cell and given a blanket, 2 sheets, and a small towel with soap, tooth brush, and tooth paste. This cell was the same as the others, except the cement was wider with a 1 1/2" mattress and small pillow.

Tori's cell was next to mine and a small room with a shared shower was in front of our cells, separating us from the hallway that we had just passed through. Soon we discovered that we would be in these cells until we were evaluated and given what they called dog collars, which were bands put on our wrists showing if we were minimum, medium or maximum security. I was exhausted physically from moving all day and mentally from everything we'd been through. it was 3:00 in the morning now and laying on the hard cement wasn't easy. I kept pleading with God to get us out of here. I fell into a fitful sleep, just long enough for a woman guard to come and get me from my cell. Going through the door, I looked back to see Tori in her cell all curled up in a ball asleep. I longed to touch her and give her comfort from the fears that I knew she was experiencing too.

Following the guard we went around a corner to a small glass wired room. Doris sat talking to a lady, who appeared to be a nurse. All along the L shaped hallway were doors with additional cells. A guard sat behind a half cement enclosure in the middle of the L, so he could view the entire hallway on both sides. There were phones, a computer, and lots of switches at his command. A dread ebbed through my entire body as the realization hit me that I wasn't in jail; I was in prison! I wrapped my arms around me trying to get warm from the cold hard interior of my surroundings. Doris weakly smiled as she passed by. Her face mirrored words of hopelessness and I knew that she was afraid to talk.

The nurse asked me general questions and took my blood pressure. I answered them as short as I could and pleaded for another blanket or for the heat to be turned up. She politely said that they kept it cool for a reason and unless I had health problems and it was recommended by a doctor, I couldn't have another blanket. I was taken back to my room and Tori sleepily walked by hugging her arms to get warm.

At six, I asked to use the phone to call my lawyer. It was Saturday, but he said that he would be in early and we could talk. During our rush of phone calls during the night, we were able to get his phone number. I explained what had happened and he couldn't believe his ears. He said first thing Monday, he would be in contact with the county attorney. I pleaded with him to get us out, but he explained he couldn't do anything until after the weekend. I hung up the phone wishing that he was in here and then he'd understand why I wanted all of us out. This wasn't fair! I'm just a mother!

Breakfast was served, consisting of a donut and a cup of coffee. shortly after we ate, each of us saw a psychologist. Tori went before I did and yelling through her cell across to my cell she explained that it was important for me to act mild and answer the questions as respectively as possible. She was being placed in minimum security along with her mother.

The guard came and I was directed to the psychologist. It was the same room I had been in before, where I had previously talked to the nurse. He was nice and I asked him if there was anyway I could find out how my kids were. He explained that Tori asked the same question and that he couldn't find out, unless we knew which social worker was assigned their case. Sighing, I stated, I didn't even know where they were, much less the social worker. I asked for a Bible and he said he could help me with that later. Trying to ease my mind over my situation, he started asking me Bible trivia in between other questions. My brain had other things on its mind, not trivia and I he-hawed around saying nothing. He asked if I was a homosexual. I said no, and he explained I would be put in minimal security. I was then taken back to my room.

The guard soon came and commanded us through the intercom system that was heard in each of the cells, to strip everything off our bed, for we were being moved to minimum lockup. Out of our rooms, we were dogged-tagged with wrist bands stating our names and ID number. Forming a line, Tori, Doris, and I deposited our first night linens and blankets in a basket and followed a guard to an elevator. We were instructed to enter and the guard left after the doors shut. Once the doors of the elevator opened on the sixth floor, a guard could be seen stationed in a half cement and glass enclosure. He pushed a button telling us to walk to the right and go through the 6A huge sliding metal door. I wondered if they knew that we were just people, not elephants from the size of this door. This led to a huge room where a guard post was stationed in front of a massive semi-circle of bullet proof glass, where 2 levels divided into 3 living areas of prisoners. This arrangement made it easy for the guard to observe all the

95

inmates in these three sections without actually coming in contact with them.

The first section was special housing with cubicles just like what we were in downstairs along with a small day room with two metal stools on opposite sides of a small table cemented securely to the floor. There were two of these special cells side by side. Later on we discovered that they were used mostly for violent prisoners under maximum security. The floor above these two cells housed eight rooms and a small day room. The second and third sections were made the same. Each held 16 rooms with a shower in the middle of the first and second floor with a bigger day room that had four metal round tables and four metal stools around each of the tables implanted in the floor. A long metal staircase with high meshed wire on both sides led to the top floor. And the 5 foot high mesh wire ran all along the second floor walkway so that the day room ceiling was two floors high. There were 2 pay phones on one side and a 19" color TV fastened to the wall on the opposite side of the room. Opposite the TV along the same wall to the inside of the day room was a small sink and an open toilet enclosed in a semi-circle of cement blocks. Tori and her mother were placed in the bottom of the first section in one of the rooms that shared the small day room and I was taken to the middle section, top floor 6A20. The middle section was full except for one bed and that was the reason why Tori and her mother were put in maximum security. The middle section were prisoners that had not been sentenced yet and the first and third section were prisoners that had jail time.

Upon entering our new rooms we were given 2 sheets, a mat cover, a pillow case, and Praise the Lord, 2 blankets. It was really cool and after a while I decided that it was a good idea, for all the girls smoked heavily and if it had been warm the smoke would have hung very heavy in the day room.

The guard opened all the doors mechanically and never entered where the prisoners were together, unless everyone was in lock down. From her perch, she could not only observe all the sections, but the inmates could talk to her via an intercom system. Every single room was equipped with an intercom, so you could get in and out of your own room and of course for the purpose of messages that concerned just you. The guard had multiple controls at his or her command which also included a computer and 2 phones. The computer's purpose was for the listing of all court dates as they were being confirmed and the amount of jail time each person had left to serve.

Tori and Doris were locked securely into their room first and then it was my turn. Walking into the day room, I passed quietly by my fellow inmates, as I proceeded up the stairs and into my room. Two of the women immediately hollered after me to close my door. I responded quickly and with much haste. I made my bed as instructed and then pushed the intercom button so I could leave my room to go back into the day room.

Glances followed my every move, but none seemed to be much interested in my existence. I guess when it came right down to it, they were just as leery of me as I was of them. Two of the girls were on the staircase writing in a small notebook and I asked if I could borrow one of their pencils. The girl with blond hair and a pretty round face consented. When we were jailed, we had no choice, but to remember all numbers in our heads, lawyers, anyone we could talk to who would help. I knew with this pencil it would make the task of recalling a number a whole lot easier. Immediately my spirits lifted and clutching it in my hand, I cheerfully asked the guard if I could talk to Tori and Doris in their cell. Without hesitation the guard agreed after looking up my name and their's in the computer and verifying that none of us would pose a threat. I found them already busy on a phone that the guard had plugged into a wall jack, just for them. It was apparent that because this was a maximum security cell, they did not trust the inmates with phones. I handed them the pencil and they were delighted. Within a couple of minutes the guard came back and explained that I had to go back to the day room, but if Tori and Doris would sign a waiver they could go to my day room, too.

Obediently, I walked out and the weight and shock of my incarceration once again pushed thoughts of desperation in front of my face. Since my cell mates didn't seem to care whether I was here or not, I decided that I might as well make the best of the situation and find out why they were here too? I hoped that this would make it easier for me to be patient while I waited out the weekend, instead of reliving the nightmare of the day before. I surveyed the room and getting ahold of myself, I noticed a lady with a devotional. I began to feel more at ease and going over to her, I asked her why she was here? Apparently she had stolen a $400 TV and when she went to return it she dropped it and broke it. Fearing prosecution, she and her husband fled to Idaho, but unfortunately for her, she was apprehended in Portland. According to the workings of the justice system she had until Friday for Idaho to pick her up before Oregon would let her go. Another lady was sitting beside her and as I talked about why I was here, she was fervently writing in a small notebook, passages from a Christian book that she checked out in the small jail library.

She explained that her crime was driving her boyfriend's car without insurance and that she had already been here for 3 weeks waiting for court. I swallowed hard, surprised that a person could be punished like this for another's failure to pay insurance. As quickly as she began her story she began to give me advice on letting my children go and that this was God's will for my life.

If only people could begin to understand that God does not will any of his children into jail, but that people who hated me for no reason were why I was here. God commands us to love, but not the world. The world is controlled by what satan wants and this is in opposition to God's love. Ephesians 6:11-12, "Put on all the armor that God gives you, so that you will be able to stand up against the Devil's evil tricks. For we are not fighting against human beings but against the wicked spiritual forces in the heavenly world, the rulers, authorities, and cosmic powers of this dark age." Later Jesus states in Revelations 2:10, "Don't be afraid of anything you are about to suffer. Listen! The Devil will put you to the test by having some of you thrown into prison, and your troubles will last ten days. Be faithful to me, even if it means death, and I will give you life as your prize of victory." God's will for our lives is for us to have life in Him. Satan on the other hand wants to defeat us in every way and steal away our faith in God by throwing all sorts of problems and difficulties our way. When we give in to satan, we allow him to rob us of our hope in God and because of this we fail the test. So do what Paul commands us to do in Ephesians and put on the whole armor of God, so you can defeat satan and his evil tricks.

We both batted around more religious concepts about the power of satan and God's love. I enjoyed the good natured talk about God. It gave me a short reprieve from constant fears of court and what they would do to us. Along with her comments she confirmed along with Doris & Tori that Eric would be on his best behavior, because the court would be watching his every action with the kids. I needed to be reassured about this for my children were continually on my mind, but I knew deep within my heart that their words were far from true, nothing could erase the fact that I loved Tori and because of this, even my children received no justice.

Some of Tori's phone calls of desperation over our dilemma, before the end of our first weekend of incarceration, made me feel even more depressed. She was trying to wheel and deal with the prosecuting attorney and CSO in Winfield and our attorney all within minutes of each other. From her in depth conversations with each party, she pleaded, even stating that I wouldn't appeal for my kids, if they would just release her parents! She was very fearful over her parents health and even though I knew she wasn't serious about what she was saying, it still hurt to hear her talk in front of her mother as if I or my children weren't of any importance to her. I felt so helpless to their situation for not only were they having health problems, but Tori's own physical condition was giving her fevers and chills, difficulty in breathing and severe chest pains. Yet in the midst of all of the confusion and fear, I was not allowed to show anymore than modest support and concern, because I was the very person who got them into this mess. I couldn't help, but feel a deep depression drawing me closer, encircling me with the cold reality that my presence in this world was only necessary for the fulfillment of pain and suffering from being what God had intended me to be, a woman who loved another woman. How I wished that God would come down from his stately throne and put a halt to our persecutors and tell them that they were wrong about Tori and I. For God made us and loved us as much as them.

But Winfield wouldn't budge, they said that the only way that they would consider letting Bill and Doris go was after Tori and I pleaded guilty to kidnapping my kids. Tori's face paled as she explained to her mother the terms of their demands and as I over heard their conversation, Doris defiantly stated that she would say she was guilty to the crime before Tori would dare plead guilty to get her and her father out. Well that solved that problem at least for now!

The more phone calls we made turned up other facts as well. Some of the checks had bounced that Tori wrote in Portland and the attorney in Winfield said that all of the parties were going to press charges against her. So in a panic, Tori's grandparents thinking that Mark was behind it all, worked closely with the Portland lawyer calling all check people to return purchases or to make the checks good. Then in order to put further pressure on us to pay up all the checks, the Portland Sheriff's department put a hold on Brad so his great-grandparents couldn't take him home to Utah. Once again the fight was on with our Portland lawyer demanding more money for the continued delay. It took until Tuesday of the following week and a $1,000 dollars later before Brad was released from Social Services and safely in the hands of his great-grandparents. Doris's dad commented that if the lawyer hadn't fought so hard and they hadn't freely given of their money to pay up the bad checks, they would have never released Brad from Social Services. He concluded, "we bought Brad back." With these words still ringing in our ears, he painted a picture of little Brad bounding out of the foster care home into his great-grandparents arms. With a sign, her grandfather said, that was all the reassurance that they needed, that they had done the right thing by coming to Portland. I had to admire Tori's family for whenever the road got rough they refused to ignore the fact that they were all united by flesh and blood, and because of this they came through regardless of the talk of people around them.

Before I left Utah, my ex-attorney had questioned the legality of the memorandum. So once again, I reminded Sean on one of my many phone calls from jail about this fact. His only reply was that he could not start the appeal until the memorandum was declared a legal document. Tori overheard the conversation and since Doris had not come with her to my day room, but was taking a nap instead, she took the phone and confronted Sean stating that he'd advised us to keep the kids and she expected him to verify this to the court. He promised he would. This made Tori happy for the moment and she hung up the phone feeling a little bit more optimistic over the future.

I shivered at the thought of how Tori had devised a plan just a week before to be able to pay the money for the retainer fee for the appeal over custody to Sean's firm. She had taken some of her jewelry along with on piece of mine and sold it to a jewelry broker. Not only did she sell the jewelry, but she also had to sign a paper stating that it was free and clear and that she could be prosecuted if the pieces weren't. Showing me the check I took a deep breath as fear once again swept into my mind over what could happen, but still I knew that there was no other choice. I knew that we would continue to make payments on this jewelry and so why did it matter that I didn't have it anymore? But now after discovering that the county attorney was trying to get Portland to press charges for bad checks, I feared the worst possible thing could happen, but thanks to many pleas to the Lord and his loving forgiveness, we were never found out.

Just knowing that she put herself in the line of fire, I knew that Tori would have risked everything just because she loved me. I even felt sure that she would die for me, she was already in jail because of me. I looked at Tori standing by the pay phone again pleading for freedom for all of us and I knew I would sacrifice everything for her love, too. Gal. 5:22-23, "But the Spirit produces love, joy, peace, long suffering, kindness, goodness, faithfulness, humility, and self-control. There is no law against such things as these." God calls us to a greater law that surpasses human legal laws; love. I am a lesbian and with certainty I claim that because of God's love instilled in me, I am justified before God.

I'd always heard that the legal system was full of holes, but that's not true. It's full of money hungry lawyers that want retainer fees before they touch your case. Then it's full of solid masses of steel and cement; Jail! The holes aren't found until months down the road if you're lucky your money hasn't run out. And on top of this you're found guilty and you have to prove yourself innocent.

Tori and I went to jail with everything we had monetarily, she had $140 in cash and I had $1.46. Doris and Bill had only $80 left after their move to Portland. We couldn't afford the expense of a lawyer for our now criminal charges from kidnapping here in Portland and because of this we were totally in the mercy of the legal system. Court ordered attorney's were our only option for the red tape we had to tackle just to waive our rights so Utah could pick us up from Oregon.

Instantly we discovered our best source of information to fight the legal system was the wide variety of knowledge obtained by our inmates. We knew nothing about the law process, but these street wise women did. Eventually, we found out that even after we signed our waiver that Utah could wait 10 days before picking us up. This didn't thrill us at all. Doris, Tori and I took turns being massively depressed and crying. In fact, most of the women in this section served their time before ever going to court. And then to an even greater dismay, we were told that the Judge didn't have to count the time served. This meant that some could serve more than the amount of time that the law required for the offense. Every girl in jail with us were too poor to pay bond and all they had to depend on were court appointed attorney's that would not accept collect calls. Many knew their court dates, but not what their attorneys were doing to help them much less free them. It was not surprising that every inmate at one time or another had tears falling from the eyes from personal fears over the uncertainty of court.

Monday shone with a promise that the miles we gained in knowledge over the weekend would win the victory in a working day. The week days started with wake up at 4:30, breakfast at 6:00 and then lock down at 7:00. Lock down was the changing of the guard. We were locked in our rooms and the guard on duty counted us and then the new guard confirmed the count by counting again. This took about an hour and happened at 7:00 and 3:00 each day, except weekends when we slept till 7:30. We were informed by the guard that we were all scheduled for court at 10:00. From our many phone calls to Winfield, we were told that as soon as we signed our waivers that Utah promised they would pick us up shortly after.

Leaving the housing that had become our bondage for the last two days was great. Finally we felt we were getting closer to getting out. The three of us lined up against the wall. We took off our shoes and the guard had us knock them together and shake them upside down before we were patted down. I tried to feel indifference to these constant bodily searches, but inside daggers were stabbing Eric and the SBC over and over again. Not only this, but I didn't see how it was possible that anything could ever be smuggled into this building, it was like Fort Knox.

Late Sunday evening, Tori talked to the attorney who rescued Brad from Social Services. Whenever you come in contact with your lawyer you go through strip searches and depending which guard was on duty was just how thorough the search. Tori didn't even come in contact with him and yet the woman guard, who searched her, really enjoyed these and put her through twice as bad a search than we had at the very beginning. She used a plastic glove and Tori came back feeling totally humiliated and dirty. After she told me the details I couldn't help but feel contempt towards the guard. The longer we were in jail the more I discovered how corrupt it was from the inside. We were just mothers, not hardened criminals! Now I understood why they took men off of the duty of strip searches for women just two years before. From this experience alone, I had grown by leaps and bounds, for I could see that our justice system was furthering the problem by lack of integrity inside its walls. And not only in the jail, but from the lawyers demanding higher pay than an ordinary person could afford to pay and Judges who are placed in a position to judge on an offense that they themselves were breaking because they didn't care about the people who came before them. This is plain sin and as far as God is concerned, the law of man is failing as miserably as the law's God handed down in the Bible in the Old Testament.

Going down the hallway again, we entered the elevator to the fourth floor, where we were met by a guard and ushered into a large room with 25 chairs. We took a seat in the back and all of the remaining chairs were filled by men. For the first time since Friday, Doris saw Bill. She was elated and whispered news and asked questions of how he was. I'd never seen two people so much in love. All weekend all Doris did was fret over how Bill was all alone and she was afraid for his health. Via her parents she received news of Bill's emotions being up and down and even conversations of him breaking down and crying. All news was met with frustration and tears of hew own. Just seeing him in court gave her confidence and put a sparkle in her eyes.

As I waited for my turn, I couldn't help but reflect on how it seemed that ever since I came to love Tori that I was met with one obstacle after another. From the fight for custody of my children to the constant secrecy surrounding the love I had for Tori. It truly seemed that now that I had found true love, I was fighting with all my might against family, friends, and country to remain in this love. How different this is from the truth of God's grace, found in the love of having His son die for our sins, from the teachings found in this world. For example, text books are pushed in our faces to make us believe that we are in control of our destiny and with this in mind, we can be anything we want to be with the right education. Gaining material wealth leads to power and power leads to fame. Following this order, we will gain friends and respect from the world. This to all appearances seems like the logical thing to do until a curve is thrown into the picture and your world turns upside down, because you love, when people dealing in the world, think you are committing a terrible sin. Yet from the very beginning God tells us this will happen, because we refuse to understand God's plan for mankind, because we are not acting within the truth that is found by loving in His word. Could it be that in our effort to do what the Bible tells us to do, by obeying the original law's handed down by Moses, that these laws were given as a tool for God to test and refine us into the people that he wants us to become? Of course it is! Romans 13:8-10, "Be under obligation to no one-the only obligation you have is to love one another. Whoever does this has obeyed the Law. The commandments, 'Do not commit adultery; do not commit murder; do not steal; do not desire what belongs to someone else'- all these, and any others besides, are summed up in the one command, 'Love your neighbor as you love yourself.' If you love someone, you will never do him wrong; to love, then, is to obey the whole Law." If we react to the different circumstances in our lives with love, we obey the whole law. For example when Tori's grandparents helped her regardless of the rumors that were being spread by Eric, they were found justified before God because they allowed love to rule their actions. My parents in turn failed the test of love when they refused to rally to my support by disregarding the rumors.

John 15:26, "The Helper will come-the Spirit, who reveals the truth about God and who comes from the Father. I will send him to you from the Father, and he will speak about me." Because of the tribulations that God's servants will go through while passing their tests, God in a super natural way sent the Spirit to guide those who would put their trust in him. John 16:7-8, "But I am telling you the truth; it is better for you that I go away, because if I do not go, the Helper will not come to you. But if I do go away, then I will send him to you. And when he comes, he will prove to the people of the world that they are wrong about sin and about what is right and about God's judgment."

The scripture was opening my eyes to the simple truth of God's love. The law in itself was good, but because people could not follow the law the Lord chose another way, which was through the death of Christ and the coming of the Holy Spirit. Since this is the case and being Spirit filled showed me what was sin and what wasn't sin, then God chose not only my life style, but He chose for me to go through the struggles that I was experiencing right now so that I would come into a greater understanding of His free gift of grace by faith in Jesus.

The chairs in our room faced a large glass wall where you could see the room on the other side where a large table with 2 public defenders and the DA of Jefferson county were safely sitting away from the prisoners. A camera was on a tripod and automatically focused on us and our public defenders as we came forward into the same room one at a time for our turn before the court. A TV monitor on the wall revealed a courtroom with a Judge seated behind a podium that was located wherever the court was regularly scheduled for personal appearances by the defendant and attorney. Two other people seated on side chairs were also in the room along with two police officers where we stood before the camera facing the TV Judge.

All inmates attention focused on the Judge as she read us our rights as a group. Then the TV screen turned to the attorneys so they could begin presenting each case. We were all tense as our names were called off 2 at a time to enter into the other room. Once in the next room each person sat by the public defender, while the Judge heard the case and set bond. Then the other person took his turn, this continued until everyone was heard. We were allowed quiet conversation as we waited. The palms of my hands were soaked in sweat. The room was stifled with tension and my comrades around me cracked jokes about our jailers, binding all of us closer together in preparation to face the enemy.

After 6 to 8 cases had been heard by the Judge, the police officer would take them back to their jail cells. The four of us were last. I was called first. Tori quickly whispered last minute instructions and nervously I left. Immediately I asked for a PR bond and to be let go on my own recognizance so I could drive my car back to Winfield. The Judge denied all requests and confirmed a $50,000 bond on me, Bill and Doris, to honor Utah's claims against us. I waived my rights to extradition so Utah could pick me up and the public lawyer said I would have to go to the courthouse to sign papers. She said she would do her best to get it done this week. My spirits dropped. Tori was next. Her crime was the same as mine along with liability crimes of another kind. Her bond was signed by a different judge and it was $22,000. Together our combined bonds were $172,000. There was no way we could pay this amount! Tori was white and all of us tensed, worrying about Tori's added crime. Was it one of the checks that were written? What was going on? It wasn't until we returned to Utah that we discover that it should have been put on Bill and Doris's as well. It was a simple technicality making her responsible for kidnapping my children too.

When we arrived back at our cells, we were searched again. We ate lunch and attacked the phone. In a frenzy we called relatives hoping to raise our bond. Tears ran in frustration as we learned that combined we needed $25,800 in cash and $141,200 in collateral. Doris and Tori pleaded, but were refused by her parents. I called my parents and to my surprise my grandparents volunteered to pay my bond, but after finding out that they would have to pay $5,000 they too refused.

The bondsman asked them was it because they didn't love me and my grandfather, who I knew had over $250,000 in the bank, said it was because he just didn't want to. Tori and I cried! So much gossip had been spreading in Winfield, that my parents were convinced that I had more than just kidnapping my own kids against me and no matter how much I denied this, they wouldn't listen. Mom got so mad at me that she hung up the phone then later she refused to except any of my calls after I tried once more to gain their support.

Ever since the very beginning when Mom marked me a sinner because of Tori, I was condemned by my family. She would consistently say she loved me and then refuse to provide for my needs. Jail is no place for family rejection! This is when you need your family to rally around you and deny any gossip! Yet the words of Sodom and Gomorrah were so firmly ingrown into their religionistic belief system that they humanly would not allow God to come in and change their minds through love. Knowing all of this, I clung to scriptures helping me in my problems and giving me comfort in my times of trouble. Matt. 10;34-36, "Do you think that I have come to bring peace to the world? No, I did not come to bring peace, but a sword. I came to set sons against their fathers, daughters against their mothers, daughters-in-laws against their mothers-in-law, A man's worst enemies will be the members of his own family."

When I loved Tori, people began to hate me, my parents turned their backs on me and the Christian world

108

of friends and church crumbled right before my eyes. All accusations were centered around Tori's and my love. Our love was unnatural, being a homosexual was a sin. If only Christians would learn the basic's of love they would have their eyes opened and understand that satan was behind this big deception. Jesus repeatedly tells us that there will be tribulation for those who follow Him. John 15:18-21, "If the world hates you, just remember that it has hated me first. If you belonged to the world, then the world would love you as its own. But I chose you from this world and you do not belong to it; that is why the world hates you. Remember what I told you, 'No slave is greater than his master.' If they persecuted me, they will persecute you too; if they obeyed my teaching, they will obey yours too. But they will do all this to you because you are mine; for they do not know the one who sent me." If Tori and I were considered pure before the church then the world would not hate us, but because we love each other as the same sex, we are hated. What better way to defeat the goal of love in the world than for satan to come in and confuse the scriptures and distort the truth of God that is found in love. Christians if you love, God proclaims that you are without sin. Of course satan wants to destroy this concept, for it is the very essence of God! For God is love.

Now if the people were good, Bible loving Christians, why did they choose to continue gossiping and trying to punish us? Their very actions condemned them as not following God! Matt. 7:21, "Not everyone who calls me 'Lord, Lord' will enter the Kingdom of heaven, but only those who do what my Father in heaven wants them to do." Which of course is to love!

As I reflected back on my life before I met Tori, I knew that I had never felt a bond with Eric like I did with her. When I married him, I had no idea that I was doing anything different than what was expected of me by marrying a man. I went into our marriage with my blinders not only securely on my eyes, but with the full intention that we would stay together for 50 years or till death do us part. But when Tori entered the picture, everything I thought I knew sharply changed, I realized that from my earliest age, I dreamed of women, not guys. I found myself from my religious up bringing denying these visions and feelings. How much easier it would have been for Tori and I to have been allowed the opportunity to act upon our sexual preference than to be thrown into a world that not only rejected this, but enforced laws against us being who God decided we would be. How blind churches are who believe otherwise. I claim with certainty and my life proves from the love that so strongly holds me fast to Tori that I am pure before God. All people who are different like me and are being called sinners by people who are calling God, 'Lord' are in sin themselves and blind to the love of God.

Later we discovered that even if we had been able to bond out in Oregon, that we would still be wanted in Utah. We may be temporarily out in Oregon, but if Utah obtained a Governor's warrant in 90 days then we could be arrested and sent to Utah on a new issued bond. I can't begin to tell you how frustrated I was becoming with the lawyers, who were suppose to know these facts, yet they were telling us to pay the bond if we wanted out. Not only this, but the bondsmen were as heartless and as big a liars as they were, by trying to get you to bond out when in the long run we could have been paying twice as much in bond money if we contested extradition. The bonds were only good for the state you were in and after talking to one good bonds woman, she further explained that if a bondsman desired, he could put you back in jail, keep the money you already gave him and there you would be all over again. After learning all of this information, it wasn't long after asking our other jail mates how much their bonds were that we understood that jails were filled with poor people. Our legal system was for the rich and the oppression of the poor and homeless. To further illustrate this point about being homeless, there was one lady ahead of me, before I came before the Judge, and because she was living in her car she was denied bail.

I felt so alone when I first walked into the day room. I was confronted with criminals, many who had been in jail several times, I was leery and afraid expecting the worst. There's so much said about the violence and homosexual activity behind bars. After just minutes had passed my fears subsided. We were all in this together and although some were more reserved than others, we were a family. We talked about our jail records, shared letters from boyfriends, gave advice on past legal experiences, talked, cried, and consoled. Bill concluded, "Once in jail, your inmates become your friends for life." I liked what he said because it was true, jail is hitting rock bottom and only those who have been there understood what you were going through and what injustices lie inside the jail house bars.

CHAPTER EIGHT

The tiny room enveloped my body sending sensations of loneliness and terror that my nightmare would never end. Closing my eyes tightly I desperately fought to erase all my surroundings and pleaded that sleep would come. The cold hard cement bed sent aches that found every bone an easy target of pain. Circles deepened in my eyes enhancing my mental anguish of fitful nights of sleep and hopeless dreams.

The fourth day of prison led to another court appearance. Tori and I were to sign the papers to waive our rights to extradition and hopefully, Bill and Doris the next day. We all signed in relief, but anxiety mounted each day as to when Winfield would pick us up and how much humiliation they had planned.

We teasingly elaborated huge crowds, ticker tapes and a troop of officers parading us down Main street in prison clothes and chains. The bond for our crime had been exaggerated and all of our lawyers and inmates were alarmed and constantly discussed over why it wasn't reduced. No one could understand why Winfield wanted us back so badly. In dismay Tori and I looked at each other fully understanding why and fearing stones and a hanging for our life of sin. Our minds were vivid with experiences of insults and threats of bodily harm by Eric and his good Christian followers.

It was 6:30 a.m. on Tuesday and again we were patted down and directed to the elevator taking us to the first floor. A police officer checked off our names and locked us in a tiny holding room with three others. Two of the inmates were from our housing and Tori asked them details of what lay ahead. Much of what they said was what we had already been told by the girls from our cell so we didn't learn anything new.

After the room fell silent, I asked questions about their lives and families. The girl with shoulder length blond hair proudly told of her life. All of her four children were under the age of five, she was just 22. Her husband and she weren't together anymore. He had taken another wife without divorcing her and she in turn was living with her boyfriend. All of her story was relayed as if she was a small child. She took a quick breath and went on to explain in great detail how her dad had set her up by testifying against her because she and he had stolen merchandise from a big Department store. She complained that they never would have been caught if he hadn't been so greedy. Furthermore, she stated quite proudly that this was not her first brush with the law. Without hesitation the next girl spoke, declaring that this was not her first arrest either. This time she was in for breaking into a coke machine and stealing $280.00 worth of pop and cash. During our entire conversation she kept insisting that she was not guilty. Only later, after court, did she quietly let us know that she had pleaded guilty and that the thirty days she had already served would be counted with the stipulation that she had 6 months to pay back the money that she had taken. Suddenly shades from my eyes were being lifted and I understood that for these young women, crime was their way of life.

My continued questions seemed to be a welcome to the silence and I prodded ahead knowing that they didn't seem to care how others might judge them for their answer. "Were any of you abused as a child or sexually assaulted?" Tori elbowed me sharply, but they all chirped up. The girl who stole from the pop machine said her dad had raped her when she was 9 and her uncles used her too. She was also battered. The second woman had been a model for child pornography. After court it was found that her car had been impounded. All of her things were investigated and listed in a police report. She had photos of child pornography and some evidence that could stop a ring of child porn operators. She had agreed to turn state evidence so she could get a lighter 5 year sentence with parole. I wondered how reliable a witness she would be for the prosecutor? Maybe this was the reason it was so tough to prosecute people involved in pornography.

The door opened and the officer called out Tori's and my name and another woman's. They quickly handcuffed us together. Six men boarded the police van first then we carefully entered trying not to pull at each other's wrists. The huge metal garage door of the jail opened and slowly our van eased out into the traffic. Looking out, I saw a world of people busily driving to work, lost in thoughts of another day. The difference in the atmosphere was strangely dramatic filling me with nostalgic feelings of life at home and at work. How I longed to be free to drive a car or just sit on the grass and look through unbarred windows at the beauty of the scenery.

Soon our ride ended at the old jail, where we were uncuffed and led to another holding cell until our time came for court. It was cold and Tori and I huddled together for warmth. Jackie, who was one of the women from our prison section, sat beside Tori shortly and then paced telling the story of her imprisonment. She was an addict and to feed her problem, she took a package for a dealer and was caught red-handed. She had been in jail for a month and a half with a $1,000 bond between her and freedom. The DA wanted her to talk, but Jackie said that if she did, the drug dealers would kill her.

Her pacing quickened and thoughts of desperation paraded on her face for she knew if she didn't talk the establishment would put her away for years. Her words angered me. She was a go-between feeding her habit and the real criminal who sold the stuff was free! Jackie continued openly terrified of court and rambled that the public attorney had waived her rights without her being present. It was the law that every person had the right to be present in a court hearing, but as usual the lawyers found away to evade this if they saw fit. On top of this, Jackie was on probation and they had given her 1 1/2 years in prison on another offense that she had committed two years earlier, but instead of imprisonment she was given probation with guidelines to rid herself of her habit.

Instead of following through with the Judge's commands she rebelled and refused to attend the classes. Today this decision was being reevaluated. Returning to our cell after court, tears were flowing down her cheeks. She had just been sentenced to Tuscany, the state prison, for a year for the probation violation of 2 years ago.

The guard called my name and my hands were handcuffed behind my back. We left the jail house, walked across the street and into the courthouse. He directed me to an elevator downstairs and then he ushered me by a throng of people into the courtroom where my hearing was to take place. To my surprise there was Eric and a member from the SBC. I was going to a hearing on child custody! Apparently since I last had custody of the children, I had to sign a waiver so that the children could be released to their father. My faded orange jail clothes shone brightly against the dull finish of the courtroom paneling and my handcuffs jingled as I held my head high while Eric and his friend gleefully watched the officer's and my procession. I was paraded to the front of the courtroom. I was then uncuffed and sat in the jury box completely on display to the entire assembly. I looked directly at Eric knowing that for four days he had to cut through red tape to get Richard and Crystal's custody out of Social Services. Thoughts played in my head of refusing to sign the papers until I had an attorney and with further defiance raging war within my being, I planned how I would fight the legality of the memorandum right here in Oregon. But as quickly as these thoughts surfaced a mother's love flowed in my heart for my children. They needed to be in school and tying things up in court would hurt them, not Eric. I didn't contest the hearing and hurriedly Eric left the courtroom with the document in his hands. Later I discovered that Oregon would have honored the paper not because it was a valid document, but because it was easier not to get involved with other state's legal battles. I had no money to buy a lawyer anyway.

Tori had indeed signed her waiver and I elaborated over the proceedings of the custody hearing. We huddled close together enjoying our short time before going back to the new jail and once again being under Tori's mother's watchful eye.

Jail took away all forms of pride. We were forced to borrow paper, pencils, combs and shampoo. They were not provided and were only bought through the commissary on Wednesday's and Friday's. And since we came in on Friday evening and it was only Tuesday, we were not given the opportunity to buy any of these things. Fortunately, four days after we came to jail, Doris's parents were able to provide us with clean underwear, socks and warm thermal shirts that could be worn under our uniforms to help keep us warm from the extremely cool temperatures in the jail. Unfortunately, this wasn't possible for most of the ladies in the jail with us for they were poor and because of this none of their families could provide for them at all. Later we discovered that after they were sentenced they were given the opportunity to work if they wanted to, but most had lost all hope in their lives and they didn't care enough about themselves to make the effort.

We were forced to scrub everything three times a day and the guards took pride on what cleaning tasks we'd do. One time everyone had to scrub by hand the high mesh wiring running along both sides of the stairs and the walkway on the second floor. Everyone was expected to help and if you were caught looking like you weren't doing your fair share you were punished; believe me it was better to clean. If the white gloves treatment had been used in our housing, they would have passed the test.

A handful of the guards were somewhat friendly, but the few that were mean sent all of us cowarding in fear. They would watch us and if we walked too much or sat too much, or looked at them in a way that they

116

interpreted disrespectful, then we would be punished by scrubbing the floor with a sponge or being locked in our cell away from our inmates. By the time the police from Winfield finally came to pick us up, we were submissive, obedient, and extremely polite.

Wednesday the same procedure of court continued with Bill, Doris and I waiving extradition. Our lawyers were informed and the dreaded fear of what Winfield would do to us loomed over our heads. We had come a long way since Friday and our impatience for Winfield to release us from jail caused more tears, posing frustration and sleepless nights more than all the other days combined. We walked around in silence with deep circles of strain under our eyes while our prayers beseeched God with pleads that He would deliver us from the mouths of our enemies.

Tori's physical condition was worsening. They refused to give her any medication until a doctor O.K.'d her prescription. When they called her doctor in Winfield to renew her pills, he said he didn't know her. We were all shocked! Tori could become severely sick if she wasn't given medication. So Doris and I prayed and huddled on opposite sides of Tori trying to keep her warm and calm. Together we took turns making phone calls and Doris's dad, with the help of a lawyer, put pressure on the jail to give Tori her medicine. Still all of their requests were refused. Tori went through Inderal withdrawal until Wednesday, six days later, before the prison doctor Okayed her prescription. This just continued to support my feelings that unless you had money or were someone high up, you were considered less than human when you were in jail!

I was amazed at how it seemed that wherever you are, people have a tendency to segregate. The Mexicans and Blacks had their clique and the Caucasians had their's. In jail this was even more emphasized. The prostitutes and drug addicts formed a clique and the burglars and shoplifters had their clique. The three of us were the church clique. But no matter who was in what group, we were all treated like hardened criminals by guards, lawyers and judges. All crimes were treated alike, whether it was a first offense or tenth.

After five days of imprisonment, I gathered innumerable information from my fellow inmates. They were all in jail, because they were too poor to pay their bonds. And to further my alarm over their predicaments, the legal system was set up to give the judges so much power. And with this in mind, many of the stipulations of the law of how long a person could be punished was ignored when it was a person who was too poor to defend themselves or were ignorant of their legal rights under the law. One judge returned from vacation and the first day back on the job, he heard 20 cases and all 20 were given years in prison, all because he was angry about the back log of cases that were left for his return. After my experience with the judge I had, it wasn't hard for me to believe these stories. Our legal system was so corrupt that even if a person was innocent it was more than likely that they would spend months to years in jail, just because of lack of money or knowing the right people.

There should be some kind of system that monitors the judges by their own peers who have the knowledge of their colleagues lack of integrity in following the laws that are stipulated through our Governments. Just like in my case my own attorney was well aware of my judges drinking problems and his mishandling of other cases. Even after knowing these facts, he was still on the bench handing down injustices! The judges have become so powerful that lawyers will not come up against them for the sake of other cases with clients that can be given heavier sentences. They know if they can't win for their clients then the clients won't pay them or want them. So in lieu of this, the judges have even more power because they can control the attorney's and thus the attorney's who are court appointed and have no big, rich, firm supporting their claim against the judges, they have the rug pulled right out from under them giving them no support but to summit to bad rulings or be treated unfairly in the courts.

118

All of the women in our section knew and talked about which judges were a prison judge and which one's were lenient. Many times in our conversations over judges one of the inmates would whisper a plea to God that he would give them another chance with a more lenient judge.

Rita was a true source of information on our justice system. Her mother was a prostitute and had 5 kids and had never married. Rita was the youngest and was born when her mother was 50. At 13, Rita gave birth to her first child and her life fell into the same pattern as her mother's. And just like her mother she was arrested many times for solicitation. Her word's often echoed through the jail as she stated emphatically that the law was an oppression of the poor. People were being thrust right back into the lifestyle of their parents with no escape, because the world wouldn't help them change. Jail was a way of life that was repeated from reform school to prison and circling back to pick up any children that might have been born from the times that they were in and out of jail. No one was ever taught a different way to live. She went on making a point by telling that the jails were no better than the streets. She illustrated her point of view by stating that if they were prostitutes, they were strip searched in jail and treated inferior by their jailers in the very same way as their bodies were take advantage of out in the streets. Just how our legal system treated them furthered the fact that there was no compassion. They were given public defenders, who are paid by the year, not by their clients and because of this many of them didn't have a chance in court because their defenders were so overloaded with cases that they didn't have the time needed to do the best for them.

Now Rita could go on and on and most of what she said made sense, for all the women that I talked to in jail returned repeatedly and were from the poorest sections of town. Not only this, but they were working the jobs that barely made minimum wage and it was impossible to make ends meet with so meager amount of money. Prostitutes, drug dealers, pimps, hustlers, organized crime, and child pornography, etc. were very active in their communities and sometimes the only way for them to get ahead. Many in desperation were forced to do anything just to survive.

Gal. 4:9, "But now that you know God-or, I should say, now that God knows you-how is it that you want to turn back to those weak and pitiful ruling spirits? Why do you want to become their slaves all over again?" As each girl left our jail, each vowed they wouldn't come back! A young 22 year old woman was released and as she passed the stairway where I sat with some of the other inmates, I cheerfully said, "Don't come back!" She did a complete turn around and faced me stating "I can't promise I won't be back, you never know what's going to happen." This jail was their home away from home. An accepted fact of their existence. Whatever they had to do to survive they would do it and if they were caught, then back to jail they would go. It's no wonder that in the United States alone, there are over one million prisoners. Obviously, we are not making any progress in reforming the prisoners by jail time alone. How can we expect to change offenders if we only want to punish and not give them a chance at a different kind of life?

Isaiah 42:6-7, "I, the Lord, have called you and given you power to see that justice is done on earth. Through you I will make a covenant with all peoples; through you I will bring light to the nations. You will open the eyes of the blind and set free those who sit in dark prisons." Isaiah 49:9, "I will say to the prisoners, 'Go free!' and to those who are in darkness, 'come out to the light!" Isaiah wrote these words under the influence of the Holy Spirit of God. For he in his own life time was seeing the corruptness of the world and the blindness of it's leaders. The more I studied the scriptures, the more God opened my eyes for me to see and understand how our world had fallen. We live in a fallen world and just from seeing the fruits of our legal system, I see the great damage that has been done and how blind we have all become to the injustices placed upon poor people. It amazes me how many people think that to solve the crime problem is to throw people in jail. These people need to be reeducated and given opportunities that allow them to better themselves. It's time for us to reach out our arms to all people and especially those who are forced to live in such a poor state that they end up being further humiliated in our jail and prison systems because they had to steal to live. Men, women and children, taught by their parents that the only way to survive is to take anything that you can put your hands on regardless if it means they have to steal to get it. Children being left to raise themselves and then expected to be law abiding citizens. Children, who had been beaten, raped and mentally abused by their parents, relatives, and friends cannot be expected to be leaders in their communities and good parents to their own children. Jesus came to open the eyes to the blind, I hope from what I learned, that your eyes will be opened and God will help you to reach out to people in need with the compassion that they deserve to be given.

Rebel had run away from home at 13. At 16 years old she was raped. At 19 she was married to man who threw her around the house, battering her repeatedly. At 26 she was divorced and at 33 remarried to another man who repeated the abuse. Now she was in jail after a neighbor had reported a family disturbance. She came with multiple bruises and bumps all over her face and on her head. The police first took her to the hospital and then finding that there were no bones broken, they brought her to jail for an outstanding warrant for failure to appear in court over a traffic violation. Her husband who had brutally beaten her remained at home with their two small children, because she refused to press charges against him.

Can you image how hard it would be for even a police officer to see day in and day out how the legal system falls short of the goal of protecting people. Television portrays these feelings over and over again by showing the lack of respect that the law enforcement people have for attorneys and judges and for government officials. It's not hard to understand why policemen with integrity would become disillusioned when the bad people go free and the innocent are treated like they're guilty. It's no wonder that some policemen take the law into their own hands in order for justice to prevail.

Another girl was just moved from juvenile hall to adult jail because she turned 18. She had been arrested for a long record of shoplifting and this time it was aggravated robbery. This was because she had been with a group of kids and one of them had a gun. With the charges combined she was looking at 48 years. Her eyes shown with defiance and Doris said she looked like trouble. I talked to her for a while and she said that she first went to court at 13. She had become hooked on heroine and she stole to feed her habit. I reached across the table we were sitting at and squeezed her hand. Looking down, I noticed scars from needle marks on both of her arms. I immediately became sympathetic and she sensed my reaction. Looking at me, I noticed for once her troubled eyes softened. Her life story quickly tumbled out of her mouth and she stated if her mother had the money she would have paid her bond. Proudly she announced that if any stranger came into their house and they were eating, whoever it was would be welcomed to sit down and eat too. Pride reflected in her eyes. It's funny how easy it is for poor people to share their last crumb and yet how difficult for another person who has plenty. She was a good person just like all the other ladies in this jail, but they were chained to a way of life.

Baby was a lesbian. She was constantly writing to her lover. She went through a big spiel of how she told her mother and her mom accepted what she said declaring that all she wanted was for Baby to be happy. Doris was sitting at the table with me and didn't flinch an inch. I was surprised. But after a few minutes of talk Doris backed away. She went to the phone and called her parents and Baby continued with saying that she had 2 relationships 2 years each and this third one was just for 1 1/2 months. She had a six year old daughter and if her lover didn't love her baby, then she didn't want her. Then she said that maybe someday she would go straight! I sighed!

Love is not sex! I wanted so much to go into Tori's and my relationship, but I didn't dare when Doris could hear my words. As it was, Baby saw Tori's and my love in our eyes and concern for each other and confronted me with what kind of relationship we had. I couldn't deny her confrontation. Immediately after our talk, Tori went to take a shower and Baby jokingly asked if I wanted to take one with her. My face turned red and I hoped Doris didn't hear the comment.

My heart was in my hands when I gazed into Tori's eyes. I'd never believed a person could love like I loved her. I took so many risks to keep her and now I'd lost my children because I loved her. Never would I trade my life for anyone else, for my life would be worth nothing without her. Touching her thrilled every feeling I'd ever had. Yes, I would have loved to take a shower with her. I ached to hold her close to my body and I was not ashamed of any of these feelings. Our sex life enhanced our love. It did not rule our love. In the sight of God we were married forever. Gal. 5:6, "For when we are in union with Christ Jesus, neither circumcision nor the lack of it makes any difference at all; what matters is faith that works through love." Love is God's law and if we have faith, then it is reflected in our love for our mate and for all of God's children.

Every lady in our day room had children when they were in their teen years. They didn't love, peer pressure pushed them into sex and relationships that they were too young to understand. Loving our Lord God, first, helps to put our relationships with other people into the right perspective by our obedience to Him. For instants, (Gal. 5:22 & 23, "But the Spirit produces love, joy, peace, patience, kindness, goodness, faithfulness, humility, and self-control. There is no law against such things as these.") Through the Spirit working in us we are given grace to handle lives situations. This does not mean that we are to do the same as our peers, but that through prayer God can direct us and teach us what is best for us. So in unity with God we can abide in His word and apply them to our everyday life situations. Gal. 5:24-26, "And those who belong to Christ Jesus have put to death their human nature with all it's passions and desires. The Spirit has given us life; he must also control our lives. We must not be proud or irritate one another or be jealous of one another." In other words, God wants us to take his guide lines found in the Bible and with it use it to help us to handle peer pressures with your brain, not your libido.

We also must be careful not to consider ourselves better than anyone that has a crime record or enjoys a different way of life, but to except all as equal and thus all are equally loved by God. For when we allow God's Spirit to work in us, we can be opened minded to why they committed the crime that resulted with them being put into jail. He calls us, "NOT" to judge people who are different, but to be patient covering ourselves in his love to protect us from the sin of judging anyone unfairly and this is especially true of our lack of understanding over the pressures that poor people go through.

In one of my many visits with my cell mates, a 28 year old women pridefully told me about her husband who was being held in the men's jail. She and her husband had 8 felonies against them. This was her first arrest. Her husband had a record full. They both got out on PR bonds and they fled the state to Nevada. Shortly afterwards they were caught by police. She was pregnant and had three other children, who are in the custody of her parents now. Their bond was set at $50,000 dollars. The police tried to make a deal, agreeing to let her go if she would just testify against her husband, but she refused. I asked her why? She grinned and replied because she loved him.

"But what about your children?" I asked. Tears quickly filled her eyes. If she testified against him he would go to prison for life and she would never be with him again. But if she could only hold out for a little while, then maybe they both could be freed. Cor. 13:3, "I may give away everything I have, and even give up my body

124

to be burned- but if I had no love, this does me no good." 1
Cor. 13:7, "Love never gives up; and its faith, hope and
patience never fail."

CHAPTER NINE

Jail could never become my home, for my confinement was constantly thrust upon my senses giving me an unending reminder of my forced imprisonment. All inmates in perfect harmony entered their rooms and pulled the metal doors closed, sending clanking echoes resounding through the building. The clashing noise was deafening and without end. Grabbing my ears I tried to block out the sound, but the banging persisted all day and night. Peace and contentment had no place within the massive correctional institution. All paths in the corridors led to rooms of pain, anguish and mental torment, a reminder that we no longer had control over our lives.

On Tuesday just before shut down time, Doris had a visitor. I'd just entered my room and clanked the door behind me when Tori bounded up the stairway to tell me the news of her grandmother's visit. She was still in special housing that was across a corridor from the day room, we all shared together. Passively I sat on my bed and glimpsed out the window into the parking lot below. To my surprise there was Brad clutching Purr in one arm and picking up and tossing small pebbles with his other hand. Hurriedly, I ran to my window and yelled to Tori that Brad was outside. She ran to my door, then down to the intercom asking if she could go into my room so she could see her son. The small window in her own room faced another wall. The guard flatly refused reminding Tori that there was no exception to the rules. Tears freely ran from her face as her pleads were ignored.

Up until now Tori had put up a very reserved and compliant front, but now her heart was in her face. She ran back up the stairs to my door and listened while I described what clothing Brad was wearing and every move

126

he made out in the parking lot with his great-grandfather. After a short time passed, lock down commenced and Tori still crying, dejectedly walked to her room. Once in her room the tears flowed like a dam being released after days of rain. The refusal of one small glimpse of her small son was more than she could bare while confined in this house of bondage and pain.

By the end of the week, sixteen women reduced down to twelve women and by Thursday evening we were down to nine. All who remained, smiled and waved good-by, while visions of their own release day played in their minds. Being left behind sent women into groups of inmates that knew that their time in jail was still far away. Hovering together they gained strength and quieted their pain with reassurance from their peers. No clocks ticked, for time didn't matter when court was still months away. For their lives hung in the balance, captives of law and justice.

The compassion I felt for these people facing a continually circle of imprisonment and release during their entire lifetime touched my heartstrings with love. The United States may have the best law system in the entire world, but it still was a mass of cold impersonal walls. People weren't treated as individuals they were just another poor person trapped in the hands of our rich bureaucracy. Now I understood why some people who have tasted prison have pleaded for reform. We didn't need longer sentences, we needed to care about the prisoner and help them change to a fairer life style so they could make a good living and have a good life for not just themselves, but for their families too.

The lady who stole a TV set, sat 15 days in jail and then was picked up to go back to Idaho to face charges. Her eyes fell to the floor. This should have been her day of freedom. Another woman sat in jail 11 days and then found out that all charges had been dropped. But since the police had impounded her car at her arrest it cost her $40 the first day and then $100 the day after that. Accumulated, it cost her more than her car was worth to get it back. Now she had no car to drive to work. Still another lady sat in jail for 2 weeks, her public attorney did not inform her that she had a PR bond. The night before her release she discovered the error and called a bondsman paying him $20 to get out. Rita on the other hand had the misfortune of going to court at the end of the day. The Judge was tired and taking one look at her, he said he didn't want to hear another excuse. He moved the court proceedings on her case to 30 days later. One hundred dollars would have bought her freedom, but her mother couldn't afford to pay.

Everyday these people sat in jail, cost them that much more in personal wealth. If they couldn't work, they couldn't pay their rent, if they didn't pay their rent then they had no place to live. The vicious circle continued until upon leaving the jail they were forced again to go right back into the crimes they had paid for the last time they were in jail. The words, money is the root of all evil, resulting in greed for more money, may be true for some people but poor people didn't steal to become rich, they stole to survive. Luke 6:20&21, "Jesus looked at his disciples and said, 'Happy are you poor; the kingdom of God is yours! Happy are you who are hungry now, you will be filled! Happy are you who weep now; you will laugh!" If only the poor people could understand that through poverty we are given wisdom, if we will only act on it and seek God to bring us up when times are hard. For God works through the weaknesses of people to change them into the people He desires them to become. When we are in need we come to Him and then through our prayers, He can help us to find answers that will help us to make it through. God is full of compassion and He will rescue us, if we will just place our trust in Him instead of taking things into our own hands and breaking the law by stealing. There is always a great reward for those who wait upon the Lord for answers for He will turn our situation into rejoicing if He's just allowed to work in our lives.

At first when people asked if they could have any

of the food I didn't want, I was surprised. We were served huge meals and I couldn't figure out where they put it. All the takers were so skinny and literally stuffed in as much as they could hold and then more. Only after a few days did I realize they were saving up pounds for when they left jail and entered into the real world again. Where being hungry was just another day in their life.

We were fortunate that the jail we were in had an active prison ministry and when church was called, most inmates gathered up their Bibles to attend. My esteem for my fellow inmates increased as each one called out to the newcomers that now was the time to follow God. So forming a small army of Christian soldiers, they walked in single file, heads high only to be greeted by the guards with commands to spread eagle against the wall for another pat down and later knowing that once again since they were coming into contact with another person, they would return to be strip searched. Nothing was untouched or left unveiled, they were jobs that had to be done by the guards, putting harassment on the freedom of worshiping our Lord. Not wanting to face the persecution of baring our bodies again, Doris, Tori and I didn't have the strength to go.

Later after shut down ended, I passed by the jail cells of inmates that remained in their rooms after shut down ended. Observing each woman in their cell, only added one more thing on top of a mountain full or sorrow. Life in jail was filled with uncertainties and huddled bundles of women faced the loneliness of fear alone. Their bodies rose and fell trembling in tears as they lay on their beds. One week in Jefferson revealed pain of people born poor, none were untouched by tears, all cried. They were people with real life problems and feelings. They were not at all like the hard core selfish criminals that were portrayed on TV. They had faith in God. They displayed love to one another. And they had hope that some day a new world would bring a promise of peace and security, a new beginning with no more pain. Hebrews 13:3, "Remember those who are in prison, as though you were in prison with them. Remember those who are suffering, as though you were suffering as they are."

Fear crept over my flesh producing goose bumps, Winfield was here. Tori, Doris and I stripped our rooms and walked into the corridors to be processed for release from Jefferson and handed over to Winfield. After yet more fingerprints, our dirty street clothes on, we waited in yet another locked room for transfer. A police officer accompanied by a woman came driving an out of date police car to travel seven and a half hours back to home. The Jefferson officers poked fun at the beat up old junk heap. The officer from Winfield just smiled and pulled out leather belts with handcuffs and 2 chains with handcuffs. Tori and I looked at each other taking a deep breath as a leather belt was strapped around her waist and handcuffs placed on her wrists. The process continued until all of us were secured. Sacks of misc. from underclothes to food were stored in the trunk. Quietly Bill, Doris, and I piled in the back seat and Tori, the woman and officer climbed into the front.

With our heads held high, we rode over the border to enter Utah. Dread instantly waved over us. We were just four people whose only crime was to love 3 abused children and try to protect them from a bad legal system.

Nearing Winfield, they informed us that the jail didn't hold women only men. So Tori, Doris and I were taken to Harper. I expected for them to take us to Harper first since it was on the way, but soon my hope was shattered as they turned heading towards Winfield first. Smiling, he announced our arrival and straightening in his seat he pulled on to Main street on the way to the police station. All of us sat up holding our heads high while people outside stared at our procession.

Once Bill was out of the car, we proceeded to Harper. In Jefferson we were allowed the freedom to make phone calls and have visitors, but in Winfield Bill was given one call and then informed visiting was only on Friday's between 2 and 4. We had made several phone calls to our pastor in the Lutheran Church, but when he

130

showed up to see Bill, he was denied. All other jails allowed visits from pastors or lawyers anytime, but not Winfield. We were big celebrities caught and now whatever punishment they wanted to give us in jail before we were ever found guilty was granted.

Harper wasn't much better than Winfield. We were given orange uniforms but this time we slept in the same room sharing an open shower and stool. I guess privacy in jail is not important. Being close to Tori at night was great, but Doris was always restless and watching us constantly to make sure we weren't too close.

Doris had changed in jail. She saw visions of a ministry to give hope to people in jail and to tell people who don't know anything about the law system. We were all dismayed over the lack of anything for inmates to do. We had all come to the same conclusion that jails were for the oppression of the poor so with this in mind, Doris kept pushing Tori and I to practice our singing. For the first time, she became a one woman spokesperson to any of the officers, who would listen, telling about how Tori played the piano and how we sang for churches. Tori and I were both pleased.

Tori and I always dreamed of totally pouring all our time and efforts into a singing and talking ministry. But Tori's parents fought it, now for her mother to push us to do it was like a dream come true.

All three of us studied our Bibles looking for hope each day that passed in jail. The Bible I'd asked for when we were first incarcerated in Jefferson was give to me on the first Saturday of our imprisonment. What a welcome it was and with some gentle pushing Tori read it and then Doris. By the end of our first week in jail, all of us silently took turns strengthening our faith in scripture and prayer. The Jefferson ministers gave everyone small New Testaments on Thursday and Doris and Tori received their own. For some reason mine was lost in the shuffle when we went to Winfield. Tori knowing I slept with my Bible, gave me hers. Later in the car to Winfield, I gave my Bible to Bill and in Harper, Doris shared hers with us.

Joshua 1:8, "Be sure that the Book of the Law is always read in your worship. Study it day and night, and make sure that you do everything written in it. Then you will be prosperous and successful."

Our incarceration took on a whole different ritual in Harper. Our room was 18 feet by 10 feet with 4 sets of bunk beds sleeping eight. The beds were in an L shape with a metal half picnic style table bench. On the opposite side of the bench was an open shower and a stool and one set of bunk beds which had a row of dusty old novels and a stack of magazines that were as old as 5 years. The walls were bars and a 2 foot walk separated us from 4 large windows opposite our bunks and bench table. The windows had bars and heavy iron screens to prevent someone from breaking any of the panes of glass. Our food was from the hospital and there was a slot in the bars where they pushed it through to us. They allowed us pop in our rooms and we welcomed a diet Pepsi feeling that this was royalty after Jefferson. The only drawback was no TV, no radio, and no phone. But Doris, a sweet checked Grandma, spun her charm and they couldn't deny her anything. They gave her special meals, because of her hypoglycemia and promptly renewed Tori's medicine prescription.

CHAPTER TEN

The morning sun broke my fitful sleep, casting shadows of the cell bars across the hard cold cement floor. Silence greeted my ears and emptiness flooded my eyes for now I was all alone. It was so quiet and still that it seemed as though time had stopped leaving me trapped in a solitary world where my thoughts paraded before me, never ending and constantly reminding me that I was no longer in control.

My spiraling thoughts recalled the quick release of Bill and Doris. The County Attorney professed in court that he had a change of mind concerning their involvement with the kidnapping and let them go on a thousand dollar bail bond each on the Monday following our return to Winfield

My heart sank at my last vision of Tori. Fear paraded across her face as she held tightly to a court order commanding her to appear in court with her ex-husband over the custody of Brad. No sooner had she received this document than the Sheriff appeared stating that a representative from the Social Services and Rehabilitation wanted to talk to her. Upon returning she nervously recited word for word how he stated that he would be talking to the DA about filing charges against her for fraud. While we were in Portland she cashed her SRS check and unbeknownst to us, it was illegal to cash a SRS check from another state. While we talked over the new developments we both decided that she needed to bond out. The same day her parents bond was reduced, her bond had been reduced to $5,000 dollars, but she didn't want to leave me in jail alone, so she stayed, but now everything had changed. She had to be free to fight for soon we discovered that Eric was rallying the creditors to not only take back their merchandise we had purchased through store credit, but also to press charges for falsifying my income.

The authorities refused to reduce my bond and my parents were so confused over my open defiance to remain loyal to Tori that they wouldn't pay my bond. They concluded that staying in jail was in my best interest. Tori finding out my dilemma tried pleading my case before her grandparents, but they too would not agree to help get me out of jail. In desperation, she started calling anyone involved in Gay Rights, hoping that someone would have an outlet to funds to help a mother who was being discriminated against. Everyone she talked with was sympathetic, but with the AIDS epidemic most funds were running dry. Besides this, all of the gay activist had prejudices to face on their own and one more distraught parent fighting for custody only added to thousands of more requests for help of the same kind. Still they gave her an address of lesbian mothers for custody that often loaned money for custody battles and in special cases they gave as much as $500 dollars. Unfortunately, this usually took about 6 months.

Months before the fleeing with our children we had placed an add in the paper for stocks in a company that Tori and I were thinking about starting and we had one man who called. In one last ditch effort she called his number and told Gene how Eric and Alan had plotted against us and had forced me into fleeing with my kids. He seemed sympathetic, but he refused to give out the money without some kind of down payment. Tori informed him about my half of the house and a small piece of land that I owned and that I would be willing to sign them over to him if he would just pay my bond. He readily agreed, but he wanted to meet with her first and view the property. So I remained in jail until he could find the time to come.

The jail bars illuminated in every crevice of my cell, sending my thoughts rocketing again to Tori and all she faced in the outside world. I felt so helpless in jail and my worry for Tori's heart condition crept into my thoughts every moment of the day. Now she was on her own to face tremendous odds of hiding our relationship once again, working with all our creditors and calming them down, and now fighting the law for kidnapping charges. I prayed for her heart, strength, and mind, trembling before God in complete surrender of my entire will. I was totally helpless, I could do nothing!

As each day passed, Tori would continue to update me on the phone as to what had happened that day. I was shocked and amazed at how much she had to do and how well she was enduring against everyone wanting to put our necks in a noose and hang us from the nearest tree. Together the County Attorney was mounting a case of fraud against us for the use of my good credit and trying with all his might to get local creditors to press charges against us. Tori keeping up with the creditors, amazingly enough was informed by them (Nehemiah 4:12, "But time after time Jews who were living among our enemies came to warn us of the plans our enemies were making against us.") what the County Attorney was doing and pleading her case before each of them and promising to return all of their property claimed them down. Soon she discovered that most did not want to be involved, but this presented another problem all of our property was in Portland. Quickly Bill sold scaffolding from his construction business to obtain the money and with Tori's help they drove to Portland picking up our furniture first. Once back, Tori returned all of the items demanded by our creditors. A flood of relief entered her voice as she praised God that the creditors were now happy.

A week after Tori's and her parents freedom she and Bill came to visit me at jail. It was necessary for me to sign a release form allowing Tori the power of attorney to handle all financial matters surrounded by our creditors and our inability to pay on the accounts, due to my incarceration. I also signed a release form allowing Sean to resign as my attorney. Since the very beginning, we had been dismayed over the lack of results from Sean.

Not only did he not get the motion for appeal over the custody, filed, but he also was unable to get a bond reduction. By now I had been in jail for almost three weeks and in this time Sean had professed to using almost the entire retainer of $3000 dollars to fight my criminal case. With no money to pay him, he was unwilling to be my attorney and he recommended that I get a public attorney.

After many phone calls at the Portland jail, Tori's pastor recommended Kathy Knox to take over as Brad's and her attorney. This of course happened only after a retainer fee was paid by her grandparents. In subsequent visits after her release she pleaded my case before her attorney requesting that she take over as my public attorney. Kathy agreed only after stipulating that a formal resignation letter was written by Sean along with my complete file over custody. She reassured Tori that as my new attorney she felt sure she could get my bond reduced.

It was so wonderful to see Tori and my eyes flooded with tears as we embraced. She looked like she had lost weight and her eyes had deep circles making her 27 years look like 40. I was shocked at her appearance and fear crept into my face as I realized that she wasn't holding up as well as her voice had reflected on the phone. She handed me a sack containing toilet items, a small tape recorder with religious tapes and my precious Bible. I was elated.

Words spilled from her mouth as she caught me up on everything that had happened since she left jail. She began by explaining what stories she had come up with to calm her parents down and cover our tracks. First she explained about how she knew of Gene, the man who she was working with to pay my bond. Next she explained how he was a distraught ex-family member with a grudge against the Zonvono family. This of course was the family that Mark was next in line to be the Godfather, too. She portrayed him as a possible boyfriend, who had lots of contacts and of course he was wealthy and he wanted revenge against the family, who had put us in jail. Her parents were thrilled at the prospect of having another family helping them and at once they started to gain back some of the strength they had lost from their experience in jail. Gene's image made them feel like someone was on their side and restored their hope that they could once again have a better life.

Tori's voice slowed as she explained how the arrangement at her grandparents was not good. Her grandparent's attitude towards Bill and Doris was cooling daily from the publicity about their family and the shame and humiliation all of this caused. Before the first week was all over they had recounted everything they had ever done wrong from their bankruptcy to the present time. Her parents were so humiliated that asking for any more money was completely out of the question. It took alot of convincing from Tori to build up their courage to fight. They were like whipped puppies after jail and any faith they had before in themselves was buried under terrifying dreams of going to prison. They were fifty years old and now all of their possessions were in Portland and all their money was gone and they had nothing more they could sell. Before long they had no choice but to agree with Tori and move to a town where Bill and Tori could find work. Within a week, Bill had found a job managing a cement business for less than $200 dollars a week. This was devastating to him when just years before he had a million dollar construction business.

Due to our quick flee from Winfield and subsequently Bill's and Doris's; many of his large construction tools were left behind in his rented shop. Going back to reclaim his property he discovered that everything had been confiscated. His former landlord admitted to taking them, but refused to give them back to him until he paid off his lumberyard bill which he owned as well. Bill went to the police and reported his tools stolen only later to be informed that their investigation was inconclusive, because no one would admit to taking them.

Furthermore in Portland, the first house Tori and I

rented was filled with all of her dad's hand tools and small transportable power tools. Upon returning to pickup our furniture from the second rented home, Tori called the former landlord's pleading for the return of these tools, but they wouldn't budge. They said that under the law until we paid them $1000 dollars in deposit, that we had formerly agreed to before they terminated our lease, they didn't have to give any of our things back. I couldn't believe my ears. If he didn't have any tools, how could he work? I quickly realized that it was God's hand that moved our former landlord to terminate our lease. For if we hadn't moved, they would have held on to everything we had and there would have been no way for us to come up with our original deposit in time to calm the creditors that were demanding their stuff back.

Eric had aroused so much concern with our creditors over the double wide that Tori's and my home was in the process of being repossessed. And to make matters worse, Tori's parents home was being repossessed too. Without any money and with me in jail, there was no way for us to make the payments. Furthermore, with additional accusations from Eric accusing us of being lesbians along with me illegally taking my children, he also made allegations that we had forged papers on my income. HUD was notified and to our disbelief and unhappiness an investigation over fraud was expected to be investigated.

Through all of this, God was opening doors, enabling Tori and her parents to move out of her grandparent's home and rent a duplex. In addition, God led Tori to a temporary telephone soliciting job selling tickets to the policeman's ball. Two weeks in jail, being handcuffed, strip searched and basically humiliated and now she was helping to promote the police retirement fund. Matt. 5:43-45a, "You have heard that it was said, 'Love your friends, hate your enemies.' But now I tell you; love your enemies and pray for those who persecute you, so you may become the sons of your Father in heaven." Tori took a deep breath and Praised God for giving her a job even though she would only be making minimum wage.

With a lump in her throat, Tori quickly recounted that Brad did not hold up very well after his great-grandparents picked him up from the SRS. He panicked, afraid that he would never see his mother again and spilled his guts over all of us living together in Portland. Tori explained that any child, under such pressure would say anything! After many convincing conversations with her parents and grandparents they seemed to believe her story. Brad on the other hand was very fearful and clung to Tori every moment since her release. When he first arrived at his great grandparent's he couldn't seem to get enough food. He complained at the foster home that he didn't get much to eat. To Tori's surprise, Brad looked as if he had gained 10 pounds. Her heart instantly went out to him, knowing that he had eaten to calm his nerves and for the comfort, he so desperately needed.

Tori continued, stating that all of our and her parents vehicles had been repossessed when we went to jail. In desperation her father and she made phone calls to all creditors on the vehicles explaining what had happened and asking for their return, but they said they were 10 days late on their last payment and they lawfully could keep them. So in desperation, Bill went to his brother's and took the estate car left after his father's death. His brother wasn't very happy with this, but rightfully he had as much claim to use it as his brother. So now at least they had a car.

The court proceeding with custody over Brad was set in about a month. Lines of worry crossed her tired face. The first appointment with Sherry, her and Brad's psychologist resulted in her begging Sherry to understand that she and I were just friends. She glanced away from my eyes as she explained that she had to lie to Sherry and tell her that she was an innocent by-stander and that she had no part of the kidnapping. I took her hand as she relived the experience of her appointment by restating that she had strongly stressed that Brad and she had been abused! Firmly she pleaded her case before Sherry

139

reminding her that any contact with Alan could very well push Brad over the edge. Her face grew deathly serious as she described the constant nightmares that taunted her memories of the vicious days of Alan's cruelty to little Brad. Her eyes lighted up with fear and a sudden burst of pleads echoed in her voice. Sherry responded immediately seeing her fear and calmly agreeing to stay impartial so that the best decision for Brad would be made. Tori breaking off from the story of her meeting, turned her gaze upon me and with confidence said that she knew that God would help her persuade Sherry in time!

Bill had waited outside for most of the visit, but now he entered the room. His face looked drawn and his voice sounded shaky. Immediately I felt compassion for this man who had been accidentally caught up in the kidnapping and now was paying for it with his pride and loss of all his worldly possessions. Quietly he motioned to Tori to come and with final farewells until the next visit he encompassed Tori and I in a big bear hug. Tears flowed from his eyes and Tori's as they left, knowing that they were free. In tears I walked back to my cell, wishing beyond hope that I could have gone with them.

Among the personal things Tori brought, she had enclosed paper and pencil. When she left she whispered for only my ears to hear for me to write about everything that we had gone through. Now with pencil in hand, I wrote.. As each day passed, I filled my days with prayer, Bible study and writing. I sang to the music of each tape she had given me and I praised God expecting him to deliver me any day from the lions den. Hebrews 10:34, "You shared the sufferings of prisoners, and when all your belongings were seized, you endured your loss gladly, because you knew that you still possessed something much better, which would last forever."

CHAPTER ELEVEN

Silence echoed through the cement and barred room creating a sudden feeling that the walls were slowly closing in. My mind immediately focused on visions of Tori and my sweet children. But as suddenly as the picture appeared a loud clash erupted exploding the image into thousands of pieces. How much longer would I wake up in this world of bars and locked doors?

Every time Tori called Gene on the phone, he would question her strongly about our relationship. The pressure of confrontation became so extreme that she led Gene to believe that she was available for dates. He eased up immediately, since he was a single man and Tori was a beautiful woman. Today she had just received news from Kathy our new public attorney, that my bond had been reduced and that Gene would bring her the money. Her voice cracked on the phone as she asked me to pray that he would give the money without her having to give him anything else in return.

Fear radiated through my body that Tori would even sleep with this man to get me out. Trembling, I commanded her not to do this and she meekly agreed, knowing that this was what I wanted her to hear not necessarily what she might have to do to gain my freedom. As soon as she hung up the phone, the reality of what she was about to do sent fear through my entire body. Taking a strong grip on the phone, I dialed my mother, both grandparents and once again pleaded for them to pay my now reduced bond. My tears flowed steadily as my words fell on deaf ears. I wanted to tell them about what Tori was going to do, but I knew that it was because of Tori that they wouldn't help. Returning to my cell, I immediately fell on the floor petitioning God Almighty! In humility

141

and tears, I begged and pleaded knowing that God loved us and was faithful to act. In less than an hour later Tori called back praising God that Gene was wiring the money!

Once hanging up the phone, Tori began her search for a bondsman who would use my property and land as collateral against the remaining $18,000 bond money. It is required that 10% of your bond money was to be paid and the remainder had to be covered in an effort to make the person further accountable if they should run. Tori scared me with this further requirement, because I had to sign the same house and land to Gene. In addition, I was homeless and I had to have a place to live. So in many conversations with her parents, she convinced them that I was pregnant from Rick (after my release and well after we had lived together, I pretended to miscarry) and that Gene would not pay my bond unless we were all together. In empathy they agreed, but they stipulated that we were never to be alone together and that I had to get a job before I got out. Hanging up the phone I easily secured an upholstery job. In excitement, I called back telling Tori the news and anxiously awaited the bondsman to come and let me out.

I had been in jail for 5 weeks and now with yet another miracle, God had provided me with a job and a complete stranger to pay my bond. In celebration, I praised God! I could hardly wait to see Tori, Brad and my children.

Since the very beginning of my incarceration in Harper, I wrote letters to my children daily in jail. I tried to call several times, but again and again Eric would slam the receiver down on the phone after making threats that I wasn't to call his residence ever again. I even pleaded my case and asked information about my kids to the CSO, but she refused as well. My lawyer was more concerned with getting me out of jail, than finding out any information about them either. By the fourth week of my imprisonment, Rich had his 12th birthday. Taking her lunch money and realizing my problem with seeing my children, Tori sent a small candy basket and balloon to school for his birthday. Now at least Rich knew that I hadn't forgotten him.

I put everything that Tori brought me on her last visit into a small paper sack and holding my Bible in my hand, I waited. Earlier in the morning she called stating that the money and she would be here soon, but now it was 8:00 in the evening. It was a matter of routine for the bondsman to check with the D.A. about my case. Apparently his conversation with the county attorney resulted in him stating that I had more charges pressed against me and he was of the opinion that I would run. Tori desperately pleaded my case to no avail. In a panic, Tori called Kathy about the problem and Kathy in return informed the bondsman that that was an outright lie and calling the D.A., she forced him to confess to the bondsman that no other charges had been filed. I had no idea of the drama that was going on and finally as the time turned to 10:00 p.m., I was called to the visiting room to meet the bondsman.

Clutching my sack in one hand, I cheerfully walked out into the reception room of the jail. I couldn't believe it! I finally was leaving. I was introduced to the bondsman and quickly I extended my hand to thank him for his support. Taking a deep breath, I stated that I would not run, that I loved my children and I would never leave. Not only this, but I was innocent and a good person. In complete confession of my faith, I verified over and over again that I was trustworthy and honest. Within an hour of pleading my case, God changed his mind. He looked me in the eye and said he liked me and with a firm hand shake, he agreed to pay my bond. To my shock, before I was let go from the jail, I was forced to sign an agreement stipulated by the court system to not call or see my children. I swallowed hard knowing that unless I signed this I would not be allowed my freedom. I had to be free to work, so I could continue to seek justice for myself and to regain custody of my children. I signed, believing that God would handle this paper in His timing.

I was shaking as I left the jail and entered into

143

freedom at last. My head buzzed and I felt very dizzy. Tori said many times on the phone how big the world seemed once you leave the jail. After being prevented from making any decisions and being given your food and told what to do, facing the outside world was a big adjustment. Even going to a store for food presented you with so much to choose from that you were easily overwhelmed. In amazement, I felt my head throbbing from the sudden change. Quietly I wondered how people who had been in prison for years could cope with suddenly being forced to take care of themselves again.

Before I was in jail, I had read articles expressing how many inmates returned soon after they left. The facts were very clear to me now that most prisoners had lost the instinct to make a life for themselves outside the bars. At the time I couldn't understand this, but now I knew how they felt. Now my learned passiveness had to be turned into fighting to survive and with the help of God, I would try to put all of this behind me and press forward with renewed hope.

It was 11:30p.m. and I braced myself as I entered through the doors to my new home. Tori's eye's greeted me brightly as she stood side by side with her mother. I wanted to take Tori into my arms, but I knew that it wasn't possible so I thanked both of them for allowing me to share their home. Doris was friendly, but I could tell that her attitude towards me was cooler. Conversation was limited to remarks that it was late and so agreeing that I was tired too, they showed me to my unfinished attic room and said good night. A mattress lay on the floor with some sheets and blankets ready for my first night of freedom. Quietly I lay in bed looking at all the nails sticking through the ceiling of the roof. I wondered if there would ever be a time when I could freely hold Tori again without worrying who was watching and what disaster they were planning to put us through.

My first days of freedom were totally consumed with how all of us could avoid jail. Thankfully, God showed me favor with my new boss as I once again resumed upholstery. During my free time most of my concentrated efforts were put on the court which was on everyone's mind. It became very clear to all of us that the law moved very slowly in criminal cases, especially when it was the full focus of all of the conversations in our home. After the three hearings I had gone to in Portland, Tori, her parents and I had 3 more additional hearings in Winfield in less than a month. One was the bail hearing, another a plea hearing, and the last was a formal charge hearing. None of these lasted very long and all resulted in yet a longer time before the final hearing that would decide what would happen as a result of my kidnapping my children.

Kathy, who was fresh out of law school and didn't have a lot of experience, tried to get Tori and I to plead guilty, which would give us immediate results, but all consisted of us being sentenced to years in prison. With this in mind, naturally Tori and I had to plead not guilty. The Lord had seen us through this far and we prayed that he would open a different way.

Soon after our decision, Kathy refused to take my custody case and after the plea hearing she said that she could no longer help me with my criminal. She professed that there was a conflict of interest. So with no further adieu and refusing to hear my pleas for reconsidering, she handed me my entire file. Once home, I opened the huge box and to my alarm, right on the top of the pile of documents, I found the letters I had written to Sean, stating that we were being persecuted because we were homosexuals. Tori and I were furious at the blatant disregard of Sean for our family and circumstances. He was a gay man and as far as I was concerned he knew that this information would do us harm in the wrong hands. I knew in my heart that God would judge him for his lack of care for his actions. This of course explained Kathy's sudden change of attitude.

By now many things had happened, Tori went to her first custody hearing and the same Judge that took my children away proceeded. He totally sided with Alan and

came down on Tori many times saying that she had
overreacted and was never really seriously harmed by
Alan. He scoffed at the so-called abuse of Brad and
immediately assigned an impartial psychologist, who later
we found out was not a psychologist at all, but a retired
minister, to monitor the visits between Brad and Alan. He
only agreed to do this because Sherry had sided with Tori,
and the CSO suggested supervised visits first. Another
hearing was set in one month. During the entire hearing,
Kathy didn't fight for Tori, but many times sided with her
opponents. Tori became petrified and our whole household
was weighted in fear.

Brad was experiencing many nightmares from the
on set of the visitations with his dad, and every night
screaming filled the house with Brad begging for his
father to leave him alone. Tori's parents had never
experienced these nightmares before and as a result of
being there when they happened made them support Tori
completely. They loved Brad with all their hearts and for
the first time they could see the fear that Brad had for his
dad. Not only did they have to acknowledge the
nightmares and fear, but Pa came with Tori to bring Brad
to the meetings with Alan. Bill in an effort to calm Brad's
terror promised to sit in the car and wait for his safe
return. Pulling up to the door of the office it soon became
clear that Brad was not going anywhere and to Bill's
further dismay, he found himself lifting Brad forcefully
out of the car and pleading with him the entire way into
the office to calm down and that everything would be OK.
Once inside, Tori sat in the nearest chair and Bill placed 5
year old Brad on his mother's lap. Brad, who usually
could be calmed by his grandfather, refused to release his
grip on his shirt and before his hands could be pulled
free, he literally had ripped holes into the shirt that Bill
was wearing. In complete helplessness, Bill with tears in
his eyes waited just outside the door listening to his
precious grandson crying and screaming to go home. As
each week of meetings continued Brad started losing
weight and becoming severely sick. The nightmares

intensified with every visit and every night's sleep was broken with screams that filled the house like a raging flood of water. Tori in desperation and in exhaustion from lack of sleep, took Brad into her bed, holding him closely in her arms all night to comfort him so that he would feel safe enough to go to sleep.

Fear continued to mount as each visit passed and the next court drew nearer, but then the most amazing thing happened. The Judge who had caused all of the problems over my custody and now Tori's, became so zealous from all of the power that he had in Winfield that he furiously went through the courthouse ripping phones off the walls.

The city council had had the phone company install phones in the courthouse during the weekend in order to monitor the long distant phone calls from the city offices. They hoped that this would reduce personal long distant calls. The Judge was out of town the first day of the week and when he returned the following evening, he tried to use the phone and found that he couldn't. In a mad rage that they had dared to install telephones without his permission, he ripped the phones off the desks and used an ax from the fire protection gear to pry off all of the phones from the walls in all of the other offices. In a further statement of anger and unhappiness, he took all of them in a large box to the city council meeting that was proceeding that very evening. The city council was alarmed at his nerve and threatened prosecution. By the time everything was said and done, he was forced to resign and to pay restitution for the damage he had done. We all rejoiced knowing that God had performed a miracle and had caused the bad judge to get just what he deserved. Heb. 10:30, "For we know who said, 'I will take revenge, I will repay'; and who also said, 'The Lord will judge his people."

Knowing God's will is sometimes very confusing. It's like rubbing your stomach and patting your head at the same time. Or facing a phone call that your son has just been killed in a car accident. It doesn't make sense and giving in to our emotions of fear that God has deserted us only makes things worse. Suffering is a way of life and in trials we learn to trust God in all situations. Many wonderful verses encourage us to believe that God loves us and that He will see us through any problems. 1 Cor. 10:13, "Every test that you have experienced is the kind that normally comes to people. But God keeps his promise, and he will not allow you to be tested beyond your power to remain firm; at the time you are put to the test, he will give you the strength to endure it, and so provide you with a way out." Time and time again when Tori and I were on our last leg, God provided a way out and direction to what we should do next. With the miracle of the Judge's resignation, a new Judge would be appointed not only to Tori's cases, but also to mine. In addition God led us to Jeff Dobbs.

God shone a bright light down on us through Tori's soliciting job. Tori worked beside a woman that was in the process of a divorce. She had shared about her custody fight over Brad and this woman just raved all about her attorney and that he really fought for you. In excitement, she copied down his number and called Jeff Dobbs. He was everything the lady had told her and in her eagerness, she professed to being me and made me an appointment for the next day.

Jeff Dobbs was a man of character and thoroughly versed in the law. Every word of Tori's and my story opened harsh criticism of his contemporaries. He loved the law and hated to hear when it had been abused. He was a good man and for the first time I felt like I could trust someone. He was not prejudice and when he confronted me on the homosexual question, I completely dropped my guard and said that it was true. By now the secrecy of my lifestyle had gone to the limit and I wanted to just tell the truth. I hated how we were being treated and I felt if I couldn't trust him about this, I couldn't ask him to fight for my kids or keep me from going to jail. To my surprise he was very compassionate and through many conversations, he not only agree to take on my case, but

148

Tori's too. In addition to this he took my case's on pro
bono and Tori's criminal case pro bono as well. This
meant that he would totally donate his time. Later Tori
and I had to pay for Jeff to take her custody case, but this
was a great deal less than what it could have been if we
had to pay for all of our court cases together. Tori and I
couldn't praise God enough. He had opened another door
and for the first time we started to gain ground with the
excellent, hard work of Jeff Dobbs. Immediately Jeff set
up a hearing so I could see my kids and before the hearing
began he set up one hour supervised visits the following
week.

Four months had passed since I saw my children
and almost 5 months since I saw Alex. Our visits were
just one hour at first and took place in the office of the
Court Service Officer. In preparation of my first meeting
with my children, Doris had bought little cupcakes from
the bakery and sent them with me to give to them. They
were as glad to see me as I was to see them. All of them
looked older. Rich had lost weight and Alex had gained
weight. 7 year old Crystal was very clingy and both she
and 10 year old Alex sat on my lap the entire visit. They
wanted to know when I could be with them and they cried
when it was time to leave. We just chatted about
everything. I didn't want to bring up Portland or anything
heavy, but it was completely on their minds. Rich started
from the very beginning of what he and his dad had done
since I was in jail and Crystal chirped in when Rich came
up for air. Unfortunately everything they said to me, I
already knew quite well, but it still brought back the sour
feeling in the pit of my stomach as I recalled the past few
months apart from my kids.

After being put in jail at Harper, Eric had managed
to gain a court order to go to Portland had pickup Rich's
and Crystal's clothes and other belongings from Tori's and
my rented house. Tori's parents had gone to Portland the
first weekend out of jail to pickup essentials and to their
shock Eric and Rich pulled up to our house at the very
same moment with the police. Doris and Bill immediately

became very angry and followed them around the house as they picked up their stuff. Rich knew where everything was and with confidence, quickly found most of his and Crystal's things, completely unnerving Bill and Doris.

From the very beginning, Tori had persuaded them to believe that we had not been together in Portland at all. Upon returning, Tori was met with a barrage of questions and in an effort to calm them down, she told them that the Zonvono family had prompted Eric and Rich only after they had planted our things. She stressed that Mark wanted to humiliate her before Winfield and them. With many tears and reminding them they were dealing with a mafia family, her parents calmed down.

Crystal's voice broke my thoughts, stating that she was very unhappy because Rich didn't get all of her stuff. Her dad and Rich had left most of her toys behind and Rich didn't get his coats. Looking at me, they asked if they could have their things back. Quietly I tried to explain to them that since I was in jail anything that Eric and Rich didn't get was still in Portland and now was someone else's.

I don't think that anyone can comprehend how helpless a person is in jail, especially when you have no money and none of your family will help you. When Tori and her father went to pick up our furniture, Bill refused to allow Tori to get any of my children's things, because of the court order. In an effort to keep up the front, Tori agreed and basically my clothes were the only things they brought home that belonged to my family. And on top of this as far as Tori's parents were concerned, I had sold all of my furniture and everything they picked up was Tori's. So literally the only thing I had left was a few pieces of clothing.

The kidnapping had made my children instant celebrities. They were interviewed and photographed and this was wonderfully exciting to them. Now that months had passed and everything was back to normal they were confused. Eric had told them that I was in jail and what a terrible person I was to have disobeyed the law. He

150

further stated that I deserved everything I got and that Tori and I were both going to prison. This only confused them more, because no matter what their father said they loved Tori and especially me. Our first hour together ended as quickly as it seemed to have begun with memories of our past scattered into little pieces, like a glass hitting and breaking into tiny fragments on the floor. Hopefully the next time I saw them, I could give them news of a new life with me that was better than what we had had before.

CHAPTER TWELVE

A different prison emerged. A hard cold invisible cell, turning normal realities into confusion. How much I wished to just let down my guard and lovingly put my arms around Tori. But amidst prejudice, this was impossible.

Tori's parents kept a cautious eye on me watching my every move and putting limits on every room that I ventured into that Tori and Brad might be in at that moment. I tried to be indifferent to this and comply with their constant demands, but after being drilled for the millionth time of where I had been or what I was doing, one day at the supper table, I just exploded telling them it was none of their business. A sudden hush entered the kitchen and later Bill quietly took me aside and warned me that if I ever talked like that again, I would have to find another place to live. Meekly I apologized, knowing that I had no other place to go and I needed the income from the job I was working at to help pay for Tori's custody fight. Not only this, but I was afraid that they would find a way to watch Tori even closer and this could separate us completely. Determined to make things work, Tori and I devised a plan to give us more time together and once again we began another front. With all the turmoil and fear over Brad's custody, Tori's parents were willing to believe anything. We pretended that Gene had our computer hooked up to phone lines in an effort to keep us informed over some under handed schemes to get back at Eric, and the SBC and anyone else that had persecuted us. By now Tori's parents had had enough and revenge seemed like a good way to get them off of feeling sorry for themselves. From just being put in jail both sides of their families were ashamed at the public embarrassment and they were quick to let them know that this was unacceptable behavior and so they punished them by totally leaving them out of all family gatherings and basically telling them where to get off. They were more or less branded, black sheep, and not worth believing or trusting. In addition, none of their former friends in Winfield would have anything to do with them either. They were completely humiliated and this opened up a solution for venting their anger. So with this in mind, I had to open the computer and monitor all incoming information. In an effort to protect her parents, they weren't allowed to see what was going on so if someone was caught and talked, they wouldn't be held responsible.

The house that we had rented was a duplex and by the time the first month had ended we occupied the bottom part too. With all of the money coming in from all of us working except for Doris who took care of the house, food, etc., we had earn enough money to go back to Portland and pickup their furniture. For the past month Tori's furniture was the only furniture we had. So a new living arrangement was made and I was given the other bedroom downstairs by Bill and Doris's.

I swallowed hard wishing that they would have let me stay in one of the bedrooms upstairs with Tori and Brad. Just the same, I was able to spend time with Tori after her parents went to bed while pretending to monitor the computer from 6:00 p.m. to sometimes 2:00a.m. in the morning. In faith that God would protect the love Tori and I had for each other, I would quietly crawl into bed with her and sleep in her arms for a few hours before going back to my room to sleep for the night. During the entire time Tori and I lived together with her parents, God fully protected our love.

The preliminary hearing began with Dobbs justifying our fleeing with my children, because of the bad rulings of a mentally disturbed Judge that was no longer a Judge. He reminded the court that this Judge had screwed up a lot and that I had acted on a mother's instinct to protect my children and that Tori was just supporting me as a friend. He further asked the county attorney why he hadn't released Tori's parents when they obviously had nothing to do with the kidnapping? In an hour's time, what had taken months to accomplish via our other so-called public attorney; Jeff had Tori's parents released of all charges and supervised visitation with my children at my parents house opened for me. I would have rather had them at my new home with Tori and her parents, but the court wouldn't even consider such an idea. Jeff kept stressing that he was tremendously pleased with our hearing and he kept reassuring us that we were doing very well.

With the passing of time my parents had eased up on my sinful life and were just as eager for the court proceedings to get over with so all of our lives could get back to some type of normalcy. Trying to somewhat show support, my mother came to court and Jeff took the opportunity to build up her faith in me. He down rated the Judge and the so-called custody hearing and he openly showed disgust for Eric. He asserted that I was a good person and that they should be proud of me. He very carefully didn't bring up Tori knowing my parents feelings surrounding her. Over all, he showed my mother how to show support regardless of everyone's opinion surrounding my case. Since I was living with the Bovard's and this was only a hearing for additional visitation, it was decided that it was best for all of us to have this take place at my parent's home.

The visitations began on Friday night and ended Saturday at 5:00 p.m. The children were very glad to be at grandma's. My mother was like most grandparents, she indulged her grandchildren and they loved her very much. Even my father, who I hardly knew as a child would play billiards with my kids and even practice shooting BB guns with my boys. Everything my kids wanted to do or some favorite food they wanted to eat was given to them. Deep down I always knew that it was a comfort to know that my parents loved my kids very much. I remember conversations with my mother before my divorce on how she found it so easy to love my children more than my older brother's children. Mainly, she reasoned that it was

154

because he and his family lived so far away and they couldn't see them quite as often. Now recalling her words gave me some solace that if I wasn't allowed to be with them that their grandparents would make sure that they would. Quickly we fell into a routine and my relationship began to heal slowly with my children and my parents.

About midnight or after, I would secretly call Tori collect from the downstairs room filling her in on what had happened with the kids and how everything was going with my parents. I knew that this was risky, but I loved Tori and every time I was away she was afraid. For invariably every time I left, Tori's parents questioned her even more about our relationship and what Gene was doing to take care of those terrible people that put us in jail. She was constantly under pressure to come up with more lies and money problems were always on their minds.

In one of her most intense discussions with her mother, her mother stated that she knew that Mark wanted Tori back and that she wouldn't be surprised if he should call her any day. Tori wasn't sure what to say and before she knew it she called the operator placing a call to herself.

Full steam ahead she pretended to be talking to Mark and her parents were eating up every word. Immediately her parents forgave everything that Mark and the family did for visions of life before the kidnapping. So again the front of Mark began. Going to a local jeweler, we purchased a ring on credit and soon Tori was re-engaged to Mark. This brought a great deal of comfort to her parents and as time passed it allowed us more freedom. The computer now was controlled by Mark and the family and even our attorney Jeff Dobbs was a member.

Since the Judge had resigned, new judges had to take his case loads until a new one was appointed. In the time being, Tori's custody hearing was to be heard in the town where we were living. And a new Judge would come from a different county to take over my custody fight which was still in Winfield.

Tori, accompanied by her parents entered the

155

courtroom. Jeff motioned for Tori's parents to sit behind her and the hearing began. The court appointed therapists came forward and gave testimony that visitation with the father was going well and that he recommended this to continue. Tori was shocked! Not once did he mention anything about Brad crying and his refusal to be even touched by his father. Furthermore he berated Tori, stating that she was trying to manipulate the therapist with information that Brad was becoming ill after each meeting. She had also stated that he was having nightmares and becoming withdrawn at his school. In his opinion Brad should be given visitation with his father without the presence of the mother.

Dobbs cross-examined showing that Dr. Stevens was no more than a former Baptist minister and a self-proclaimed counselor and had no credentials to make any sort of evaluation. He reminded the Court that the state of Utah required an accredited psychologist to make an evaluation concerning minor children. In response the Judge acknowledged this as being true and he threw the testimony out. Relief flooded Tori knowing that if she had been before the other Judge they would have already handed Brad over to Alan on a silver platter.

Sherry took the stand and testified that Brad was having problems and that he was not ready to handle visitation with his father yet. She said that sometimes it takes years before a child is emotionally able to deal with the other parent. She recommended that supervised visitation continue. Tori took a deep breath. Sherry had come through again.

Alan took the stand next and his attorney brought up immediately that he had been newly remarried since October. His wife had two boys, one that was a year older than Brad and the other that was exactly the same age. He gave a complete picture of the wonderful family life that Brad would have with his new family. The Judge seemed to be quite impressed. Until Dobbs cross-examined Alan and quickly brought up that he had committed himself to the state hospital for trying to commit suicide. He also produced the paper that showed that Alan had been found guilty of child abuse. He confronted him on physically abusing Tori and especially Brad. Alan squirmed in his seat, but still maintained that nothing had ever happened, stating that he was forced into admitting that he abused Brad. Still Jeff continued bringing up that Alan had lived with his new wife for over a year and only after the custody hearing was made did he marry her. Alan angrily stated that he married her because he loved her and after having a bad marriage he wanted to make sure that he was doing the right thing before committing himself to another one. Jeff questioned him further, showing proof that he had broken the restraining order time and time again when Tori was living in Winfield. He also brought to light that the counseling office that Alan had obtained a report stating that he was a well adjusted person, was the same office that his new wife had been an employee for the last 11 years. Alan acknowledged that this was true, but it didn't have anything to do with his wife working there. Every question Jeff asked Alan was quickly reputed. Quickly he left the stand and Tori took a deep breath praying that the Judge could see through Alan's smooth cover up of lies.

Immediately Tori was called to the stand and testified in her behalf as a fit parent and Brad's reactions to the continued visits with his father. She produced papers of testimony from Brad's teacher and a witness paper from a former doctor stating that Alan had abused her physically and sexually. Both were entered into evidence and Alan's attorney took his turn cross-examining. He of course brought up that I was living in the same house with Tori. Tori quickly stated that it was a duplex and I was living in the other half with her parents and she hardly saw me. Quietly she exited the stand and Jeff gave her hand a reassuring squeeze that she had done very well.

The Judge left the room to consider the testimony. And then after the recess he entered the following findings into fact. He denied change of custody and set up supervised visitation with the father to be conducted with Sherry. He also set up a future hearing in 6 months to reevaluate his decision.

Rejoicing Tori and her parents entered the house. I stayed away from court not only to alleviate talk about Tori's and my relationship, but to watch Brad and pray. Now I praised God with them. Thank-you Lord for once again testing our faith and bringing us through the fire. 1 Thess. 5:16-18, 'Be joyful always, pray at all times, be thankful in all circumstances. This is what God wants from you in your life in union with Christ Jesus."

CHAPTER THIRTEEN

The constant secrets that kept our relationship alive, sprouted hard steel bars in an invisible cell. The cell surrounded us as a continuing reminder that the slightest movement in the wrong direction could turn the courts against us, if they should hear the smallest word of love from our lips.

A month after Tori began her first job, she was offered a new job as an office manager. This was a brand new company and with Tori's expert help, she organized the office staff and hired additional workers. She made quite a bit more money and secretly kept the knowledge of how much she made from her parents in order to occasionally provide money for emergencies. Some of this money went to paying Jeff Dobbs in her custody case. Jeff had taken my cases pro-bono and Tori's criminal, but her custody case we had to pay a beginning retainer fee of one thousand dollars. With the additional money being brought in by Tori's new employment and my job, we could pay this without the knowledge of her parents.

From the very beginning my upholstery job brought in more money than Tori's and Bill's combined jobs. I had worked out a 50/50 rate with my employer and with wonderful blessing from God, I soon had his furniture upholstery business running smoothly and efficiently. He had a car upholstery business that he enjoyed doing himself and so the furniture part became basically my responsibility. After I had worked for him a couple of weeks and he began to see my work and was beginning to place trust in my abilities, he began to share that I called him just in time to get the job. Apparently a man who was just released from prison applied the very same day I called. I swallowed hard as I noticed his complete disgust for such a person. He continued telling me he tried to get ahold of the referral number I had given him, but the phone was busy. I praised God knowing that once again, He had protected me, for in a panic that the job was about to slip through my hands, I had given him Eric's number.

From the start of my marriage with Eric the only job I had was upholstery. I liked working with furniture and soon I was as good as him. When I had given Eric's number for referral, I prayed that he wouldn't call the number. Eventually, I told him that I was recently divorced and that now I was in a custody battle and that the number I had given him was Eric's and I exclaimed about how glad I was that he never talked to him. Unfortunately business slowed down just after the holidays and unexpectedly he fired me. I couldn't believe it, for the first time in years his wife and he were excited about how much money they were making on their furniture upholstery business. Later, on one of my visits with my children, Rich said that Eric called and talked to my employer. He recited word for word everything that had happened from me being a lesbian to running with the kids. To my surprise Rich said that my employer thought I was a terrible upholsterer. This of course was an out and out lie, but as usual it was my word against their father's. But this sure explained the reason why I was fired and why he refused to even think of giving my job back even though I had pleaded with him, asking him why?

When we had run with the children, I left my upholstery sewing machine and sample books behind. There was no room for them in the truck and since Bill did all of the packing we couldn't put them in. Later after being brought back to Winfield and eventually released, going back to the owner of the apartment I formerly rented, I asked for the return for my equipment and they refused until I paid one month's rent. I had no money and no building in which to do my upholstery work in and so I left defeated.

Now I had a terrible dilemma, I had no job and I knew no other occupation than upholstery. I was very

160

discouraged. My mind kept recalling the loss of my children and being thrown into jail. Hopelessness crept over my entire body sending panic in torrents of humility and tears. I was so defeated that I was sure that I would be sentenced to prison and never have the freedom to take my children anywhere with me again. Waves of terror consumed my heart that I could lose Tori as well. I was to the point of believing that my life was completely useless. Mentally I started preparing myself for suicide by justifying that everyone would be better off without me. I was sure that Tori and Brad could live a normal life and without me around they wouldn't have to constantly be forced into hiding. My children wouldn't have to go through ridicule because they had to see me and I wouldn't have to face another day in that awful house with Tori's parents watching my every move. In desperation, I called Tori at work and demanded that if she really loved me to come and help me. I warned her that I felt that my life was not worth living and death was the only way out. Immediately, she came giving me the needed encouragement that I so desperately needed. It's amazing how a little love can completely erase the power of fear. I had allowed my armor of God to slip and Satan had come in and demanded my life for payment. But Tori's love lifted me up and put my feet back on the firm foundation of God. Ephesians 6:10-18, "Finally, build up your strength in union with the Lord and by means of his mighty power. Put on all the armor that God gives you, so that you will be able to stand up against the Devil's evil tricks. For we are not fighting against human beings but against the wicked spiritual forces in the heavenly world, the rulers, authorities, and cosmic powers of this dark age. So put on God's armor now! Then when the evil day comes, you will be able to resist the enemy's attacks; and after fighting to the end, you will still hold your ground.

So stand ready, with truth as a belt tight around your waist, with righteousness as your breastplate, and as your shoes the readiness to announce the Good News of peace. At all times carry faith as a shield; for with it you

161

will be able to put out all the burning arrows shot by the Evil One. And accept salvation as a helmet, and the word of God as the sword which the Spirit gives you. Do all this in prayer, asking for God's help. Pray on every occasion, as the Spirit leads. For this reason keep alert and never give up; pray always for all God's people." Two weeks had passed since I lost my job and the very next day after I again surrendered my entire body to Christ a bright light shone on the newspaper for an opening as a CNA at a local care home. I went down for an interview and immediately I got the job. Two weeks after that I took on a second job and two weeks after that my upholstery equipment was released.

Just before the return of my tools, Tori and I made a deal with our former landlords in Portland for them to give back all of Bill's tools. We had left several expensive items of our own in the house that we weren't able to remove before the police arrested us. It was agreed, after many phone calls that they would except our things in addition to $200 dollars. I was amazed with as much money these people projected as having, how they had to have what little we had too. She was a head nurse at a huge hospital and he was a bridge architect. They had the house we had lived in and a new house that was twice as big. On our many phone calls I had pleaded with them stating I was a Christian and that I had made a mistake taking my children, but I had no choice. They in turn stated that they were Christians too, yet they refused to show us mercy. You can tell a Christian by their actions and from my experience with them they were no better than the people that Jesus was constantly berating in the Bible because they lacked compassion for the widows and orphans, or for the blind beggars who constantly sat in front of the gate leading into the temple. It is important for all of us to be willing to back down whether we feel justified or not by allowing God to direct us with compassion and mercy for our fellow man. God loves people and God would never lead a person to take revenge on another and if a person defies God's will in this and

162

takes advantage of someone, he is being deceived by Satan and he is walking in sin.

Bill went and picked up his tools and Tori and I began to rent a building where he could do carpentry and I could work in upholstery. We continued our front by paying the rent and installing a phone. It wasn't long before our newspaper ads provided us with jobs and after some time passed, I let go of my second job in an effort to spend more time on upholstery and on my CNA job.

From the very first, Eric and the county attorney threatened to rally my creditors to press charges against me for falsifying information for credit. Once out of jail, Tori and I were able to make some payments, but not all because of lack of money. I had good credit before I went into jail, but again when I couldn't work, I couldn't pay and by the time of my release the interest had accumulated to a point of no return. I hoped that with time I could pay, but I couldn't. So taking my attorney's advice and laying my pride aside I went to a bankruptcy attorney and filed. The first court for bankruptcy was a month away and another miracle was performed by our Lord with not even one creditor contesting.

In my Bible studies, I encountered the book of Nehemiah. I identified so much with Nehemiah when he was in the midst of rebuilding the wall around Jerusalem. This took place shortly after the 70 years of punishment ended, because the kings and people of the Jewish lands had practiced worshiping the false gods of the surrounding nations. In chapter 4, Nehemiah found out time and time again that his enemies were plotting to keep him from rebuilding the wall. And over and over again the Lord would inform him through the Jews that were living among their opponents what their enemies were about to do. Because of this, Nehemiah 4:15, "Our enemies heard that we had found out what they were plotting, and they realized that God had defeated their plans. Then all of us went back to rebuilding the wall." Nehemiah was able to stop them and because my creditors informed me of what Eric was doing, God enabled us to intervene with the truth.

It seemed that when I lost the support of other people, I gained new and firmer ground in the protection of God, who was my only refuge. God pushed me forward when I thought and felt that I could not last another day with the tremendous oppositions that I faced as a lesbian woman.

During the winter months between the strife within our home, which seemed almost as worse as prison itself, and constant court appearances, we began once again seeking support from gay activity to aid in our predicament. Tori and I together, had written a very explicit and intense letter about what had happened and most importantly that we were closeted lesbians. And because of this, we knew that "they" would understand. But before I could mail the letter, I wanted Tori to read the finished product for she was at work and I was scheduled to see my kids for the weekend. So in an effort to hide the letter, I left the letter under my lingerie in my dresser drawer.

No sooner had I reached the front door of my mother's home, a person to person phone call was placed for me from Tori. She was sobbing and frantically telling me that Doris had found the letter and she was ready to kick me out of the house and that she would see to it that I would never see Tori again. Whispering in fear that Doris was listening on the outside of her door, she rapidly explained that she had been able to cover the letter with the idea that we didn't know what was in it! In an effort to silence her mom, she took the letter from Doris and tore it up discarding it with disgust, while keeping Doris from showing it to Bill or anyone else. She further stated that we had been instructed to put it in my drawer by Mark! Period! And that there was no truth in it's content!

Common sense told me that Doris didn't buy this story, but what else could she tell her? That we had really written the letter? That it was true? Oh dear God, what do you want from us here? What is the answer?

Deep-rooted fear slowly started creeping all around me and I could only seem to see prison bars shrouded in hopelessness everywhere I looked. I was careful to act as if nothing was wrong in front of my mother and when the weakened had passed, I quickly headed back for town. I could just imagine the problems that Tori must be facing all alone. Would they let me in or would I have to sleep in my car? My fingers implanted themselves even deeper around the steering wheel as I pleaded for mercy with God Almighty. You are the Creator of the Universe. I beseech you. Please fill their hearts with love and compassion for me and please don't take Tori away from me.

As I tiptoed up the front stairs and quietly opened my bedroom door, I saw a glimmer of Tori's parents faces reflected on the mirror of the living room wall. Everyone looked OK. Had Doris really kept her mouth closed about the letter? Where was Tori? But before, I had even had a chance to take off my coat, Doris had found a way to leave her company, for her parents were visiting for the weekend, and confront me about the letter. I looked her in the eye and denied knowing what she was talking about, except to back up Tori's story, that the computer had printed off notes and that I was supposed to keep it safely inside my dresser. "Why were you in my room anyway?", I asked. she exclaimed that she had a right to be in any room in this house because it was her house! To my surprise, I realized that she completely excepted Tori's explanation. She was so totally against the relationship that Tori and I had that she would believe anything so that she would not have to face the truth. I couldn't help but praise God, that for at least now, Doris had no wish to carry out her threats of eviction. " The Lord is good; he protects his people in times of trouble; he takes care of those who turn to him." Nahum 1:7.

A few months later, our attorney received a $500.00 check from the gay organization that we had sent this same letter to help aid in the fight for custody of our children. Once again we praised God, acknowledging that He helped us to conquer the people who opposed us.

CHAPTER FOURTEEN

The prison bars were becoming less eerie and a light shone through the windows just before the sun fell behind the horizon. My spiraling thoughts eased momentarily at the sight of the wings of a beautiful white dove. Hope emerged with a gentle peace of knowing that in all my struggles against man, I had not been forgotten by God.

In the middle of March, a job opportunity opened up for Tori at the largest restaurant and motel chain in Town. We prayed over this job for one week, before the fringe benefits that came with the great salary pushed their way into our needs for immediate cash to help in all of the expenses that were being thrown at us daily. Tori was so worn down both physically and emotionally from the stress that her other managerial job possessed that this seemed like the answer to our prayer. But within only 48 hours of accepting the position, I was receiving the strangest and most nerve-racking phone calls from Tori. She said, "You won't believe what God has done here! He has shown me a way that I can dub the books and take up to $400 cash daily and no one will ever know. Please Tori, don't do this, I begged. But she insisted and it worked for 6 days until she went to work the following Monday morning and her boss with a very worried look on his face said, "Tori, Mike discovered over the weekend that there $200.00 missing out of the vault! You need to call in everyone who has had access to the vault since Friday and seriously question them about it and I'll contact the police if you can't resolve the issue first." Before the day was up, Mike and Adam had gone over the book's for the last 2 months and noticed that since Tori had begun, the same irregularities were there. Tori was a nervous wreck! What was she going to do? Through God's gracious love and forgiveness, Tori admitted to the crime and was fired that same night, but no charges were filed against her.

In the crossroads of life we are faced with situations that seem beyond our ability to control. The still small voice inside of each of us beckons us to draw upon the Bible for answers to our everyday dramas. What may seem like a mother's love for her child could be the very trap sent by satan. The Bible teaches us: James 1:12-13, "Happy is the person who remains faithful under trials, because when he succeeds in passing such a test, he will receive as his reward the life which God has promised to those who love him. If a person is tempted by such trials, he must not say, "This temptation comes from God.' For God cannot be tempted by evil, and he himself tempts no one. But a person is tempted when he is drawn away and trapped by his own evil desire." Tori wanted the security that she thought money could buy now, but God wants us to have faith that he will protect His people and that breaking the law and stealing was not his way. God had a better way! I still don't feel that knowing all of this, that Tori really knew how to just completely let go and rely upon God. For her faith constantly wavered each and everytime she looked back on what had happened to me and my children within the court system.

Hebrews 11:6, "No one can please God without faith, for whoever comes to God must have faith that God exists and rewards those who seek him." 11:33-40, "Through faith they fought whole countries and won. They did what was right and received what God had promised. They shut the mouths of lions, put out fierce fires, escaped being killed by the sword. They were weak, but became strong; they were mighty in battle and defeated the armies of foreigners. Through faith women received their dead relatives raised back to life.

Others, refusing to accept freedom, died under torture in order to be raised to a better life. Some were mocked and whipped, and others were put in chains and taken off to prison. They were stoned, they were sawn in two, they were killed by the sword. They went around clothed in skins of sheep or goats-poor, persecuted, and mistreated. The world was not good enough for them! They wandered like refugees in the deserts and hills, living in caves and holes in the ground.

What a record all of these have won by their faith! Yet they did not receive what God had promised, because God had decided on an even better plan for us. His purpose was that only in company with us would they be made perfect."

Taking all of the scriptures above into perspective, we can understand that our life in this world will be full of problems and pitfalls. But by remaining close to God in every situation, we are able to over come the obstacles that litter our paths to get us to disobey the Word of God found in the Bible. God wants us to play by His rules and succeed down the slippery paths of life with victory by doing it His way.

It wasn't long after this that everything came to a head with the living arrangements. Tori's mother was placing so many demands on her about me being in their way that Tori was completely becoming worn out from the constant fighting. The more stress that she was under the more worried I became over her heart condition. I literally was afraid to go home or even sit down to a dinner with the household for fear that I would do something or say something that Doris didn't like and Tori would find herself once again smoothing out my mistakes. From the instant I entered the house, I was given boundaries and conditions that for any normal person would have thought were completely unreasonable! I couldn't go into Tori's part of the house unless Doris was there too! I literally couldn't talk to little Brad or Tori for that matter! I was expected to stay in my room and give them all of my money! But never the less, I loved Tori and no matter what these sacrifices were, I didn't care, as long as I knew she was close by. It wasn't necessary to touch or even talk, for a quick look from her always reassured me that I was loved and cared with words that were beyond expression. It wasn't that I didn't build trust with Tori's parents, but they were so overwhelmed with court and not having any money that every time they saw me it just accentuated why they were in this mess. Still with their continued unreasonableness, I felt it was best that Tori and I both move out. But how were we going to do this with no money?

During this same emotional upheaval, Tori was struggling with her next new job and boss, who was an attorney. It seemed that she was unable to do anything right and just when she figured out what he wanted, he changed it. Tori was not one for patience and after being on the job for only days, she resigned. I was dumbfounded. We had talked briefly about this just the night before, but I didn't realize or I just didn't listen, to what she was trying to tell me!

The following day I was scheduled with my weekend visit with my kids at my mother's. In a brief weakness, I told Mom I just couldn't take living with the Bovard's any more. She took me very seriously, and at once excitement lit up her face as she said that she would be willing to buy me a mobile home to live in with the agreement that I would pay her a certain amount a month until I had paid it back to her in full. Her words illuminated my thoughts with a brilliant plan that would assure not only the escape from Tori's parents watchful eyes, but also this way when I went to court I would have a place to live with my children after my custody hearing. Eagerly I grabbed at the offer. Together we hunted down one mobile home and then another. Mom was becoming more excited by the minute and she called my grandparents who agreed to loan me $3,500.00 for a used mobile home. I could see that the more we looked and discussed the home the more that mom was certain that she could get me away from Tori. I played into her hands praying all the while that God would show me what to do.

Tori completely came unglued fearing that I was leaving her behind, but having faith in our love she joined the search for a mobile home without mom knowing. Going through the newspaper we located a mobile home for rent and quickly ideas formed in my mind giving me visions of how to pull off a scam on my parents. By now I had met Gene face to face, and he and I had started a strong friendship. From the very beginning I used my Christian background to assure him that the agreement he and Tori had entered into for my release from jail was a true contract. Continuing to build his faith in me, I went with him to the courthouse and signed over my half of the house just like what was agreed. Calling, I told him that I had to get this money from my parents and I asked him what he would charge me for him to cash the check. He was immediately eager to help and once we agreed on the amount, I put my plan into action. Tori was completely amazed. She had never seen me push forward with such assurance and determination. I quickly rented the home and taking the plunge, I called my father and told him about the great home I found and if I wanted it I had to act fast. He immediately came and fell hook, line and sinker. Once the check with Gene's name on it was in my hand, I prayed that Gene in turn would come through on his end. By the end of the week Tori and I were ecstatic that God had come through with the money. Now we both moved out to separate houses and for the first time in months we were together at night! Even though my parents did not personally know that I had deceived them, there was no harm done for in the months to come I paid back every cent I had borrowed from them. With God as my Judge, I knew that they would never have lent me a dime if I hadn't covered my tracks.

Shortly after this Tori devised a plan to use my parents credit. It seemed that ever since I began loving Tori I was put in the position to lie, cheat and steal. I hated this profusely, so swallowing my moral values once again, I plunged ahead. Going to my parent's home, I used the key they had given me and I rummaged through their papers until I had all the information to apply for credit. I felt a chill of fear, but Tori had assured me that we didn't have a choice and even though my conscience was bothering me, I didn't know how else to get the needed car for reliable transportation and a piano so Tori could give

170

lessons.

Entering my parents home on another visit with my children, I was immediately stopped by my mother in the doorway with her demanding what I had been doing with her credit. I was startled. I quickly defended myself that I hadn't done anything and I didn't know what she was talking about. But to my bewilderment she recounted word for word a car salesman saying that she was approved on a car loan. My mind immediately envisioned this morning's departure of Tori to Wichita to see if she could get a car and a piano. Mom continued with her words sending chills through my entire body as she stated that the salesman had given a complete description of Tori. Furthermore, she confessed to the salesman that she had not applied for any such loan and that she was calling the police.

The last detail of this story sent my mind frantically searching for a solution out of this mess. I must have sounded like I was babbling as I half convinced her that neither I nor Tori were involved. What seemed like hours was just actually minutes until a few private moments could be spared to call Tori.

"Oh, thank God, you're there, Tori!", I exclaimed! "You've got to stop using my parent's credit. A car salesman called here trying to firm up a deal with mom over the car. What am I going to do? Mom's threatening to call the police and the D.A. on you and your parents."

"Calm down, it's going to be OK! Just tell your mom that Eric is doing this, because you're gaining grounds with charges being lessened with the DA and it's not making him look very good. Remind her that he hates you and he hates me and he'll stop at nothing to make sure that they hate us too!" Tori had always been a quick thinker and seemingly knew how to get out of any cubicle that was put in her way. I hurriedly hung up reminding Tori to play it safe.

Hebrews 10:22-24, "So let us come near to God with a sincere heart and a sure faith, with hearts that have been purified from a guilty conscience and with bodies washed with clean water. Let us hold on firmly to the hope we profess, because we can trust God to keep his promise. Let us be concerned for one another, to help one another to show love and to do good." It is so easy to allow satan to come in and deceive you into thinking that you can do anything you want to other people when actually he is moving you in a direction separate from the one that God is leading you. This happens when we allow our want for more things now, to get ahead of God's timing. Being out of God's will brings punishment. Hebrews 12:5-6, "Have you forgotten the encouraging words which God speaks to you as his sons? 'My son, pay attention when the Lord corrects you, and do not be discouraged when he rebukes you. Because the Lord corrects everyone he loves, and punishes everyone he accepts as a son.' " Unfortunately, Tori and I were not quite ready to understand this verse and apply it to the situation we were in with my parent's credit.

By the time my weekend was up at mom's and I had reached Tori, I was mentally exhausted from the fear that my mother had placed over me and not knowing just exactly what Tori had been up to after my call to get her to stop. I did trust her implicitly when it came to her love for me, but with money, my faith in her was faltering because I knew that she was desperate to make her front with Mark stay alive in her parent's eyes! As I gazed upon Tori, I knew everything was going to be OK and I felt ashamed of myself for ever doubting that I couldn't trust her being alone.

Together, we quickly reviewed the past day's events and decided that the piano she had coming out on the following week on my mom's credit would be OK. Tori had purchased it on time from a 'shady' company, whose only concern had been money! They had not even questioned her bizarre story about how she was Louise's daughter and how Louise was home with a broken leg and she was doing the leg work for her. Not only this, but she was asked to sign Louise's name for her on the loan!

That night holding Tori, I had horrid dreams of

both of us being locked behind prison doors for life and visions of guards beating us for doing nothing wrong at all, I knew instantly that God was letting me know that we were not to do this, that we needed to be patient and let Him provide for us. When morning came, I expressed my concerns to Tori and we stopped the piano from coming. Later God rewarded us for our obedience to Him and led us to some people who were more than willing to take payments for a used car. The piano situation was not resolved, but the car was even more important.

CHAPTER FIFTEEN

It seemed no matter how hard we tried to pretend that the prison we were placed in was normal, the more that we saw that we could never lie enough or hide enough to please the people who surrounded our cell. For the people didn't care if we were good, hard working, loving parents, they just wanted us to be like them and if we couldn't, then nothing we could say or do was enough for them to give us support.

By the end of May, it was apparent that Tori was on sinking sand and that Alan was atop the highest mountain gleefully jeering from above. Sherry's good conscience and her strength to do what was best for Brad had been blown to the wind. She lived in Winfield and the rumors of Tori and I being homosexuals, had placed too many doubts in her mind for her to stay on Tori's side. Urgency followed panic when she announced that she felt Brad could handle an evening on the town with Alan and his family in just 3 weeks. This would take place just before the next court hearing!

We not only begged, pleaded, and cried for mercy and intervention from our Heavenly Father, but Tori began an immediate search for a new large city to escape to and fast! Bay City quickly came to her mind for we had gone there numerous times on excursions keeping up the front of Mark. After many phone calls and trips to the library, Tori diligently read the want ads in the Bay City papers.

The following weekend, we took some of the money that we had hidden from Tori's parents and presented it as a gift from Mark. It was really hard for me to swallow and not spit out the jealousy and anger I was feeling. Why shouldn't I go? It was my money! But quietly and instinctively, a quiet voice from within gave me the peace

174

that I so desperately needed. It prodded my faith along whispering, "It'll be OK. I haven't brought you this far, to let you be alone again. I will pave the way."

Tori and her parents drove separate cars to Bay City. This way Tori and her dad would both be able to go to job interviews and look for housing for they knew that a weekend was a very short amount of time to accomplish anything. We had made reservations at The Embassy Suite Hotel which was quite luxurious, but SO very expensive to keep the front going. I'm sure her parents were impressed, but I knew that they were more interested in finding a job that would pay more than the pennies they'd been making here. If only they could look back and see how far God had taken them. But they allowed their wants to creep in over and over again by complaining verbally that they wished they were never born, that all their so-called friends weren't really friends at all, or that they were tired of eating "bread and butter!" We uplifted them in prayer continually, but a person has to be willing to allow God to lead them. They needed to put aside their own prejudices and allow Tori and I to love like we were meant to love. That was the reason they were feeling unhappy and abandoned by their fellow man. Because they refused to stop judging us, they couldn't see the truth of God helping them on a daily bases. All they could do was fall back on what they had been doing in the past unwilling to yield to change and see how things can be different when God hand is in it. When God brings us into a new way of thinking, we must be willing to see it but since they weren't willing to submit, they were still in darkness holding onto the past and treating us like we were the scum of the earth.

Acts 28:25-27, "so they left, disagreeing among themselves, after Paul had said this one thing; 'How well the Holy Spirit spoke through the prophet Isaiah to your ancestors!' for he said, 'Go and say to this people: You will listen and listen, but not understand; you will look and look, but not see, because this people's minds are dull, and they have stopped up their ears and closed their eyes. Otherwise, their eyes would see, their ears would hear, their minds would understand, and they would turn to me, says God, and I would heal them.'" How well this scripture speaks to us today when even the church has been blinded to the truth of the Gospel. For if people love, they are doing the will of God.

Today Ministers and lay people look for the bad in people, while reciting pieces of chapters found in the Bible for the purpose of causing us to hate certain characteristics found in people. For instance: it is easy to quote Romans 1:26-27, This talks about the lust of woman and man for the same sex, but they completely deny what the scriptures captions in Romans 1:18-25 which is found before this scripture, "God's anger is revealed from heaven against all the sin and evil of the people whose evil ways prevent the truth from being known. God punishes them, because what can be known about God is plain to them, for God himself made it plain. Ever since God created the world, his invisible qualities, both his eternal power and his divine nature, have been clearly seen; they are perceived in the things that God has made. So those people have no excuse at all! They know God, but they do not give him the honor that belongs to him, nor do they thank him. Instead, their thoughts have become complete nonsense, and their empty minds are filled with darkness. They say they are wise, but they are fools; Instead of worshiping the immortal God, they worship images made to look like mortal man or birds or animals or reptiles. And so God has given those people over to do the filthy things their hearts desire, and they do shameful things with each other. They exchange the truth about God for a lie; they worship and serve what God has created instead of the Creator himself, who is to be praised forever! Amen."

Listen to these words of truth! The scriptures directly following these words and including Romans 1:28-32, are referring to practices that were done in 'satan worship!' Never was this passage designed to condemn homosexuals in a whole. It was created for the sole purpose of pointing out the harm of worshiping idol's

176

like Bail, Dagon, etc.; gods that were worshiped by the Gentile nations! As a result of disobeying the first commandment, "Worship no God but me", people did the things that were written in the first chapter of Romans as rituals in their pagan idolatry. Please do not be deceived! Sex in all forms was used in disgusting practices while engaging in worship of man made god's.

It still amazes me when I look back, how God always works out everything, even to the smallest detail. Regardless of what people thought of Tori and I, God uplifted, loved, and directed our path for our best interest. As a result, before the weekend was up, Tori had been hired as an accountant's office manager. But her father had only interviews and a more dejected feeling of self-worth than ever before. The situation was becoming so tense for Tori that each time we spoke on the phone, all Tori seemed to know how to say was, "I just can't handle seeing my dad like this; or when we were looking at the last rental house today, Dad didn't even bother coming in with us, he just laid his arms and head on the steering wheel and wept." "How am I supposed to stay strong when everything around me seems to be hopeless?"

I know that my empathy should have gone further than saying, "I'm sure that your dad will find a job and that a house would become available" but I couldn't because inside me, I didn't want them coming along at all! I wanted Tori and Brad to myself! I immediately gave these feelings to God and gave strength to Tori in a silent uplifting to God. In 1Peter 2:2-3 it also says, "Be like newborn babies, always thirsty for the pure spiritual milk, so that by drinking it you may grow up and be saved.' As the scripture says, 'You have found out for yourselves how kind the Lord is.'" But Tori's parents didn't crave the milk nor the pitcher it came out of, they wanted cream and the land of honey, and then some! When a person is not open to the will of God, satan can easily come in and discourage and thwart their plans. And as long as Tori's parents refused to allow us to be who God wanted us to be, it was not His plan to have them come to

177

Bay City! And because of this, He would not make it easy for them in the process.

After what seemed an eternity, they arrived home tired and dejected. Nighttime rapidly approached and I had the time alone with Tori and Brad that I had been craving all weekend. But Tori was at her wits end! "What are we going to do? We just can't pack up and move to Bay City when my parents don't have a house or a job to support them. My parents absolutely do not want you coming along. Tori kept repeating over and over and over again.

I quietly embraced her on the sofa, all the while listening for her mother's footsteps coming up Tori's front porch of her tiny apartment. I seethed silently, yet fervently praying that God would open another window that would supply us with His will in such a way that all our unanswered questions could be resolved. And suddenly, I knew! I knew that Tori and I alone must go to Bay City at the end of the week. God would supply the means and the excuse for which to go. For we were walking in the will of God and not her parents and because of this, we had to be the ones to pick and chose what jobs we would take and where we would live.

By now it was old hat for Tori to tell an elaborate story to calm and assure her parents that Mark was still in control. She explained that Mark was going to make connections with some realtors in Bay City and that she was supposed to go by herself this upcoming weekend. Her parents were immediately leery of this idea. They always thought the worst of a situation and sensed that I would also be going. Tori denied that until the very day we left. Even though we both knew and had prayed for God's knowledge and will in our move, we still had to deal with their human way of thinking that love is only for a man and a woman.

I had just finished up reupholstering a small chair for an individual and he was planning to meet me in the shop that I shared with Bill. When calling him and making arrangements to meet him, I had slipped and told him that

I was going to Bay City and because of this, I needed payment. During the short time, which couldn't have been more than 4 or 5 minutes, Bill had slipped in the back of the shop and was silently listening to our conversation. I panicked! I hurriedly picked up the chair to take to the man's truck, but not before he said loud enough for the whole world to hear, "Well, I hope you have a good time in Bay City!" "Why God? Why did you let him say that?" But I knew it wasn't God, it was satan!

When I came back in the shop, Bill had disappeared. I drew a big sigh of relief, because I felt that if he had heard my customer, that he would have surely stayed around to confront me. I hurried back to my mobile home according to our plan. I locked it up securely for Tori was to pick me up and then we were leaving town via the country roads. We planned to try and get back the cash deposit Tori had used to take out a loan on the piano. I tried to talk her out of it because I felt that the people in the piano store would be suspicious if I said that I was Tori's mother. Who was I trying to kid? I was 33 years old! Tori kept saying over and over that it would be OK, and that we needed this money to aid in our move. If only I had listened to the still small voice of God and not let my human nature rule my better judgment. For what is human nature, but our need to control our future, which always has to do with money and what it will buy.

I tensely entered the store and tried not to appear nervous. But, I was never any good at lying and this time did not prove otherwise. After what seemed like an eternity, a man appeared from a cubicle and asked how he could help me. I began talking quickly about how I was Louise Barrett and that I was here to get my cash deposit back. He said that he could not give it back without proper identification. "No problem," I said, "I've got my purse out in the car, I'll go get a credit card and be right back."

I felt like I was running the marathon in speed style when I walked out of the store. Tori immediately sensed that something was awry. "What's wrong?" she

179

asked. I quickly explained that I needed something that would show identification. I thought of the phone card but we were so nervous that we couldn't find the right one. So Tori came across the new Harrison's charge card with Louise's name on it and neither one of us felt there would be a problem with it, because I had signed the name on the back and our signatures would match to a tee. He made a copy of the card and then came back to me to say that his boss would have to authorize this and she was out to lunch. Could I come back after one? What could I do but say, "Sure, that will be fine."

Heading down the road our next plan of attack was to buy new spring clothes for the both of us, with my mother's charge card. I knew that Tori was sensing my insecurity about this, because she always rambles when she's nervous and for the last 15 minutes she hadn't seemed to take a breath. I wanted to just forget the piano shop and Harrison's and just go on to Bay City. Tori on the other hand kept pressing that we needed to keep on track and so reluctantly, I agreed.

No sooner had we begun looking over the racks of clothes in Harrison's, that Tori's name was paged over the intercom system. We both froze! What should she do? "Oh dear God, what's happening?" Tori had just begun to sign a charge slip with Louise's name on it, when once again, her name was paged. I knew exactly what she was thinking if she asked to pick that up, they'll know that she wasn't Louise, but if she doesn't answer it, what will her mom do next? So quickly deciding that the first was the lesser of the two evils, she answered the page.
Fortunately, the cashier was so busy tallying her clothes that she didn't even listen to whose name was being called over the intercom.

It was her mom, crying and screaming on the other end of the phone, pleading for Tori to tell her that I wasn't with her and that we hadn't done something awful. She related a conversation that she had just had with my mom about a phone call from a piano shop. Louise said they questioned her about a piano and when she was hesitant on the other end, they knew that she didn't know what was going on. Immediately they described both Tori and myself and how we'd been in to try and collect back a cash deposit on a piano. They warned her that if we should show up again, they were prepared to have us arrested for fraud. Both Louise and Doris quickly started cruising the town trying to find me. And to make matters worse, Bill came home when this was all taking place, and explained how he had heard me tell someone that I was on my way to Bay City. Immediately, Doris called my work place to discover that I was off all weekend. And to further our problem, she said that she had called the State Highway Patrol and gave them complete descriptions of both of us. She went on further to say that Tori shouldn't be surprised if they stopped her while attempting to go through the toll booth. For Doris had lied and said that there was an emergency at home.

I could see from the intense fear on Tori's face that something was terribly wrong and that they were pressuring Tori to tell the truth. She hung up the phone and we quickly left the store behind. She had promised to call her mom back from a pay phone where she could freely speak and this gave us a few minutes to get our p's and q's together on what in the world we were going to do!

I was mad at myself for not realizing that we should have never tried to use my mother's name. I should have listened to my conscience, which was telling me all along that we shouldn't be doing this and that God would provide us the money we needed in His timing, not ours. Still because of all the problems that Tori and I were facing, I was confused and didn't listen to my heart which was telling me no! And as a result we were now in an even worse mess!

Tori could always find the peephole to squeeze out of it and once again I could see her mind buzzing. "Why not tell my parents that you've been saying too much about what's been going on in our life to people at the rest home and that the family (mafia) told you were going to Bay City, only to come pick you up and take you to another state where you were being practically brainwashed on the fact that you do not talk, unless spoken to! And that you're only being warned once, and if you screw up again, then you're dead meat." I knew instantly that it was going to take something like this bizarre and outlandish story to work and that it would work, because they would just as soon not believe that their daughter was in love with another woman.

Inside my heart, I felt such despair! Why couldn't everyone just let us love each other openly and let us be happy? All of this mess was still happening because of our love. Everywhere in the Bible it tells us to always love each other as deeply as you love yourself. But today, that word had to be changed to hate! Tori told her parents that she would get word to the 'guy's who had me that I needed to call my mother and calm her down and that they were not to worry about what I would say to her, because the guys would have a gun at my head and believe me, I would say exactly what I was told.

When she finally hung up the receiver, Tori's face was ashen! Neither of us spoke a word; the silence was only pierced by our cries for mercy! Tori started the engine and began what now seemed like 'our drive in 'hell'!

Miraculously, nothing happened! We peacefully drove through the toll gate and on to Bay City. We must have met over 10 state patrol cars and nobody stopped us or even looked at us suspiciously. Once again God intervened on our behalf and not only did God safely get us to Bay City, but He once again kept us from the grasp of the law. Romans 8:29, "Those whom God had already chosen, He also set apart to become like his Son, so that the Son would be the first among many brothers." Even though people were letting us down all of the time and forcing us to come up with one more lie after another, God was faithful to us, helping us and blessing us because our love was in His will.

In order to follow the right path, we must understand how God works with people. God commands us in many passages in the Bible that he will test us to prepare us to be worthy to be called His sons. When Cain killed Abel and God confronted him, God proclaimed in Genesis 4:7, "If you had done the right thing, you would be smiling; but because you have done evil, sin is crouching at your door. It wants to rule you, but you must overcome it." Daily we face the question of whether or not we will follow God's direction in our life. God tells us that we must not only know the difference between good and evil, but we must learn what pleases Him and do it. Cain refused to do what was right, and as a result the land that Cain loved so much was cursed and he became a homeless wonderer. This was his punishment for killing his brother. From the story of what happened to Cain we gain the wisdom of how God uses his life as an example of what happens if we don't master sin and allow love to rule. If Cain had only loved his brother, he wouldn't have been lead into the sin of murder, because of his feelings of jealousy over Abel's sacrifice being approved of by God. God continues in Exodus 15:25b-26, "There the Lord gave them laws to live by, and there he also tested them. He said, 'If you will obey me completely by doing what I consider right and by keeping my commands, I will not punish you with any of the diseases that I brought on the Egyptians. I am the Lord, the one who heals you.'" The laws that were to be enforced by the Jewish people, were laws that helped the people to get along with each other so that they could live in harmony and peace with there fellow Israelites. The Ten Commandments, if followed, produce order that stop people from doing what comes natural through human desires. For all human beings are self centered and want their own way. All are motivited to If we understand the law's purpose then we can know what is the right way to behave towards our brothers.

When Jesus came, He brought a new law that makes it easier for us to follow which is found in grace. In grace we find that love conquerors the sin in our lives and enables us by just trusting in Jesus that we can be cleansed from our pass sins. When the Holy Spirit enters our lives, our way of thinking about our fellow man changes, and we learn from our pass mistakes instead of hurting from them. In our lives in this world we are on a journey that takes us through valleys of decisions. Which road we travel determines how we pass the tests that God puts before us in our travels. God trims and breaks off every part of our way of thinking that does not follow His plan for our life, and through this, He directs us and teaches us the truth concerning the world. I know that as I go through each day and conquer each situation that arises that I am becoming more like Jesus, when I pass these sometimes very difficult tests.

Tori and I had a lot to learn on our journey; God was changing our way of thinking and He was becoming our strength when we were facing such tremendous odds because of people's prejudice. Still through our persecutions, we had to learn to follow the truth found in honesty, even over money. Thanks be to God that when we did make the same mistakes by using my mother's credit once again, that He was faithful to us and He helped pull us through. He knew about the fight we were in and understood that we were just trying to give her parents what they needed to stay on Tori's side for Brad's sake.

After we checked into the hotel, I used the phone in the room to call my mom and Tori called her parents outside in the hall way. She was not nearly as believing as Doris & Bill. Everything I said, she questioned over and over again. Pictures of the jail in Portland kept crowding my senses as I tried to secure my mom's faith in me, but nothing seemed to be working. All she wanted was Tori behind bars and persecuted because she was a lesbian, who had corrupted her daughter into an ungodly lifestyle.

I frantically denied my feelings for Tori and after one hour of continuous rambling, I knew that I had no choice but to put most of the blame on myself for the piano, car and now Harrison's. But how? "Dear God, please work through me, calm my mother down and help me! Please, dear God! Hear my prayer." Everytime I looked up, all I could see was Tori's worried expression begging for me to tell her everything was going to be OK. Why had

I agreed to all of this? Didn't we ever learn?

As the night progressed, both Tori and I were at least able to stop our parents from banding together and lynching us. If only Tori or I had been a man, both of our parents would have aided us and supported us in the move to Bay City. Morning came only too quickly and immediately we put aside the night before and turned towards the want ads in a beseeching way. Should we look for a home? What part of town? What county? Should we look at schools? Or jobs? Quickly, we prayed for a peace and guidance, because God is a God of calming love, not anxiety, and He could only pave our way if we allow Him to have control. Immediately, different prospects for homes just seemed to be raised in dark print on the page. And you know what else was equally amazing? Each and every telephone call we made was personally answered. On a Saturday morning, in the city, they could have easily been answered by recorders or endless ringing. But God's will for our lives reigned once again!

At 10:30 our first appointment was too good to be true. Not only was this duplex really nice and in a secure part of the city, but the landlord did not require a credit check. Wow! We didn't want to seem too eager, so we made tentative plans to meet at her home right after lunch. The only remaining problem was where were Tori's parents going to live?

The day was quickly beginning to fade when we both came to the realization that the choice was obvious. Doris and Bill were going to have to live with Tori for at least a little while until Bill was able to secure a decent job and find a home. There was just no way that we could afford to foot the bill for two homes. And if we even attempted to do so, Tori's parents wouldn't have tried to live on their own unless they thought Mark was behind them and would support them if they failed. Not even solitary confinement in jail, caused me to fear never seeing Tori as much as this did. Over and over, I beseeched God from the very depths of my soul, that there could be another way to handle this situation, but I knew

185

that if Tori didn't provide some kind of front for her parents that they would immediately take Alan's side in court and he would get custody of Brad if we didn't play by their rules. I knew that I had no choice but to accept this solution and trust that God would get them out!

Still it was very hard to listen to yet another cover story by Tori. I questioned how Tori could be so bubbly to her parents while empathically stating that I would not be going and that Mark was planning a grand life for them in Bay City? Her words echoed over and over filling my very depth with uncertainty and fear that it would never be possible to ever have a normal life with her.

On our third and final day, and as our trip spanned the windy plains, our souls together reassured us that our love would see us through to a bright tomorrow without the lies. We had stopped for a brief rest, when I began to feel uneasy about how hot the car seemed to smell. Tori shrugged it off, with the fact that she'd been pushing the speed limit and reminding me that the car was several years old. "Just quit worrying, the gauges would show a problem if there was one," she kept saying. I prayed for protection over the car, the road, anything that came to mind when BOOM, SZZZ, and instantaneously Tori was screaming that the car was losing momentum and the accelerator wouldn't work! What should I do? Oh my God, what's happening? Poured out of our mouths at the same time. Carefully, Tori maneuvered the car to the shoulder of the road.

The tumultuous wind and hovering rain clouds gave way to a flash of lightning illuminated a sign revealing that we were still 150 miles away from home. I got out of the car and opened the hood, only to be met with a loud hissing and white hot smoke spurting from around the heads on the engine. "Dear God please help us, please fix our car. I don't think I'd ever prayed so frantically before. There was no way on earth that we would ever be able to explain to Tori's parents why we were together! About a mile and a half in front us was a by-pass and so wrapping my jacket securely around me, I left Tori and successfully located a tow truck. Minutes ticked, then the hours ebbed away as finally our car was in a mechanic's garage. The engine had become so hot that it had blown all of the gaskets and they were unable to get the proper parts until at least tomorrow or the next day! What were we going to do now? Suddenly a bright light from heaven shone down and a grandfatherly man appeared and said he'd drive us to a nearby town where they had rental cars.

We excitedly hopped in his truck not even stopping to think we didn't even know him and headed down the road. I have always been ill at ease around strangers, but not Tori! She immediately began chattering about our move to Bay City and our kids, just anything to keep the silence from penetrating into our minds and further frightening us with the possibility of blowing yet another cover. What seemed like hours since our car broke was actually only two, and God once again sent us the help we needed to prevail.

"My brothers, consider yourselves fortunate when all kinds of trials come your way, for you know that when your faith succeeds in facing such trials, the result is the ability to endure. Make sure that your endurance carries you all the way without failing, so that you may be perfect and complete, lacking nothing. But if any of you lacks wisdom, he should pray to God, who will give it to him; because God gives generously and graciously to all. But when you pray, you must believe and not doubt at all. Whoever doubts is like a wave in the sea that is driven and blown about by the wind." James 1:2-6. There was no doubt that Tori and I were praying in unison and because of our faith in God, He was faithful to us and gave us success once again.

Upon reaching our destination we quickly rushed in and explained our desperate situation to the rental car owner and not only did he not require a credit check, but he agreed to just take $100 total as credit towards a 1986 AMC Eagle. God indeed was faithful! Tori and I were grinning ear to ear, giving thanks to our God!

Reaching home Bill and Doris were so exhausted

from taking care of Brad and worrying about what Tori was up to that they hardly pressed for answers for the rest of the night. I'm not sure if they were fearful to know the truth or they just didn't want to know so they wouldn't have to face it.

CHAPTER SIXTEEN

No matter where we went or what plans we made, we were unable to break the incredible disgust that society placed on us, because Tori and I loved each other. It was an unbendable, iron clad, wall, that was so firm that all truth ran away and hide way down in the hearts of innocent people who were sentenced to love in secret. It was a lifestyle that was condemned to the point that the world wanted to kill and destroy and annihilate, all who would dare to be who they were meant to be by God! It seemed that the whole world could do anything they wanted to us without any conscience. Justifying there every action for denying us justice by beating us without fear of prosecution while feeling fully justified that we were receiving exactly what we deserved. It was a massive cell, encircling throngs of people just like Tori and I, and swallowing us up and devouring our every ability to try to find a balance in a world, where hate was accepted and our love was despied.

Days and hours all began blending into minutes and seconds as the time rapidly approached for our new life to begin. I desperately wanted to be there for Tori. I wanted to be able to say, "Don't worry, I'll be just fine until I can come up and start our new life together, " but I didn't even know when I would see her again or if we'd be able to talk freely on the phone to one another. How could I give her the support, I knew from the look in her eyes, that she so much needed? Throughout the last few months, God always spoke to me in a very matter of fact way. He just kept reminding me then as He was doing now, that He would never give us more than we could handle. When we are weak, He is strong. But the problem was, I just wasn't willing to let God give me the peace and endurance to handle this; I wanted to be in control.

189

I begged and pleaded that God would let this week tick slowly by, and quiet the clock inside my heart, but it seemed like the hands on the face only bended in surrender to the truth. I wanted more time to memorize Tori's face, her hands, her words. I wanted to say over and over again, how much I loved her. I wanted to assure her how quickly the time would fly until we were together again. And once again say, how much I would miss her, but my lips were silent.

As we awoke to the sunshine pushing itself through the shade of the window, I knew there was no turning back and nothing to stop the ticking of the clock. We arose silently being careful not to talk, knowing that all our words would be nothing more than forlorn words of love. We couldn't afford to shed tears that would lead to suspicion in the eyes of Bill and Doris that we were indeed lovers and linked to one another after all.

How was I going to say goodbye to Brad? He had warmed my heart when no words Tori said could comfort me. God had given me a love for Brad comparable to my own children. Who was going to fill my void now? As if knowing my innermost feelings, Brad, who never crawls on my lap without an invitation, promptly cuddled into my arms grasping for his own security that everything would be OK.

All too quickly, a knock sounded on the apartment door and Bill and Doris were there ready to begin loading her furniture into the U-haul. Bill and I were the strongest, so Doris and Tori simply stayed out of our way. Doris, who hadn't spoken to my face, for the last week, couldn't stop talking. And Bill, who was never a man of many words, just gushed with courtesy and eyes of emotion. But I knew they would never break down and say that they'd miss me and I knew more than ever, that they would not leave me alone with Tori to give her just one more quick hug before she left. "Oh Heavenly father, please wrap your arms around me. I need your peace. My heart feels like it's being crushed between two trucks. Please protect Tori and Brad. Guide their way easily. Oh

Lord, watch over all of us!"

As the wind whipped around my face, my arm slowly sank to my side after the last wave of goodbye ended. My insides ached in despair as I wondered if Tori really would be OK? In my inner most thoughts, I knew that God was with me, and He once again was molding me and showing me that he would see both Tori and I through this time apart.

I slowly drove away from our apartment and made my way back to the mobile home as we had planned. Tori promised me that at her first opportune time, she would call me. Call me! I didn't want a phone call. I wanted her! But I needed to hear her voice, and so I began my wait. Using my mother's permission, we had already established a phone line at our new residence in Bay City, and I knew if nothing else, that I would be able to hear from Tori by bedtime.

Bedtime came and passed. I had already been pacing the floor for hours. I must have dozed off, for the shrill tone of the phone ringing off the hook made me jump with fright! Tori's voice was tired and excited on the other end of the phone. She had so much to say, but all I could do was say, "Tori, I miss you. I love you. What am I going to do with myself for the next two weeks?" Over and over again I repeated my words. Her words of encouragement and confidence immediately bolstered my own patience and endurance to the level I knew God wanted it to be until we could be together again.

Their trip went without incident and upon arriving, she and her parents were immediately greeted by several neighbors on the block. Tori described them in detail and quite emphatically stated that they had been enjoying themselves a lot (by drinking) before they had arrived with there moving van, and so the idea of offering to help unload seemed much like a fun escapade to them. But I knew that it was the Angels of God over looking them and answering their prayers. Tori was to begin her new job as an account executive in downtown Bay City, which was going to be at least a thirty minute drive one way. The car that had broke down on us was so expensive to fix that the owners willingly took it back understanding that we didn't have the money to fix it. So in the mean time, Tori was forced to drive a dilapidated 1979 Jeep that would not with stand the intense trip, day in and day out that her job would have demanded.

From all of the trials we had endured, I had become keenly aware of the leading of the Holy Spirit in my life and I immediately sensed that God wanted me to push Tori to let that job go and look for a job that would be a lot closer to our new location. It would be easier on everybody and she would be able to get to Brad if an emergency should arise when he started school instead of expecting help from her parents.

At first, she gasped in surprise! "What? Quit? I can't quit! This is a good job with good benefits. It may not be full time yet, but it will be when fall comes. I can't afford to let this go, when my dad hasn't even been able to confirm the connection with the construction company he made before we moved up here. Are you crazy?" I held my ground. I guess I didn't realize what a corner this had put Tori in, because she still had to find a way to rationalize her quitting before she even started, to her parents. Before the weekend was over, Tori had submitted to my way of thinking. "God is our shelter and strength, always ready to help in times of trouble. So we will not be afraid, even if the earth is shaken and mountains fall into the ocean depths; even if the seas roar and rage, and the hills are shaken by the violence. The Lord Almighty is with us; the God of Jacob is our refuge." Psalm 46:1-3,7.

Tori immediately began secretly reading the want ads in the paper. And lo and behold! God again answered our prayers! She called the number, even though it was pushing 10:00 in the evening and it was answered on the first ring. The Doctor on the other end immediately liked Tori and before their phone call was finished, Tori had practically been hired just from the call. I couldn't believe the bounce that was back in her voice when she called later that night! God is just so wonderful! And to

192

top everything off, her parents were actually relieved when she told them what she had done, and they were supporting her all the way! "For the Holy Spirit will teach you at that time what you should say." Luke 12:12.

Throughout the following 10 days, life flowed as smoothly as it could. Tori's job was demanding with long hours and Brad was fighting her tooth and nail about never being with her anymore. At Bill's job, he was being treated like a carpenter instead of a contractor; demeaning sums it up in one word. Doris was constantly harping to both of them how she was homesick for her own furniture and her own home and when would Mark provide the money for them to move out? I so feared that they would become content to live under one roof and Tori and I would never be a family again. In John 14:27 it says, "Peace is what I leave with you; it is my own peace that I give you. I do not give it as the world does. Do not be worried and upset; do not be afraid." I prayed fervently that Bill and Doris would let Tori witness to them, but within their own hearts, I knew that they felt their prayers were only answered if it had to do with wants and prayers that were in the form of demands that they would never see me again!

During this time as well, I continued to work weekends at the nursing home, ran a very successful garage sale, and surprised Tori by reupholstering the living room furniture that they were unable to take with them because the Uhaul wasn't big enough. I was becoming excited for I knew I had only to make it through the next 24 hours before Tori would once again, be not only in my thoughts, but in my arms too.

The morning sun awoke my senses with joyful anticipation. Tori had convinced her parents that with the Scout being so unpredictable that it only made sense that she start out a day early for her court date. It's hard to believe that almost an entire year had passed since our nightmare began and now we would have our day in court. Just the same, since money was very limited, she convinced her parents that naturally she would be staying

with me! Yeah! I had received a call just before bedtime
last night asking me to substitute at the care home today.
It couldn't have come at a better time. Not only would it
be more money in the pot, but it would help pass the time.

As the day progressed, I actually had butterflies in
my stomach and sweaty palms, just like high school! What
was wrong with me? It was just Tori! Would she still want
me when she saw me? Would things still be the same
between us? All of these thoughts kept muddling my mind
as I thoughtfully walked to the break room at work, when I
happened to look down the hallway and there she was! I
tried not to run, but every wave of containment that was in
my body was swept away with our love! Immediately her
eyes in unison with mine filled completely with love and
spontaneously assured me that everything with us was OK.

During the evening, I filled Tori in on the intense
conversation that I'd had with our lawyer, Jeff Dobbs. To
sum it up, he felt that everything at our criminal court
hearing tomorrow would go fine. He kept reiterating to
only answer the questions that were asked with a short, to
the point answer and to let him take care of the rest. Tori
began pacing, and I knew that even though she had as much
faith in him as I did, the Judge could deny our agreement
with the prosecution and rule differently.

All too quickly, the wonderful night of loving Tori
ended and the reality of the unknown greeted us by the
buzz of the alarm clock. It was so unbelievably hard to let
each other out of the warm embrace we had encumbered
around ourselves throughout the night, especially with the
not knowing what would happen or whether we would see
each other again after the verdict was in from me
kidnapping my own children. I reminded Tori of Hebrews
10:33-36 which says, "You were at times publicly insulted
and mistreated and at other times you were ready to join
those who were being treated in this way. You shared the
sufferings of prisoners, and when all your belongings were
seized, you endured your loss gladly, because you knew
that you still possessed something much better, which
would last forever. Do not lose your courage, then,

because it brings with it a great reward. You need to be patient, in order to do the will of God and receive what he promises."

Naturally, it would be too easy if we had been allowed to just park and walk into the courtroom, but that was impossible for the stares of onlookers seemed to penetrate our every move. "God was in control", I quietly spoke to Tori. "To have faith is to be sure of the things we hope for, to be certain of the things we cannot see." Hebrews 11:1. We quickened our steps and took a huge sigh of relief as Jeff waved us into the court library for a quick update.

On all other court appearances, our attorney was usually the first one to arrive. He liked to set the tone for the court proceeding and he felt this gave him somewhat the control, whether that be actually true or not. But just the same it gave him the opportunity to speak privately with the Judge in his chambers and to hopefully gain his favor to his point of view over our case. Today proved no different except for the fact that the Judge was not here yet. So Jeff quickly briefed us on how he felt today was going to go, and that we basically would have to admit to the charge he had agreed to with the prosecuting attorney. Mine being a misdemeanor and Tori's a diversion. He assured us that court would be short and to the point over why we had kidnapped my children and not to worry. He also explained that we needed to say how sorry we were to not let the court process handle the situation. My insides just seethed! By now, I knew how well the court did not favor lesbians, even when we had been denying it for the last 2 years! But neither of us wanted to be behind bars and if it took biting our tongues, then that's what we'd do! James 4:12, "God is the only lawgiver and judge. He alone can save and destroy. Who do you think you are, to judge your fellow-man?"

The Judge that was to sit at our trial, had been given our case, not by his choosing, but for the fact that Judge Alburn was forced to resign, and he was late! Can you imagine how uncomfortable it was to just sit in a small court room, with your ex-husband, ex-pastor, and special prosecutor, all whom just seemed to be licking their lips for our blood, that they "just knew" would come from the lynching they had planned? The clock seemed to stay motionless.

Within an hour,we began. Both attorney's reiterated their version to what brought on the kidnapping charges. Thank God, that the Judge had agreed to let Tori and I stay while the other one testified! Jeff felt that was a small victory and that the tug-of-war was being pulled easily to our side of the room. Unfortunately, that lasted for only a split second!

Tori was called to the witness stand first. She rose assuredly from her chair next to mine to take her solemn oath. The examining chair was placed within a few feet of the Judge's presence, thus making it of vital importance that our emotions were kept inside our heart and not on the cuff of our sleeve.

"How old is your son Brad? Does he enjoy school? Are you and Brad close? I mean do you get along good? Does he trust you implicitly?" Jeff Dobbs asked Tori all in one breath. Her surprised look of what do these questions have to do with anything, quickly were suppressed before she turned confidently to look the Judge in the eye and answer each one in the order asked. "Oh, I just wanted to mention one thing, so that everyone understands my involvement in this case. I've taken your case on 'pro-bono' from day one, isn't that true?" he asked as he casually sat on the edge of the table. "Yes, it is." Tori replied.

At first, Jeff had denied accepting our 3 cases, that of Tori's custody, my custody, and the criminal charges due to monetary reasons and the fear of the unknown pertaining to the rights of homosexuals and their children. But after a great deal of talking and explaining our cases, he was alarmed over the injustices we had suffered and he wanted to show us that the law that he loved so much could be just. Because of this, Jeff wanted the court to know that he felt we were treated unfairly by everyone involved in this case and to further make his feelings about our case heard, he let them know that we were "freebies" to put it mildly and he was proud of helping us!

I could see Tori's face becoming ashen with fear as questions to mine and her relationship came out. Jeff seemed to pick up on her uncertainty and continued to take his time working his way from surface questions to in depth ones that directly pertained to why we had kidnapped my children. Tori took a deep sigh and looked straight into my eyes. I glanced quickly away, for the fear the Judge would notice the love that I felt for her. Her words came forth, "I love Elizabeth as a very dear friend. A friend, who was there for me when I was going through a very nasty divorce. One filled with physical and sexual abuse to not only myself, but to my son as well." I couldn't help wondering, what in the world did our relationship have to do with the charge at hand?

My oldest son, Rich, when he arrived back in Winfield, with the help of his father, had tape recorded and later his words were transcribed, as if it were a diary of the events of what we did when we took them out of state. We knew that this report existed and had even read parts of it, even though it was supposed to be court documentation only. My ex-husband had not allowed Rich to just tell the story, but he had filled in all of the details from police reports he'd read and basically asked Rich whether they were true or not. This was one of the main theories that the special prosecutor held against us, as to why would a 12 year old boy lie against his own mother?

Rich's story played on the fact that Tori and I shared a bedroom together while we were gone, and that we slept in the nude. That he often saw us saying we loved each other, and kissing and hugging in front of him, Crystal and Brad. So what? Yes, we loved each other, was this a sin? But I knew in my heart, that it was a terrible sin to Eric and now he had turned even Rich against me. For time and again, I was hit with passages in the Bible pertaining to homosexuals from Eric and his friends and

197

now even Rich.

There is so much misinterpretation of the Bible that no wonder people are leaving the church because of all the rules. The Bible is being picked apart one verse at a time and because of this chopping process, gay people and others are being denied the right to raise families with people who believe in God the same way that they believe. Let's set the record straight when God destroyed Sodom and Gomorrah, it was because of satan worship that resulted in sexual immorality which was stipulated in homosexual behavior, not because these people were homosexuals. 2 Peter 2:6, "God condemned the cities of Sodom and Gomorrah, destroying them with fire, and made them an example of what will happen to the godless." In other words it was their unbelief in God that condemned them. But because of false teachers in the church today, people who love God are hated for the very reason that these same people are not seeing the example set by God of two entire cities being destroyed, because they refused to worship Him. If you read everything in the scriptures containing the passage of Sodom and Gomorrah and not just the initial story, you would understand.

When the clock struck 12 o'clock noon, the special prosecutor had completed his cross-examination of Tori. She had held her ground seeming nothing less than the best friend a woman could ask for and the perfect motherly image. Before adjourning for lunch, the Judge asked Tori if she would be willing to work as a court-appointed mediator for children whose parents had either abused them or were going through a divorce. "Of course, I would." Tori replied. Smiling for the first time that day, he casually remarked that he wanted to accept her diversion, but the sentencing would commence after he'd heard from me. We then recessed for lunch.

The only way to the third floor of the courtroom is to walk 6 flights of stairs or take the elevator which rose and declined at a snail's pace. My mother, Tori and I instantly decided we needed the exercise when the special prosecutor and his supporters entered the elevator. I only hoped that we would not run into them face to face as the elevator and outside door were only 1 foot apart.

Naturally, the inevitable happened. But much to my surprise, my mother swept Tori up in a big bear hug and told her in a very loud voice, how much she cared about Tori and how mean and vindictive my ex-husband was being. I only wished that a newspaper photographer could have jumped up from the bushes and recorded their mouths hanging down to their chin from utter shock! Not to mention that I was in shock too, but at least for now my mother was coming into the light of God's love and seeing that our love wasn't some gross, scary monster.

We had only less than an hour to try to eat something for strength and for Tori to call and explain to her parents why she would be running late. Tori and my mother began talking about the morning escapade as if it were a soap opera. Neither one had any trouble devouring their food and each and every time, I put the fork to my mouth, extra saliva came rushing to my tongue and I knew that I would be sick to my stomach if I ate much more. Mom kept saying, "Elizabeth, all you've got to do is to tell the truth. Let God take care of the rest." But I knew how powerful hate could be and this was to be no exception. It was not cut and dried like our attorney expected. It was like we were being thrust in the mouths of lions. Oppression, fear that our attorney was starting to be on sinking sand, and sadness that Tori would be leaving once again dominated my innermost thoughts. I tried to make idle chitchat, but my heart just wasn't in it. I could only quietly rub my leg against Tori's under the table while praying that I wouldn't say anything that I would regret.

"And the tongue is like a fire. It is a world of wrong, occupying it's place in our bodies and spreading evil through our whole being. It sets on fire the entire course of our existence with the fire that comes to it from hell itself. Man is able to tame and has tamed all other creatures-wild animals and birds, reptiles and fish. But no one has ever been able to tame the tongue. It is evil and uncontrollable, full of deadly poison." James 3:6-8. The special Prosecutor, immediately felt my distrust for him. His eyes became hardened and determined that he was going to destroy me, if it was the last thing he did! And he practically did! What do people do, who do not have God on their side? Or a public defender that could care less? We had the best attorney that money could have bought, had it not been for being pro bono, and it still wasn't good enough.

I quickly decided that there is no such thing as allowing the court system to run its course, or to assume that the Judge would not succumb to pressures of society. Less than 45 minutes had passed from the interrogation being thrust into my face by the special prosecutor, than I knew we were indeed not only on trial for the criminal charges at hand, but for our lifestyle. Each and every time, he would slip in a question about my relationship with Tori, questioning whether we slept together, Jeff would immediately become irate and state his objections, and time and time again the Judge would use a lame excuse as to why it was relevant and overruled the objection.

"Are you aware that it's a federal crime to unlawfully apply for credit cards by falsifying your income, or any other part of the application?" demanded Ryan. "Yes, I am" my voice whispered to him. "Is it true that you ran up over $150,000 worth of debt for items too numerous to mention? But I'll mention the new mobile home, two cars, Dodge truck, grand piano, appliances and who only knows what else. And that you just recently filed and was granted bankruptcy for the above stated amount?" "Yes, it is." I replied defiantly. "But, there were valid reasons using the credit cards and until I was arrested in Oregon my credit rating was A+++ and absolutely no payment was past due." Ryan just ignored this last comment and continued on his quest to violate us by public humiliation.

It was hard enough to control my anger over this rampage, while trying to find a way to keep my eyes averted from my mother, who kept crying silently, Tori, who was white with fear, and my ex-husband and ex-pastor, whose eyes were filled with gleeful indulgence and complete disdain. Jeff kept using his right hand in a stroking method to make my voice subside. He had instructed us both before even entering the courtroom that it was very important that we presented the perfect picture to the Judge. I just never realized how difficult it was to keep my control!

God's Spirit within me, churned, vehemently, silently acknowledging that He was with me, but satan indeed was a mighty foe. As the afternoon progressed into early evening, rarely did the questions that were posed before me, even begin to touch upon the reason why I ran with my children or what had happened over the last year that would make me want to do it. They just continued to press that I was guilty, because I loved Tori and I had left Eric for her, I had unlawfully used credit (as far as they were concerned) to live a life of luxury, and that I was an unfit mother for all of these things were not a good influence for my children.

The Judge, who through the day, had really said very little, except when he was overruling for the prosecution or growling at me from behind his wire-rimmed glasses. All at once, he just seemed to come to life from behind the bench, and said in a gruff voice, "I've heard all I want to hear from Ms. Barrett about this matter, Mr. Prosecutor. Please ask her whether she understands what she's been charged with and what her plea will be." Ryan immediately argued that he wasn't finished with me yet, but for once God intervened and his motion was denied. Ryan, read from the criminal docket entry, "a class A Misdemeanor, in violation of Utah A. 21-3608, Penalty 21-4502, How do you plead?" I glanced at my attorney and he nodded his head to proceed. "Guilty", I answered. The Judge in return, repeated the charge and did I fully understand the penalty for pleading guilty to this crime? He then reminded me that I had the right under U.S. law to plead not guilty and be tried with a full jury present. I nodded that I understood. He leaned back in his chair pleased with my answer.

I stepped down fully prepared that Tori and I were basically home free. But no! Ryan calls Eric to the stand. What in the world could he say that hasn't already been said? My mind queried. As Eric took his oath, our attorney could only shake his head in disgust. Any other court situation where there had not been the undertones of lesbianism would long have been over and forgotten.

"They also learn to waste their time in going around from house to house; but even worse, they learn to be gossips and busybodies, talking of things they should not." 1 Timothy 5:13. My ex-husband, if he knew nothing else, should know that here was not the place to expand on his quote wisdom in this matter. But instead, he assuredly positions himself in the witness stand such as a king splendidly sits upon his throne, to watch a betrayed person stand execution. To any impartial listener, Eric's story would have had them easily believing his version, as his gentle voice swooned, "I really hope that in the future that Elizabeth and I can get back together for the kid's sake. I still love her. The church still loves her. God still loves her. I just believe that she's strayed off the path and that given time, God will bring her back to us. The kids need a mother!"

At that remark, my attorney slammed his fist down right in front of Eric and he literally lost his control. He began ranting and raving about how Eric had permanently damaged my leg by ramming it inside of a car door and how he was constantly running to the DA and the CSO every single day with more letters that stated vindictive and untrue facts about me. And that persistently he was having his church friends take shifts following my every move. How? Just how, could he get up on the witness stand, under oath and say that he wanted me back? Eric's face turned every color of red under the sun and began stuttering nonsense, all the while the Judge told Jeffrey Dobbs to refrain from any more outbursts!

Ryan seemed to pick up where Eric left off, only it seemed that one more surprise was still in the bag! It included paper that he used to write different organizations for help in locating the children, hotel rooms and food for himself and a friend when he came to Oregon to pick them up, a welcome home party when the kids were found in Portland, newspaper articles about the kidnapping, clothing, and last but not least over $800 in loss of wages for time off of work, etc. He concluded his polished testimony by saying how he felt that Tori should be punished in jail, but that I should receive probation because it would better serve the children. For it would be embarrassing for them to continue to explain to their friends that "mom" was in the county jail!

"Did you or did you not send out several hundred letters to friends, relatives, mere acquaintances requesting their help through donations of money, food, advertising, etc. during the time Elizabeth and the kids were in Oregon?" Eric stuttered as my attorney questioned him once more. "Well, yes I did but," echoed as Jeffrey Dobbs faintly smiled and said, 'Nothing more. I am finished with this witness, Your Honor."

"We'll recess for 15 minutes. When we reconvene I'll allow each attorney 5 minutes to provide closing arguments" and at that Judge Raymore exited quickly to his chambers. By looking intently at Dobb's face, I still felt that today had been like an old-fashioned stoning except the rocks consistently bounced back to the throwers. Yet when I looked at Ryan, I felt uneasy. Like the final hurl of a sharp rock had yet to be aimed at us, but this time it would seriously maim if not fatally! I repeated my fears in a quiet whisper so that Tori and my mother could hear me. "Oh, that's nonsense," Tori firmly said. I so wanted to believe her, but my Spirit was not at peace and I couldn't quit shaking. What if I went to jail? What if he said I could never see my kids again. What if he said I couldn't move to Bay City?

"Calm down! Everybody got their laughs. We've learned that to love God, we sometimes have to be humble. God is with us and he won't let us down.

"All rise." echoed off the stark walls as a piercing thought entered my mind. Oh dear God! Tori could lose

everything!   She could lose Brad to Alan if they feel she's
not stable because of what she did to help me.   Please
protect Brad too, God!   Please!

"Do not allow yourselves to be condemned by
anyone who claims to be superior because of special
visions and who insists on false humility and the worship
of angels.   For no reason at all, such a person is all puffed
up by his human way of thinking and has stopped holding
on to Christ, who is the head of the body.   Under Christ's
control the whole body is nourished and held together by
its joints and ligaments, and it grows as God wants it to
grow.   You have died with Christ and are set free from the
ruling spirits of the universe.   Why, then, do you live as
though you belonged to this world?   Why do you obey such
rules as, "Don't handle this," "Don't taste that," "Don't
touch the other?"   All these refer to things which become
useless once they are used;   they are only man made rules
and teachings."   Colossians 2:18-22.   Listen to what God is
saying in these verses, could it possibly be true that all
the churches are making up their own rules so that they
will be more important than God?   Of course it is: for God
is love and any teaching that is hateful and precludes any
people from God's love is false!   Just looking at Eric and
hearing his testimony revealed that he was not following
God, but painting a pretty picture for the D. A. and his
own pastor and church friends.   He wanted their respect
and approval and he conveyed this by stating that he was
still in love with me and that for the children's sake, I
shouldn't have to be put in jail.   This was his show and his
opportunity to put made up human morals above God's plan
for loving people.

My ears ignited in fire when I heard Ryan say "and
Your Honor we are requesting that Elizabeth receive 2
years in the Johnson County Jail, no probation, community
service hours, and a fine of $2,000 to repay her ex-
husband, Eric."

Up jumped Jeffrey Dobb's practically yelling at the
top of his voice. "Are you crazy, Mr. Prosecutor?   We've
already agreed on a plea bargain and there was no

agreement as to jail time only to probation and possibly court costs, period!"

"Excuse me, counselor!" the Judge ordered. "But, I believe that I have the final say and that because I sit before you, that I will do what is in the best interest of serving the State of Utah and the charges set before me. If you do not wish to accept the punishment, I will incur to these two women you represent, then you have the right to request that I reject the plea of guilty and you will then be furnished with a new trial time with a jury for all evidence to be reiterated. Otherwise, calm down and let justice serve!"

However, it seemed like an eternity before Jeff finally calmed down and the arguments ceased. But my insides were in turmoil. What if the Judge listened and succumbed to the pressures that Winfield had put so intensely on the D.A.'s office that he would have stepped down rather than take flack from his course of action.

The Judge's gavel ramified the verdict he'd just handed down. I was humiliated, relieved, irate, and frustrated all at the same time. Mom and Tori were both hugging me and our attorney could only sit at the table and run his hands through his hair. I'm not sure who had really won! Yes, I received a 1 year jail sentence and after a harsh tongue lashing it was reduced to 2 years probation. Tori received a 1 year probation and her diversion was granted if all probation requirements were met. We both were to pay $1,000 each to Eric for his expenses and all courts costs which were $199.00 each, plus expend any time we would have after working 40 hour weeks by supplying an additional 500 community service hours to be completed by the end of our probation period. The Judge said he saw no problems with my moving to Bay City, especially since I didn't have a job that could support me in this area at this time, but it still must be Okayed through my CSO.

CHAPTER SEVENTEEN

I wanted to come out of my cell of solitude. I wanted to be able to love Tori with the peace and safety that the law could afford. I wanted to not hide from society. I wanted to be looked at with respect by my peers. I wanted to live in a world that had no place for me, but a closet. A closet filled with boundaries, that if not followed would be enforced with punishments of abandonment from family, friends and especially the freedom to love without fear. The courts were unfair and if we continued to pursue our love then we would be forced to a life of silence. A life and home behind the front of lies, because now we knew the truth about our laws for homosexuals, the truth was revealed through the verdict of hate, they felt they had to punish us with to keep us in our place.

As Tori and I left the parking lot of the courthouse, life as we'd known it for the past year was now at a standstill. I was numb. Tori was shaking, crying, and talking faster than I could comprehend. "How in the world are we going to be able to do 500 community service hours in a year and still hold down our jobs? Where are we going to get $2,000? We'll never get off of probation! What are we supposed to do? Pick-up trash? I don't want everyone to know what we're doing! I want to start our life clean in Bay City!" she demanded. Now was definitely not the time to agree with her! From deep within, an instant peace overcame my thoughts and even though I didn't know how we would manage, I just knew that things were going to be OK. But for now, after once again returning to my home, I could only pull Tori close to me and cherish the little amount of time we still had together, before she began the long journey back to Bay City. "See to it, then, that no one enslaves you by means of the worthless deceit of human wisdom, which comes from the teachings handed down by men and from the ruling spirits of the universe, and not from Christ. For the full content of divine nature lives in Christ, in his humanity, and you have been given full life in union with him. He is supreme over every spiritual ruler and authority." Colossians 2:8-10. God was teaching us about this world by showing us the injustices that befall people in this world. He revealed to us how people had taken the rights of other people in an effort to control anyone that was different from the small accepted society. He showed us the prejudices and the corruptedness of the courts. He helped us to understand that the law was controlled by wealth and power; not by justice.

I had been praying with as much strength as I still had in me, that her parents would quietly and calmly just accept the story Tori told them about court and that I would no longer be in the picture. It was still so very important to them, that Tori and Mark would marry, and that I would be "put out to pasture" so to speak. It hurt me to think that I could have lived with them for so long and practically known every thought that they thought and yet be treated like I should be trampled on as dirt. And yet I knew without a doubt, that if Tori ever broke down and told them, that there was never a Mark and that I was Mark, they would fight her tooth and nail for Brad.

During court and on the way back to my mobile home, neither one of us brought up the fact that Alan had filed another motion to take Tori back to court for custody of Brad. There had been no time for panic and for thoughts "Oh no, what am I going to do?" Our attorney had expressed concern over the fact that our courts seemed endless and that he didn't know if he could continue. Especially since during all the times he represented us he had inquired a lot of expenses through traveling and preparing for all of our different cases and he thought that it was just time for us to part company. He was becoming defeated over the tremendous fight that was

207

involved in our cases and how the law in his own eyes wasn't holding up, like he had expected.

Tori instantly grabbed his arm and made Jeff face her eye to eye. "You can't just leave me up in the air. I trust you. I trust you completely. You are the best. Please, I have paid you each time I've gone to court for Brad and this will be no different. I need you!" Jeff reluctantly agreed as long we furnished him $1,000 in cash only on or before her next court date, which was only 3 weeks away. Silently, I trembled. Where could we possibly come up with that kind of money in such a short amount of time? There just was no stone humanly left unturned that we hadn't looked under for money. Isaiah 40:25-26 reads, "To whom can the Holy God be compared? Is there anyone else like him? Look up at the sky! Who created the stars you see? The one who leads them out like an army, he knows how many there are and calls each one by name! His power is so great- not one of them is ever missing!" We needed no one else but God! "He strengthens those who are weak and tired. Even those who are young grow weak; young men can fall exhausted. But those who trust in the Lord for help will find their strength renewed. They will rise on wings like eagles; they will run and not get weary; they will walk and not grow weak." Isaiah 40:29-31.

Over the next few weeks, Tori searched in vain for a duplex or home that fell in the income bracket for her parents, that also had some inkling of "class" bestowed upon it. After spending hours looking at different homes, Tori finally found a small but acceptable home. She secretly met with the landlord, convinced him that a credit check wasn't necessary, and made arrangements that the rent and deposit could be paid every other week until it was completed. She said it was like pushing a mule uphill to get her parents out of our house! But God was indeed victor! Within 24 hours of their move, the car that I had purchased for $600 from my first upholstery job, was so fully loaded with my upholstery tools and clothes that the frame practically drug on the road. But my heart was joyous! I was going home!

By this time, summer was in full swing and Tori's custody case, which had already been continued twice, was scheduled for a hearing in just 5 days and so far we had only sent Jeff $300. Fortunately, He had agreed that he would see me through my custody case' pro-bono' only because he intended to make headlines with my case and because it was more of a challenge to him than Tori's, I suppose. That indeed was a relief, but it still didn't help us find a money tree for Tori's court.

Tori was always very good at reading people and on the phone before I had moved in, she had suspected that the two ladies that shared a duplex across from us were gay. She was always guessing as to peoples sexual nature, but this time even I was inclined to admit that she was right. We became good friends with Andria and Dee in a very short time, as our "hello" from across the street, became nightly talks with one another after our children were asleep. It soon became apparent that Tori was right. They too were closeted as Andria was a school teacher and had visitation rights with her two children during the summer and every other weekend during the school year, because of the accusations from her home town that she was a homosexual. Dee on the other hand had sole custody like Tori, and didn't care if she was accepted by society or deny her sexuality to anyone. The only difference was that their families knew they were living together, but just as 'friends'.

The evening of Tori's court, Dee had accidentally walked in on Tori sobbing in front of the fireplace. Tori explained that all day she had counted and recounted the money she needed for court and she was still short $500. Dee, not knowing quite what to do, quietly knelt beside her and asked if there was anything she could do! Tori of course, said there wasn't, but she shared her concern that tomorrow when she arrived at court, that her attorney would up and walk out of the courthouse, as he had threatened to do, if we did not have the remaining $700 in cash! Dee listened and left only to come back over shortly with Andria.

As I answered the door, Andria was ashen and seemed fidgety. Brad was outside playing with Andria's children on the porch, so Tori's emotions were quite obviously on her sleeve. Andria began to speak in a soft but determined voice, "You know that we've only known you for a short time, but I know more than you'll ever know, the scared feelings that you're feeling right now. And I know there's nothing I can say to make them go away, but I've just received my paycheck from school and I want you to use this $500 towards your lawyer's bill. You've just got to promise me that when you complete your work for next week, that you pay me back first above all other bills. OK?" We were speechless! If ever an Angel came down and surrounded us with God's love, it surely was right now! Praise God!

Tori and I arrived back in Winfield 2 hours before court so she would be able to meet with Jeff before it started. Jeff threatened her on the phone the night before, that it could be detrimental to her case if I should be seen with Tori at court, so I decided to wait in the library which was directly across from the courthouse. I hoped it would give Tori encouragement just knowing I was close and that I would be praying that the Judge would truly listen to what she had to say.

It was 4:00 p.m., a very long and exhausting 6 hours, since I had seen Tori. Jeff Dobbs's cowboy hat caught my eye along with Tori's graceful canter through the pained window of the library. They were acting quite casual and spirited, and I just felt that God had been victor. As I ran out to meet them, I also caught a glimpse of her ex-husband and his new wife, Lori, who were also walking with a bounce and I grew concerned that my initial perception was wrong.

Upon seeing me come out of the library, Tori gave me the thumbs up sign. She turned and thanked Jeff for everything he'd done and stated lightly that she would keep in touch. Hopping into the car we began our journey home, as Tori began filling me in on the details of court.

210

Court was held in the small courtroom that ran adjacent to the Judge's chambers. When the proceedings began, Jeff Dobbs immediately stood up and requested that everyone including Alan's wife be barred from the courtroom! This encompassed Helen, the CSO, Sherry, the Licensed Counselor, and any onlookers. Of course, Alan's attorney asked that the Judge deny this request, but the Judge quickly granted his wish. Tori praised God immediately, knowing that this would keep all of the above from blending their stories together for a better case.

During a brief recess the Judge made it quite clear to Jeff in the privacy of his office that Helen would soon be out of office. The Judge even went so far as to ask Helen to come in before everyone and questioned her to find out if she had anything pertinent to add to this case, and when she answered no, he told her that she was free to go home early and that he'd see her on Monday! Shocked she bowed her head and quietly retreated. After Tori finished her words, I couldn't help smiling at knowing that this was God's favor shining down on my family, remembering all the lies this lady had told the court over my running with my children. "Vengeance is mine saith the Lord!"

Alan took the stand first, since it was his motion and he began telling what a wonderful father he was to his two stepsons, and how much he enjoyed the time he was spending in counseling with Brad, and that he felt Brad was ready to be alone with him! Jeff was able to counter all of this and shake his testimony on the stand, when he refreshed the Judge's memory, that Alan had been admitted to the State Hospital and that he had even attempted suicide when Tori filed for divorce. Not only this, but that she had to place a restraining order on him as he had attempted to kidnap Brad, and in addition to this, he sporadically paid child support, just to mention a few things! By this time, the Judge was sitting straight up in his chair and his lackadaisical manner was now attentive and serious!

Tori's hands were sweating and she felt like

211

everyone could see her trembling as she took the seat behind the witness stand! The Judge gave her a reassuring smile that quickly melted away her nervousness. Jeff quickly asked her to give a summation of what had happened over the last few months. Immediately she felt the calm assurance that only God's presence could provide and she began by vividly portraying what had happened over the last 2 years and more importantly the last 6 months since their last court date. She expressed her fears over allowing Brad to be with Alan for not only had his behavior changed upon the visits with Alan, but that he was waking up screaming in the middle of the night, for the 'bad man' to go away. He was also refusing to eat at the table for he was absolutely sure that he saw his dad and so under the table is where he hid. Tori told the judge, that Dr. Robert Allen, whom Brad was now seeing was an expert on child abuse and that the letter she had brought along from him would express his views on the situation. Immediately Alan's attorney objected, and the Judge had no choice, but to grant the motion. According to the law, a witness had to be present to testify and he must personally submit any letters for evidence. Thus it could only go into the court file for future reference, but the Judge could not lawfully read it at that time!

Next, Alan's attorney Mr. Reuben, asked Tori mundane questions like where do you live, and where does Elizabeth live from you? Tori swallowed hard as she gave them a brief scenario of my living several miles away and that she had very little to do with my life. Jeff quickly butted in stating that he found this question was not relative, oddly enough Alan's attorney didn't put up a fight and the Judge ruled in Tori's favor.

When she finished testifying, Sherry was called to the stand. Frustration filled the entire room as each attorney in turn tried to persuade her to take their clients side and she gave wishy-washy answers on every question. It didn't matter who asked it, even the Judge. Sherry seemed totally confused on what was best for Brad and simply stated that she no longer wanted to be apart of this

212

case. The Judge's expression reflected with stern words as he relieved Sherry from her position as counselor. Shaking his head later in chambers, he told Jeff that he felt it had been a mistake to let her be the counselor that supervised the visits, because her own emotions were torn.

Since the very beginning Sherry had been Tori's first and only counselor as well as Brad's. She had heard Tori's confessions of sexual abuse and physical abuse and in the very first court case, she had recommended sole custody, with no visitation rights for Alan. Now she was cast in the role to be an impartial professional! Apparently from her testimony she couldn't handle this. And not only did she still live in Winfield, but she heard the rumors and her curiosity, since the kidnapping had definitely been aroused! But Tori knew the truth over why she was confused! The truth was that Tori was the better parent and that Brad proved that his father wasn't the good person he was pretending to be for the courts, from his fear during the supervised meetings. She was confused, because she wanted to do what the world wanted her to do and condemn Tori because she chose me over Alan. But God would not let her follow her peers recommendations, because he knew that Brad could not be with his father and live. For God knows what goes on behind closed doors and he knew that Alan didn't really want Brad, but he wanted to punish Tori!

As both attorneys presented their closing arguments, Tori prayed with all her might that God's will would be victor. A total sense of well-being and peace invaded her whole body at the exact time the Judge began his determination by saying that "pertaining to the custody issue, sole custody is hereby granted to Tori." Mr. Reuben jumped up and before he could even say anything, the Judge quieted him by saying, "Your motion for visitation had nothing to do with changing custody. Now sit down!" He went on to say, that he felt no one knew exactly how Brad would react until their actually was a visit. But he didn't feel that Brad could handle just being left on his own with Alan; so therefore Tori would be

213

allowed to be there. She had to make arrangements to go to Prescott, where Alan lived with a 3 week time period and spend the day there with them and from thence on, Alan had to come up to Bay City to visit Brad. He also requested that Tori have Dr. Allen contact him by phone within the next few days, as he really wanted to hear, what Robert had to say about Brad and visitation with his father.

CHAPTER EIGHTEEN

Bay City proved to be a wise move for Tori, but for me it was a new kind of prison. Bars shrouded in every direction limiting me to never answer the door or phone, or even being able to go outside for fear that Tori's parents would suddenly be upon us. Not just this, but the reality of my children being 250 miles away sent new problems with me making 12 hour trips back and forth every other weekend to Winfield. And working 12 to 14 hour days in the upholstery shop to just stay in the black! My alarm button sounded ringing with fear that something could happen to one of my children, when I was so far away and pleads to my Heavenly Father was my only comfort that He was watching over them daily.

It wasn't long before Tori's heart condition and the stress that she succumbed to on a daily basis with her parents was wearing her down completely, that you only had to look at her and she'd cry. I was so fearful that this constant secrecy was going to cause her to have a heart attack that I begged her to quit her job, especially now that her court was over, and just help me in the upholstery business. Amazingly, it helped Tori tremendously with her parents, for they were once again reassured that Mark was still in the picture and that the 'money tree' would grow again.

Alan was already tiring of the so-called visits with Brad. He halfheartedly tried to see Brad once each at McDonald's and Hardee's for maybe 30 minutes as he went through the city to a job. Brad did not respond in anyway except to completely ignore Alan and tell him verbally that he just didn't want to see or be around him.

The morning dew shown over the yard and mesmerized my thoughts as anticipation surrounded my every waking moment of court, which was quickly approaching. Tori and I had gone over and over every detail of the last year, Alex's behavioral disorder, the security I could now provide with my home and job, and of the complete psychological evaluation that Dr. Robert Allen had recently done, which showed that I was a perfectly normal human being! Nothing had been overlooked. I was ready. I loved my kids and I just wanted to be able to express that to the Judge, without him feeling that I might take the kids again if court did not go to my liking.

I praised God that he had removed Judge Alburn from this case, but I was still skeptical of Judge Smith. Only because Jeff had discovered that he was like a twin of my ex-husband right down from his thoughts on child rearing to leading the teens in Bible study; except he was a Catholic. This just reinforced my belief that fighting open would be a losing battle. 1 John 3:10, "Here is the clear difference between God's children and the devil's children: anyone who does not do what is right or does not love his brother is not God's child."

I so much wanted to be able to spend the eve of court with Tori, but the distance involved left me no choice available, except that I spend it at my parents home. Even though Mom was trying to support me and love me just the way I was, it was still very hard for her to give me public support. So it came as no surprise that Mom practically begged me to not force her into going to court. I desperately wanted someone on my side, for I knew that Eric would not only have his parents there, but as many of the Southern Baptist Church members as possible. But in my heart, I knew that if she were there, Eric would be encouraged to put her on the stand, and I just couldn't trust her under pressure. She was just too wishy-washy! Revelation 4:15-16, "I know what you have done; I know that you are neither cold nor hot. How I wish you were either one or the other! But because you are lukewarm, neither hot nor cold, I am going to spit you out of my mouth!" God wants us to do what is right and when we become confused over the truth then we are of no use to Him. Satan breeds confusion and if we can not make up our mind, then you can guarantee that he is behind these feelings.

The time throughout the night ticked so slowly that my burdens were ladened even deeper in my thoughts. How I wished Tori were here to hold me. With a start, I arose from my bed. Dad's alarm was louder than the rooster on the fence post! Looking into the mirror, dark circles were apparent that last night was not restful at all and applying my makeup didn't seem to make them look any better. With a deep sigh, I quietly bent on my knees and gave my burdens to God in prayer.

The courtroom was filled with Southern Baptist Church members, Eric's parents, Helen, the CSO, Bud, the therapist who had been working with the kids, especially Alex, and each of the children's teachers from the past year in school. The harsh echo of the gavel brought me instantly to an alert frame of mind as the proceedings began. Immediately upon the end of the sound, my attorney asked that the courtroom be cleared and the Judge refused. My heart quickened as the Judge announced that Eric's side would be heard first.

"I call Eric to the stand," announced his attorney, Barbara. Her questions to Eric were to the point. "How do you feel the kids are doing at school? Have they adjusted well living with you? Do you feel that custody terms should be changed?" And he answered as you would expect. 'No further questions, your Honor" she assuredly spoke.

"Now Eric, isn't it true that when you were in high school that you had a homosexual affair with another boy whom we'll call 'Jake'?", asked Dobbs. Stuttering, a slow definite creep of red started appearing from his neck on up, as words of an embarrassing "Yes, but" came creaking out of his mouth only to be met by another question from Dobbs. Just exactly what kind of sexual acts did you perform, Eric? Also, weren't you called the town bully and disliked by the small town that you grew up in?" At

217

that, Barbara scooted back her chair in a rage and shouted an objection while stating, "Your Honor, what Eric did when he was a boy has no relevance in this case, Objection!" Judge Smith by this time did not even bother covering up his obvious curiosity when he said, "I feel that this is indeed relevant. Overruled." Eric was stunned and by now it was lunch time and his attorney asked for an immediate adjournment so she could confer with her client and the Judge agreed. Romans 2:1, "Do you, my friend, pass judgment on others? You have no excuse at all, whoever you are. For when you judge others and then do the same things which they do, you condemn yourself." Matthew 7:1-2 "Do not judge others, so that God will not judge you, for God will judge you in the same way you judge others, and he will apply to you the same rules you apply to others."

Smugly, Dobbs continued as court began again. He had achieved his goal by flustering our enemy. Half the time when I told Dobbs about incidents like these, I felt like he was half-listening and he'd never remember them. It's not that I desired to try Eric as a gay person, but rather as someone who could not judge me for the very things that he did too. I was shocked over how attentive the whole court was when it came to Eric answering these questions. They hung on his every word as if wanting more. The subject matter changed abruptly and Jeff continued with questions about, "Did you feel Elizabeth was a good mother during the time you were married? Was she well liked and active in her church up until the time of your divorce?" Of course, Eric admitted that I was a very good Christian until Tori came into the picture.

How dare he! Why was everyone so interested in the relationship I had with Tori? It was of no importance to the fact that I was a good mother, a good friend, and a good God-fearing Christian. Dobbs, immediately backed off from that line of questioning so that he would drop my sexual preferences. One and a half hours later, Eric stepped down from the witness stand, ashen and knowing that Dobbs had deeply hurt his testimony.

218

Unexpectedly, Barbara said, "Your honor, we call Elizabeth Barrett to the stand." I grabbed Jeff's hand, looking for direction. "It's OK, we're keeping even. We might as well dig in and get it over with." he whispered. I stood up self-consciously smoothing the sides of my skirt in nervousness. " Dear God, please be with me and don't let me say anything that can hurt Tori's custody of Brad. Just help me to say the right words to convince the Judge that I should have custody of the children!" I prayed.

Daring a glimpse over to Eric's table, my eyes met head on with a vicious Barbara, who just seemed to gleam with, "Just wait until I work you over the coals. We'll just see what you're really made of!"

I shook it off and waited for Dobbs to ask his first question. "Elizabeth, tell me about what's happened in your life over the last year. Tell us in your own words, why you felt that it was necessary to run with the kids and why you deeply regret your decision today." Frankly, I felt that it was a sin to lie. But, as Dobbs had told me many, many times over, that it was imperative that the Judge feel that I was truly sorry for my endeavor and the disruption to the children's lives and that no matter what happened, it would never happen again.

So, I began: "I love my children very much. All three are so special to me and I love them from the depths of my soul just like any other mother loves her children. But when we had court a year ago, I just could not act like everything was all right and that the court was looking out for the best interest of my children. Although, I am very sorry for my actions now.

Alex had always been a difficult child, but his behavior changed drastically after our divorce. He was out of control not only at home, but in the classroom too. Sharing this with my therapist, she recommended that I take Alex to his pediatrician, the only doctor we had ever used, for an evaluation."

"And who was the therapist who recommended that you do this?" interrupted Dobbs.

"Sherry, from the mental health center, she'd been

seeing me and the other kids as well. But because of some testing she'd done on Alex, she was concerned that there was a possibility of brain damage. previously, I had shared with her how Eric had handled Alex's difficult behavior by physically hitting him on the head with his fist, to twisting his ears and spanking him hard with a homemade wood paddle all over his body. Not only did he do this, but he would smack him on his face for not responding to his commands promptly. I can't begin to count the amount of arguments that erupted in our home from Eric's abusive behavior in the form of discipline towards our children." My throat tightened as the story unfolded and tears came to my eyes as I relived the nightmare of Eric's bullying of the kids, but especially Alex, who alone defined his father on an every day basis.

"From the doctor's examination of Alex, he referred me to a neurologist, who recommended further testing after an examination that agreed that Alex had indeed suffered brain damage from the harsh physical treatment of his father. I love my children and from all of the information that was gathered from the doctors, I knew that Alex needed help and with this in mind, I persisted in presenting this issue in the next court hearing over custody.

I was shocked, when Judge Alburn's decision came back totally one-sided. And after contacting my attorney, he informed me that it would take up to two years to appeal Judge Alburn's decision. I was frightened for my children's safety and I felt there was no recourse except for me to run." The memory of that moment of panic sent my body trembling and tears running freely down my cheeks. "Eric had not even asked for a custody change, and he changed it to sole custody, with visitation to be only once a month, but he would leave it up to the father's discretion." I sobbed uncontrollably.

Jeff quickly came from his sitting position behind his desk and offered me a box of Kleenexes. "Judge Smith, at this time I would like to reinstate evidence that was presented at the court hearing now in question,"

220

interrupted Jeff "that pertains to the Doctor reports including Sherry's report on Alex. These reports confirm that Elizabeth is telling the truth. Also, I would like the court to note the MMR and parenting testing results that Elizabeth voluntarily took. I might add that it was said, that she received the highest score ever given on the parenting exam.

"Now Elizabeth, about your relationship with Tori. Do you live with her?"

"No," I said staring defiantly at Barbara. "I live in a duplex 25 minutes away from Tori." I lied while brushing away the tears from my eyes and using another kleenex to wipe my nose.

"OK, fine, now...", pausing for effect, Dobbs says, "It's been stated in your eldest son's report, I believe that's Rich, correct?", I nodded my head in accordance. "that you regularly left him and Crystal alone in the apartment to go and be with Tori way into the wee hours of the night. How do you respond to that?"

There was instantaneous silence in the courtroom as all eyes were on Dobbs, who was resting his body on the end of our table and then quickly rising to come closer to me. "Elizabeth, were any charges filed against you because of this incident?" he challenged. "Yes, but no charges were pressed against me. An SRS investigation found that since Rich was 11 1/2 years old that he was quite capable of babysitting."

"Could you please tell us about the night of March 3rd, 1988," questioned Dobbs?

I trembled as I quickly recalled for the court the nightmare of being attacked by Eric viciously in front of my apartment and once again my emotions from reliving this experience sent tears from my eyes. Surely the Judge could see that everything that I said about what Eric had done to the kids were true after what he did to me? I questioned deep within my being as I finished up my description of that night with the results of the injury to my leg. "The doctor who treated me, said that I would always have a permanent disability in my leg. From this my last attorney recommended that I press charges civilly against Eric for punitive damages over my leg. Not just for the money, but mostly to get Eric to leave me and the children alone. But I later dropped them at Mr. Dobbs request in an effort to calm down the fighting and to resolve the custody matter over our children."

Dobbs once again presented the letter from my doctor over the injury of my leg so it could be put into evidence for my defense. " One final question, do you want your children to live with you? And do you feel that it's in the best interest of the children to have residential custody with you?" "Yes, to both." I replied. "Nothing further, Your Honor." Dobbs enunciated.

Before I could even take a deep sigh of relief, Barbara had attacked with her first question. "Ms. Barrett. You provided the court with phone numbers and addresses of the two upholsterers that you are currently working for and I took the opportunity to call them up just to verify your statement. Not that I doubt you, but you must agree that several statements you've made in the past are certainly questionable especially when it pertains to Tori?"

OBJECTION!, Your Honor!" Jeff yelled.

"Sustained!", bounced off the walls as she hastily withdrew and rephrased the question by now repeating a quote from the phone conversation. "Sheila acknowledged that you did work for her, but that the address that her company dropped off and picked up the furniture was in fact, the address that Tori had given the court for a home address. Would you explain why you lied to the court and committed perjury when you said you didn't live with Tori?" She snidely quipped.

My heart raced as the words came from my mouth to once again cover up my relationship with Tori. "I do not live with Tori. The address I gave you is mine. But I do not have a basement or a garage to do the work in and I cannot afford to rent an office space right now. So I work out of Tori's garage during the day." Barbara scowled in disbelief and continued with a barrage of questions for the next hour trying to trip up my testimony at every turn over my fleeing with my kids to my finances, but most of all over what kind of relationship I had with Tori.

After a short recess, the afternoon session seemed to just fly by. Naturally, Barbara called many character witnesses as to Eric's parenting and church standing. The children's teachers were called and they all said what wonderful children we had and that Eric was very attentive to them and always stayed on top of any problems that might arise in school. At that final remark, Dobbs cross-examined by demanding from Alex's teacher, "Mrs. Cole, isn't it true that you received several letters from Ms. Barrett expressing concern over Alex's grades and how his attitude was in school? And isn't it also true that you did not respond to these letters?"

She shook her head up and down as she in turn looked sheepish over her neglect to concur that I was likewise a responsible parent to my children. Her face turned red as she replied. "Yes, I received the letter. But, I'm a very busy person and I just didn't find the time to respond."

I took a deep breath knowing that she was one of Eric's best friend's mother. Why would she say anything but nice things for Eric's sake and her own sons approval. But Dobbs wasn't so easily fooled as he questioned her further by asking, "Would you please describe the problems and disruptions that Alex was causing in your classroom last year?"

"Well, with Eric's daily involvement in the classroom most of his disruptions stopped." she lied. I hoped from her remark that the judge would see that Alex was not doing well under the care of his father, when he had to show up for school every day to keep Alex in line for his teacher.

"Come now, Ms. Gleason, let's be truthful here, didn't Alex continue to receive detention because he even went so far as to give his best friend a bloody nose at recess? And didn't his grades sporadically rise and fall just the same way that they had previously done the year

223

before?" Immediately Dobbs presented a slip of paper that she had signed indicating that Alex had indeed disrupted the classroom on several occasions and as a result been put under detention after school. Her face once again turned bright red as the evidence was presented. I prayed, hoping that the Lord would embed this into the Judge's mind that Alex truly did need some kind of treatment and that I had been telling the truth about the problems Alex was having.

"Well, I suppose that would be true." she stammered.

"Nothing further, Your Honor." Dobbs gleefully announced.

The Judge's eyes rose to meet the solemn face of the courtroom clock which gestured that it was already past five. "I feel the urgency that we should keep going, no matter how late it gets, so that all evidence will be fresh in my mind, but unfortunately it has been a long day. Therefore, I ask that the Plaintiff call just one more witness as of today and we will continue court at the very earliest day that both counsels and I have as an opening. In addition, I wish to speak with the children privately in my chambers on that same day. Council, please call your last witness."

"Your Honor, I call Bud to the stand." Barbara said. Her questions to him were mundane and seemed to center around his thoughts of me. How would a therapist feel qualified to answer questions that pertained to hearsay? My thoughts questioned. But not to fear, Jeffrey Dobbs is here! "Bud if I may? Have you ever met Ms. Barrett?"

"Yes, I have. At a divorce class that she was assigned to take by the court." he answered.

"Have you ever counseled her or had any in depth conversations with her?" Jeff continued.

"Well, not exactly," Bud replied.

"OK, Bud. Was it court ordered over a year and a half ago, that Alex specifically receive therapy on a regular basis, and that he and Ms. Barrett were to receive counseling together; that is to work out any supposed

224

differences that they were having? And please would you look back over your records and tell me how many times that you've seen Alex, and how many times you've seen him by himself?"

Agitation pierced Bud's face as he proudly stated that he had forgotten to bring along the file and could not answer the above questions. And to his best ability, he just could not recall specifically how many times or what they talked about, except that the children wanted to live with their dad.

At that remark, Dobbs said no further questions, except to add, "Bud I want it stated for the court record, that I feel you are perjuring yourself and that I will not only be subpoenaing you for the continuance, but also your file."

Shame, amazement, and embarrassment all seemed to caress Bud's face as he quickly walked out of the courtroom door, letting the door close loudly.

DOWN went the gavel. "Court is adjourned! Counsel, would you please come to the bench so that we can clear a court date?"

Court was set for the following Friday. A mere 7 days away. Dobbs walked me to my car and excitedly squeezed me around my shoulders. "I feel really good about today. I know we're going to win this one!" With his words still ringing in my ears, I made the long drive back home; I just couldn't wait to get home to tell Tori, Andria and Dee about today's events.

It was 2:00 a.m. before I arrived back home, but Tori was wide-eyed and bushy tailed. She thrust a Diet Pepsi in my hands, shoved me onto the sofa, took off my shoes and began massaging my feel all the while demanding that I had to give her a complete and detailed run-down of court. I was so tired! But Tori was relentless and I knew she'd never sleep peacefully until I filled her in and so that's exactly what I did.

CHAPTER NINETEEN

The chirping of the birds outside the garage door, where I worked, broke the silence of the melancholy day I had settled into. Again emotion over the loss of my children brought memories of days gone by that in my present life could never be played again. Silently, I prayed that the nightmare my life had settled into would vanish, just like the scary thoughts that I had when I was a child when I was suddenly awakened by a bad dream.

Tori and I had begun our daily routine down in the shop, when the phone rang. My heart just seemed to want to burst out of my chest and I knew that whoever was on the other end of the phone, had something to say that I didn't want to here. Dear God, please don't let there be any problems, went through my whispered prayer, before I took the end of the receiver from Tori, who had just said that it was my lawyer.

Apparently a relative in his family had just passed away and he would have to leave the state immediately so court would have to be postponed. Unfortunately after a 3-way phone conversation between himself, Eric's attorney, and the Judge resulted in a court day that was two months from today's date! "Two whole months? Jeff, can't it be any sooner than that? It's really hard financially and car wise to be able to see my children when I have to make the whole trip back and forth?" I said.

"I'm sorry, Elizabeth. This was the soonest that we could agree on a date. I'm sure that they're stalling, but my hands are tied. In the meantime, it's very important that your visitation is prompt." Dobbs said as he quickly hung up. He had never been known for his lengthy phone conversations!

The months passed quickly. I thanked God daily that He had seen fit to bless us with work. My only worry

226

was that my car, which was very old and dilapidated, would succeed in me arriving safely to and from Winfield on my every other weekend visitation with my children.

Finally the day once again arrived and with my seat belt securely buckled, I leaned out the window to give Tori one final hug before I was on my way. I really felt confident from how well court had gone the first time that when I came home tonight, that I'd be bringing along with me, either the kids or a date when they would be coming. As I drove, I savored the quiet time that six hours of driving gave me to converse with God and pray over court. I arrived in Winfield extremely stiff from driving, but filled with hopeful anticipation. Much to my surprise, not only was my mother sitting on the bench up by the courtroom door, but so was my sister! Thank you, God! Excitedly, I hugged them and I knew that this was indeed a joyful celebration. For once, since the long ordeal of the custody fight, I had someone sitting on my side of the court.

Together we waited for my attorney and Eric's supporters to finish arriving before court was in session. Within 10 minutes, Judge Smith had hastily rushed in with his robe still unzipped and harshly pounded the gavel on its pad! Jeff Dobbs quickly began appraising the courtroom unabashedly, all set to reel the verdict into our side and completely in my favor. The whole mood of the room was filled with anticipation. The Judge had just announced that he didn't even want to be here today because his son was sick at home. He urged the attorney's to make this quick and to the point! I couldn't believe how uncaring and rude his behavior was to all of us present. It was as if he had already made up his mind and that the testimony was not going to make any difference.

Dobbs worriedly glanced at me and then quickly stood up and called our first witness. "Your Honor, I recall Bud to the stand." As he hurriedly approached the stand, I praised God that Bud had obeyed the court's order and brought along his file on the children. Judge Smith reminded him that he was still under oath. "Bud, now that you have your file to remind you of what's been happening in your sessions, would you please tell the court just how many times you've seen Alex since January?" Thumbing through his papers as if searching for the answer, the Judge prodded him to quickly find his response. "4 times that are documented." Bud announced.

"4 times in the last 12 months? Weren't you ordered to see him on a regular basis of at least twice monthly?" Dobbs quipped, appearing appalled.

"Before you answer that, Bud, would you look at your file and tell me of those 4 times, how many times did you see Alex alone?" Red again began to creep up Bud's face for he knew that if he didn't answer, Dobbs indicated that he would simply take the file from him and look it up himself. "I never saw him alone, but Eric never interrupted our sessions, and when the other kids were there, Alex never varied his story."

"And just exactly, what was his story?" insisted Dobbs.

"That Alex didn't like his mom and that he didn't want to have to see her. That he wanted to continue to live with his dad and brother and sister." Bud blundered.

"Are you tell me as a professional social worker that you feel that Alex would really tell you the truth in front of his father? Especially when there are allegations that his father physically abused him?"

"Objection!" yelled Barbara.

"I'll restate, Your Honor," Dobbs hastily smirked. "Do you feel that having had all sessions with Alex and his father that you completely know him and whether he's telling you the truth about his relationship with his mother?"

Bud began squirming in his seat, but he replied, "Well his story matches the story that his dad says he tells him at home."

"And you believe Eric?" Dobbs disgustedly asked.

"Why shouldn't I?" Bud retorted. "I feel that Alex's problem completely stems around his relationship with his mother."

228

"Excuse me, Bud, but couldn't his behavior problem stem from the actual pain and frustration over the abuse from his father and not directly from the relationship with his mother?"

"I suppose that's possible, but I don't really know." Bud nervously replied.

"Have you ever had a session with Alex and his mother as ordered by the court? Have you ever spoken with Ms. Barrett regarding Alex?" questioned Dobbs.

"I spoke with his mother at a divorce class that I gave. And I have to say that I felt she was obsessive over her feelings that Alex needed to be completely evaluated. She listed instances when Alex was there for visitation and how Alex seemed to be withdrawn and depressed to the point of doing harm to himself. She also asked about what happened at the sessions and if she could be apart of them. I refused to even discuss the situation and I walked away from her before we could finish the last of our conversation." Bud vehemently explained.

"Don't you feel that any mother in the same situation would show a lot of concern and love for her child and want to know when joint sessions were going to be held? Especially so that the counselor could hear both sides of the story?" Dobbs questioned.

"I suppose so, but,"

"Just answer the question, Bud. So you're saying now, that you don't really know what's best for Alex?" questioned Dobbs.

"I haven't seen Alex that often to have made a complete psychological evaluation."

"Well, have you run any tests or made an effort to schedule the sessions any closer together?"

Bud replied, "I have no control over my schedule, the secretaries handle that and as for testing, I didn't feel there was any need."

At that note, Jeffrey Dobbs shook his head in disgust as he could see that we were simply playing round robin. It was up to the Judge to see that Bud was lying. As Barbara said she had no questions for Bud, I glanced

229

back to see how my mother was handling court for she was to be our next witness. With all the strength I could muster, I silently prayed to God Almighty that she would back me 100% on the witness stand.

I sat staunchly in my wooden high back chair as mother nervously tripped into the box that held her chair for questioning. Naturally, Dobbs presented me 'on a pedestal' and mother supported the facts that I had reason for running with the children, that I was a wonderful mother, and that she felt it would best serve the children to be living with me. She also voiced her concerns over Alex's behavior and reiterated the fact that Alex had had a behavioral problem ever since he was born and that his 'acting up' as she called it was certainly nothing new. Pleased with her assured behavior, Dobbs tipped his pretend hat towards Barbara as he made his way back to our table.

Barbara just glared through Dobbs as if he were a ghost. Her own eyes looked murderous! "Mrs. Barrett, I'm quite curious about something. Isn't it true that up until your daughter's divorce became public, that you had hidden the fact that you were not actually deaf? That for the last 24 years of your life, you've been covering up the fact, that you can hear everything, even whispers, that occur in your presence?" Barbara questioned viciously.

"Yes, that's true, except my husband has known for quite sometime." my mother replied as she looked towards me for reassurance. I smiled and nodded to go on. My Spirit was going like a whirlwind within my soul, and I knew that subconsciously, the Angels in Heaven were hovering over my mother with protective gloves made of love.

Barbara seemed surprised at her response, but nevertheless prodded on fiercely. "Well then, Mrs. Barrett, would you please tell the court how we are supposed to believe you now, when you stand before us and tell us that your daughter is best suited to be the residential custodial parent?"

Even the Judge who up until now, had been

impatiently unbending a paper clip, abruptly gave his undying attention to her reply. "I've been Elizabeth's mother for 32 years. I don't expect anyone except my family to understand why I've pretended for all these years. But I'm simply telling you the truth, when I said she was and she still is a wonderful mother."

Although the answer was not what she wanted to hear, Barbara's dart had already hit the bulls-eye and after relentlessly badgering my mother for another 15 minutes, she abruptly halted questioning and stated that she was ready to call her first witness.

At that remark, the Judge questioned her on whom her witnesses were to be. Dobbs had no problem agreeing with the Judge when he related the fact that he'd already heard enough character witnesses on Eric's behalf to last a lifetime, and that he wanted to recess for lunch. But before his gavel adjourned court, he reminded Eric, that all 3 kids were to come back with him, as he would be speaking with them privately in his chambers before handing down a ruling on the motion before him!

Lunchtime seemed like an eternity! I wished out loud that I would have the chance to visit with the kids before the Judge questioned them, but as I should have expected, mother and my sister were only concerned with the fact that mom had looked 'like a fool' and that 'if I had just worked out my problems and submitted to my husband' I wouldn't be in this predicament! Neither of them had the courage to stand by my side for the afternoon even though they felt their excuses could cover up the truth. My sister's husband would be home soon from work and she needed to be there when he got home because he didn't know she was at court, and mom felt that it would be better if the Judge didn't see her and was reminded that 'craziness' ran in our bloodline.

But only through the grace of God, did I convince them that it really was a dire emergency that they stay to show confidence in me! We quickly hurried our pace to the courthouse in hopes that I could have a chance to talk to the kids before they met with the Judge. As a mother, I felt it was very unfair that Eric had been given the lunch hour to convey to the children, what they should say to the Judge and what he might possibly do if they didn't say what he told them to say! It's just so unfair that any child should have to make a choice and feel guilty towards one of their parents when they choose the other.

This was just one of those times when I simply had only one option available to me, Prayer! Immediately my prayer was answered almost before I finished. My children were unattended in the hallway outside the courtroom while their father went to talk to his lawyer and I welcomed this opportunity to give them courage for choosing my side. Just before their father reappeared, I reminded them through tears that I loved them, and no matter what happened today, I was still their mother and no one could take that away from us!

Before court started up, the Judge took the children aside and casually showed them the courtroom. He explained where the witness stand was and what his bench and gavel were all about. By doing this he hoped to ease the tension from the children's faces and at the same time gain some trust with them so that they would open up to him in his chambers with 'how they were really feeling'.

While we waited, over an hour lapsed. I just felt a sinking desperation fill my soul as each minute ticked by. Dobbs had made enough snide quips to Barbara to fill his cowboy hat to the brim, but when I asked him what he felt the verdict would be, he seemed very optimistic. "We've presented our case as well as we possibly could. We only have to hope that the Judge will not let the lesbian issue blind his rationale!"

At that note, the Judge quietly closed the door to his chamber and ordered court in session. I could tell by the look in his face and the way that he would not look towards our table, that it was not going to be good news! The tears started welling up and flowing down my face silently. I heard the Judge begin, "There's been a lot of evidence presented over the last two sessions, some has been truthful, some has been very confusing and contradicting from each of the parties. However, after hearing from the children in my chambers, I feel convinced that for the following 9 months it's in the best interest for the children to remain in residential custody with their father. But I am granting the Petitioner's motion for custody to be changed from sole back to joint custody; that the mother be allowed 3 days before school starts with the children at her new home in Bay City and the following visitation schedule:

Every other weekend from 6:30 Friday to 3:30 on Sunday. Both parties are to find an amiable meeting place between the homes.

Petitioner will pay $100 a month in child support.

Petitioner will receive the children on Thanksgiving, Christmas and Spring Break for the time they're out of school.

Petitioner will receive the children for 3 weeks in the summer for an extended visit.

Additional visits are optional and the above may vary if both parties are amicable.

Petitioner is not responsible for any medical bills of the children.

I am informing Ms. Barrett that she is not to allow the children to be in the presence of Tori Bovard during the visitation period.

I am also instructing the court for the record that one of the main reasons I ruled the way I did was because I did not feel that it was fair for the children to be placed in a new home, a new neighborhood, and a new school when school will begin in less than 2 weeks from now. Therefore, at the adjournment of today's session, I wish both attorneys to approach the bench and we will set a hearing for June of next year, when we will permanently establish residential custody. At that time, we will review the findings of both parties and how the year went at both homes, as well as revisiting the children in my chambers."

I think I only heard half of what the Judge actually

said because my feelings took over my senses and all I could do was let down and cry! I was the better parent not Eric! Why was it so bad to love Tori? How dare they tell me who I could see and who I couldn't! Dobbs kept shaking my arm telling me to 'get a grip' that even though I didn't get the kids now, there was no reason presented today in court that said I should not receive permanent residential custody next June. It was just very important that I abide by my probationary terms and did what the Judge requested and absolutely make no waves!"

That was easy for him to say! But I knew he meant well and that he had to be as disappointed as I, for Jeff never took on cases unless he could win them. I had completely forgotten that my family was here, but when I got up to go be with them, they had practically nothing to do with me, except to say that I should have stayed married to Eric and make things work out. Where was the motherly hug and understanding I so desperately needed right now?

"Instead, in everything we do we show that we are God's servants by patiently enduring troubles, hardships, and difficulties. We have been beaten, jailed, and mobbed; we have been overworked and have gone without sleep or food. By our purity, knowledge, patience, and kindness we have shown ourselves to be God's servants by the Holy Spirit, by our true love, by our message of truth, and by the power of God. We have righteousness as our weapon, both to attack and to defend ourselves. We are honored and disgraced, we are insulted and praised. We are treated as liars, yet we speak the truth; as unknown, yet we are known by all; as though we were dead, but, as you see, we live on. Although punished, we are not killed, although saddened, we are always glad; we seem poor, but we make many people rich; we seem to have nothing, yet we really possess everything." 2 Corinthians 6:4-10.

Alex and Crystal looked pleadingly my way, as I stood waiting for the elevator to open. I opened my arms for them to embrace me, and when they hugged me back, they both said, "Mom, we told the Judge we wanted to live with you, but Rich said he wanted to live with Dad!" I instantly reassured them that everything was OK and that they'd done just fine. Looking over their shoulders at their father gloating at this temporary victory, only made me more determined than ever to run the race God had set before me and be Victor through His grace! Hebrews 12:2, "Let us keep our eyes fixed on Jesus, on whom our faith depends from beginning to end. He did not give up because of the cross! On the contrary, because of the joy that was waiting for him, he thought nothing of the disgrace of dying on the cross, and he is now seated at the right side of God's throne."

Finding a pay telephone that was unoccupied took driving over 75 miles before I was finally able to contact Tori and let her know briefly the outcome of court. Just hearing her voice, dropped all of my defenses and made my words stumble over one another in sync with the tears that were making puddles around my feet. Tori just lifted me up right then and there in prayer. Her voice was surprised and defiant all at the same time, but she knew now was not the time to question, why! I purposely hung up quickly, for what I really needed was Tori in person, the only person who really understood me.

Tori's eyes met mine in one accord and simply and deftly wrapped me in her arms while stroking my hair in a calming rhythmic motion. "Why didn't the Judge listen to me? Why didn't he listen to Dobbs destroy all the evidence they had so carefully made against me? I kept asking Tori over and over, only to hear her say, "Elizabeth, no one knows why God allows things to happen and it's not up to you to question Him, but to accept His Will. I know it's difficult. It's hard for me to accept, but I know that God is here right now and that He will reveal to us His purpose in this mess, when He's ready!"

So many times people say that it's God's will when things do not turn out for that person, and that you should just accept it, but this isn't true! God helps people who are being subjected to man's will, for the best for the person who is suffering under man's will! God did not

235

take my children away, rather people who misconstrued the scriptures, took them away. For instance when Adam took the first bite from the apple was this God's will? Of course not! Gold told him not to eat the apple, but Adam did it anyway. Thus all men alike were given free wills. Because of our free will's, satan was given the opportunity to bring in corruption to our world and we were given the chance to become a part of it. Because of the activity of satan we became blind to God's love for mankind, and wars evolved, misunderstandings among people, and every sin that could be thought up by the human mind.

Then God in His perfect understanding of the hopelessness that man created for himself, proposed a new way by setting apart a whole nation and giving them the 10 commandments and over 600 other laws that would help them govern themselves in harmony and peace. But man was unable to follow these laws, so God did away with the laws and sent His Son to be the Savior of the world.

From the free gift of Jesus all of the laws written in Deuteronomy became obsolete. The new law shone down in love inspired by grace! Romans 8:28, "We know that in all things God works for good with those who love him, those whom he has called according to his purpose."

Knowing all of this, still did not make my life any easier, but it did enable me to acknowledge that I was not alone in my despair from the loss of my children, but many gays in the world were also suffering just like me! I could not help but pray that God would shine His light down on them and help them to know that God loves them and calls them His sons.

CHAPTER TWENTY

I prayed that with the dawn of a new day that my prison sentence would end, and I would be free to go through life like I had before all this mess had begun! I loved Tori so much, but it caused me so much pain to hold on to this love through the midst of the demands of the courts and now with the impending visitation of my children the bars ignited in a fire that lit a path for my enemies to further devour me from my stubborn refusal to deny my feelings for Tori. I hated what they were doing to my family, yet there was no one in the justice system that would help me. In many prayers filled with tears, I begged God to see my dilemmas and to rescue me so that through all the persecutions, I would be able to stand firm with a sure faith that He would see me through in the nick of time.

It was extremely difficult making Eric play by the rules that the Judge had given us. He refused to let me have the kids until the last 4 available days before school started and then he would only meet me at Fenton, a mere 100 miles to my 155! But that was OK. My heart was joyous and I just couldn't keep smiling as Tori and Brad waved me on my way.

The children were careful not to show any emotion as we drove most of the way to Bay City in silence. It quickly became apparent that their father had drilled into them that I was a sinner and that if I would just admit that I had made an awful mistake, that he would forgive me and let me be his wife and their mother again. Just like it used to be!

As the garage door closed down behind us, Brad's excitement plunged him down the stairs as fast as his legs would carry him and he literally hugged them as tight as he could! Alex & Crystal's eyes showed how much they'd missed all of us, but Rich was quiet and reserved. He made it very obvious that he was his dad's son, and that whatever we said or did was going to be elaborated on to his dad immediately upon his return.

I explained to them before we went home, that we would be staying with Tori and Brad for their visit, because my home was being sprayed for bugs and that the odor was toxic to people during the first 48 hours the spray was drying. This story developed as Tori and I discussed what was the best way to handle the situation for the first visit. As a result, Rich was greatly relieved that he could see Tori and I had a valid reason to back up what he was going to tell his dad.

Tori and I planned many wonderful activities for the kids to experience for their first time in Bay City. We rode the trolley, went to a movie, we even went to the Mall, which all of them felt was exciting. We did everything that a normal family would enjoy, except we just couldn't be normal for Alex erupted with constant problems. He was out of control and he simply exploded with no provocation by shoving any of the kids or me for that matter, or verbalizing his frustration with slang and hateful bantering! It was never ending! Tori and I were both physically exhausted and even though the whole time that my kids were with us we kept an open prayer line to God going in full motion, it still didn't seem to be enough.

I showed love and extreme patience with each of the children, but Eric's constant pressure of condemning me verbally to my kids because of my love for Tori was tearing them apart. They loved me, but they were afraid to show it for fear of not only what Rich would say when they returned, but what Eric would do to them if I won their approval. So they were creating a barrier that would guard them from being happy in my company and Tori's and this took the form of hate. They hated my house, my car, my work, and most especially they hated Brad and Tori. I could not begin to comprehend all of the damage Eric had done to them by teaching them that it was right to hate what they didn't understand. In defiance of all that Eric

238

was taught in the church, he had put aside the most basic principle of all, which is to love. For God is love! When he forced them to hate, he purposely caused them to sin and because they were too young and inexperienced to handle the pressures that this put on them, their emotions took over and especially Alex's behavior changed. Matthew 18:6, "If anyone should cause one of these little ones to lose his faith in me, it would be better for that person to have a large millstone tied around his neck and be drowned in the deep sea." I wondered how Eric could read the Bible and not be convicted by this passage. Satan works in hatred, not God!

After dropping the kids off, I felt my whole body go limp as if my entire being had been wrestling with 'demons' in the lions den. Yet to my surprise, Tori was standing in the yard talking fervently with 2 women and a man pointing at our home and throwing her arms up in the air every few seconds. Cautiously, I drove past our home hoping to divert Tori's attention so she could let me know if it was safe for me to stop. But she was so intent with her conversation that she didn't even see me! Quickly, I parked the car and jumped out just in time to hear Tori's parting remarks that she would not budge from this house until she had talked to her lawyer and/or the lease was bought out!

Eventually upon reaching the house, Tori calmed down enough to tell me what was going on. She had been cleaning house after I left and when she began starting supper there was a knock on the front door. She didn't answer immediately and suddenly she started hearing strange voices from the living room. To her surprise she was met by a man and a woman. The lady was a realtor and she was taking the man through our home for his final walk through before he took possession of our duplex. Supposedly, the landlord was to have sent a letter explaining that she had sold the duplex.

Tori immediately stated to them that she had a year's lease and in the lease it said, that the home was not on the market and that since she was current on her rent, it was not possible to sell the house. The realtor met her statement with a warning that even if she did go to court and win this round, it would make for very bad relations with her landlord and that she would only find a way to have her evicted! Tori took a deep breath and signed.

Michael, who was the man who had purchased the home seemed genuinely sorry about the mess. But his realtor informed him that he could not let her live in the home, because his loan would be denied if he himself did not live in the house. So Michael then proceeded to tell her that he would be willing to rent a U-Haul truck and bring along some friends of his and move her free, no strings attached.

She told him that she realized this wasn't his problem, but she still felt that until her landlord paid her back her security deposit and moving expenses, she was not going to budge! And with that, they left.

Caressing strokes of sunlight played upon our faces, while thoughts of moving invaded our thoughts and consciously the heartache of satan attacking us once again was indeed discouraging. "Israel, why then do you complain that the Lord doesn't know your troubles or care if you suffer injustice? Don't you know? Haven't you heard? The Lord is the everlasting God; he created all the world. He never grows tired or weary. No one understands his thoughts. He strengthens those who are weak and tired. Even those who are young grow weak; young men can fall exhausted. But those who trust in the Lord for help will find their strength renewed. They will rise on wings like eagles; they will run and not get weary; they will walk and not grow weak." Isaiah 40:27-31.

Glancing over at Tori, who was so very quiet this morning, I became determined that God would be victor if it killed us trying! Over the next week, negotiations between our lawyer and our landlord became exhausting and frustrating. Without question, God became victor when she finally backed down and agreed to return our security deposit along with $400 for basic moving expenses. Michael also came through and helped us move to yet another new home. Truly God's own strength came and renewed our weaknesses with the power of God's gift of strength.

Life started to fall into a routine and even though Eric made a big stink over the kids being around Tori, the court did nothing to stop me. I silently thanked God for not allowing me to be dragged back into court over this defiance, and I began making the regular visits with the kids that the court allowed. At first everything went smoothly until Eric refused to bring the children part of the way and once again my lawyer became involved and contacted the Judge, and basically the Judge enforced the decree he originally handed down forcing Eric to meet me. Once this was solved, my problems continued with Alex until I finally put my foot down and refused to allow him to come for one of the visits. When you have such limited visits it's hard to discipline your children and as hard as this was for me, I could not put up with his continued hateful behavior to his sister, brother, and of course Tori and Brad. His next visit resulted in a complete change in his attitude and I just couldn't Praise God enough for giving me the strength to hold firm. For once again God gave me super natural strength to do what was right.

I began my probation requirements and I was assigned an officer of the court for monthly visits. Immediately, I was informed that I was responsible to meet the community service hours on my own. Earnestly, we looked for several months and made call after call to places like the Red Cross, hospitals, volunteer services, but there were always long waiting lists that stopped us dead in our tracks. My probation officer began really putting pressure on me about when I would get these hours completed. It was by a stroke of luck that Tori called and inquired at Prison Fellowship. Todd, the administrator of Prison Fellowship, who served a nine year prison term himself, was certainly willing to help out others in need. He gave us office work that could be done at home and we kept prisoner's wives at our home for marriage weekends at the penitentiary. We were also involved in soliciting donations for the prison ministry which resulted in endless telephone calls. It was so interesting the way people treated you when you said you were calling for 'Prison Ministries.'' Either we could feel the love and compassion of true Christian brothers or we felt aloofness and condemnation. Within a few short months we completed the much needed hours! Praise God!

Brad was doing exceptionally well in school, was well liked, and had adjusted to the move remarkably well considering that this was his 9th move in his six years of life. Tori was happy working at home and catering to our customer's fanciful whims, while I joyfully worked and Praised God for our upholstery business taking off and prospering. Not only this, but we were able to purchase a car that was my first reliable transportation which made my trips a whole lot more worry free, especially since I had two previous break downs with my old car. Even my kids began to lighten up and settle into the routine of making the lengthy trips back and forth and for once since the kidnapping and court, they actually began expressing feelings of love and gratitude.

Standing in the doorway watching the sunset had put my thoughts into a tranquil state. The last few days had been especially hard as Tori's lower back was causing her extreme pain and she had literally been flat on her back unable to help me at all with shop work. My silent cries to God asking for him to heal Tori's back abruptly ended with the shrill ring of the business phone. It was not unusual to receive phone calls in the evening because our customers knew that we worked out of our home.

Tori had the gift of gab and loved working with the customer's and taking great care to become their friend as well, but I became somewhat curious when Tori said the phone call was for me. She didn't know who it was, except that it was a man and he'd asked to speak to Elizabeth Bartell. I was surprised for I hadn't gone by that name for over 3 years!

My Spirit took flight inside my soul as I put my mouth to the receiver and heard the deep resonate voice,

"My name is Kirk Barnes and I'm investigating alleged criminal actions pertaining to the mobile home that you purchased and allegedly falsified the income tax statements. I'd like to discuss this with you and also I'd like to speak with your friend, Tori Bovard at the same time." Flustered, I said in a numbed monotone voice, that I would be glad to answer his questions after I'd spoken with my attorney. At that, he gave me his telephone number and said that if he hadn't heard from us the following day, that he'd be calling back.

As I slowly put the phone back on the hook, I could feel Tori's presence in the room. Without saying a word, our eyes met. Calmly, I tried to assure Tori that everything would be OK and that Dobbs would handle everything and I just knew that Eric was just trying to get revenge no matter how much mud-slinging he had to do.

Tears started cascading down Tori's face as she started screeching that she was going to lose Brad and that we were going to be jailed again, all the while I was trying to reach Dobbs at his home. Psalm 70:1-5 says, "Save me, O God! Lord, help me now! May those who try to kill me be defeated and confused. May those who are happy because of my troubles be turned back and disgraced. May those who make fun of me be dismayed by their defeat. May all who come to you be glad and joyful. May all who are thankful for your salvation always say, 'How great is God!' I am weak and poor; come to me quickly, O God. You are my Savior and my Lord-hurry to my aid!"

It was past 9:30 the next morning before contact was finally made with Dobbs. He quietly listened and then said that he didn't want to get involved in yet another case as he just couldn't afford to go 'pro bono' anymore. Tori grabbed the phone from my hand and pleaded tearfully for mercy! Dobbs reluctantly agreed only after we promised that we would send a total cash amount of $5,000 to him certified and within the next 10 days! He promised to get back with us over the next 24 hours after he'd made a few calls, but in the meantime we were not to speak with anyone; just refer them on to our attorney's office. Each and every time the phone rang, our hearts seemed to stop beating which only made our adrenaline shoot jagged darts into the air. When Dobbs finally got back to us, we had received over 4 phone calls from Barnes insisting that he must speak with us. Dobbs strongly suggested that this case was nothing more than Winfield still drudging up mud to sling and that we were to trust him because he'd never let us down and he wouldn't do so now!

All we could do is pray with every ounce of strength we had to God Almighty to have mercy on us, to forgive us for our wrongdoing, to provide us with an overabundance of work to meet the retainer fee requested, and to let us begin a new with all of our past closed behind sealed doors. And our prayers were indeed answered! After a week had passed, Tori's back was healing nicely and from all angles it seemed as if Dobbs had stopped HUD dead in their tracks; at least for now! God once again renewed our strength and met our retainer fee!

CHAPTER TWENTY-ONE

I have always been someone who holds my emotions inward, like a time capsule where only God and I knew the real me, while Tori talks her emotions out non-stop, often acting like a record that is stuck in one place! But the two opposite ways we dealt with life, just lit an ever glowing bright light in our souls that allowed us to deal with every day problems as one. Problems that many people like us had to deal with inside the prison of being gay.

As every new dawn broke it seemed as though we were always treading on thin ice and constantly praying incessantly that the nightmare of being hated by everyone would be over. It seemed as soon as one problem ended, yet another one would appear. And for every mother this next problem was almost more than I could endure. We had just started our first 3 week summer vacation with my kids and the air was filled with tenseness from Tori and I trying to attain a balance with our kids and work. The first evening as the kids were getting ready for bed, Tori went into Crystal's room to put away some laundry and Crystal blurted out that she was tired of Alex always pulling her underwear down and trying to touch her when her dad was gone and Rich was left babysitting Alex and her.

Later on that night, Tori quietly explained to me the situation and what Crystal had said. We had both noticed that Crystal's behavior seemed different, but with everything that all of us had been through it was only normal to have problems with all of the kids. Now, I could understand why Crystal was constantly locking the door of her bedroom and screaming hysterically every time Alex even came near her.

Just three months before, I had complained to Eric that Alex was constantly hitting Rich in his private area and that he needed to have a talk with him and to inform

Bud his therapist about this as well. Eric laughed and stated that he never had problems like this at his house and that as far as he was concerned it was all my fault! That ended our conversation.

After discussing the problem thoroughly with the limited information Crystal had given us and taking in consideration the lack of support that Eric had shown in the past for the children's problems, we decided to ask for direction from Robert, Tori and Brad's therapist. Our suspicions about the truth were quickly turned into concern when the visit Crystal made to a sexual abuse counselor for children, confirmed our innermost fears that he felt she was telling the truth. After the interview, Robert took us aside and reinforced what Crystal had said. It wasn't just what she said, he continued, but also her subconscious acts like pulling her dress down well below her knees to protect herself while she spoke; that supported his theory. He stated that not only was sexual abuse occurring, but Crystal was also being terrorized in Eric's home. Often she was left alone and the boys were left in charge. He elaborated over a terrifying story of Crystal being in bed and Alex holding a pillow over her head, while Rich looked on. Not only this, but both boys would verbally threaten and hit her in addition to Alex touching her private area. Tori, after glancing towards me, knew that I was in no state to figure out what our next move was, but she didn't have to figure that out either, for Robert simply said, "You have two choices. Either you can call and report this to the SRS or I will. Anytime there is suspicion of abuse of any kind, it's the law that it must be investigated."

Hearing Robert's words just sent my emotions into orbit! I felt as if I was swirling in the clouds, oblivious and unable to obtain a safe landing when all of a sudden, I hit the earth with a thud! What am I thinking? How must Crystal be feeling right now? How could I begin to assure her that this was not her fault and that she was doing the right thing by telling us about it and whoever else that could help this situation at her dad's house to stop? But

246

most of all, how on earth was I going to get Eric to understand that he had a problem at his house that needed to be handled promptly.

We drove home in silence with her between us in the front seat! Tori spoke what my heart didn't want to admit. "I think it's best if Alex goes home to his dad's and doesn't finish his vacation with us; at least for now." It was just so overpowering. Not only was this nightmare in 3-D color, but Richard, who now was almost 13 had elected to run away from our home just two nights before. Later I found out that he had set up a prearranged safe house with one of Eric's friends in town. Eric had so twisted his mind with interpreting the scripture's wrong that he was determined that he couldn't and wouldn't enjoy spending 3 weeks with his mother, whom in his eyes was a sinner doomed to hell! And to my horror, he left in such an act of defiance that he put his fist through the wall.

Not only had Tori and I spent a sleepless night, because of this, but so had the other 3 kids until Rich finally called us and said that his dad had picked him up and that he was back in Winfield. Yes, we called Dobbs, but frustrated as he was, he felt that it was in our best interest to wait and confront Eric at our final custody hearing, which was only a few weeks away.

The red tape surrounding the SRS was disheartening with the Bay City department unwilling to make anymore than a courtesy interview to Crystal and submit their findings to Winfield. Basically, they felt that she was being assaulted, but there was nothing they could do, but forward all information to Winfield for it was not in their jurisdiction and so it was out of their hands. By law, Winfield had to investigate it, whether they chose to be brief or thorough, was not relevant. And of course as the days passed, they only questioned the boys and their father. They did not contact me, speak with Robert or question Crystal, who at the time was with me.

It was extremely hard to let Crystal go back when

summer visitation was over, but I had no choice or I would have been found in contempt of court for breaking the last court decree. With court being so close, I just couldn't chance them using this as a weapon against me. I was still reeling with anger over the result of the phone call I had with Eric. All he seemed to be interested in was how I could accuse the boys of such a terrible thing. From this alone, I knew that Crystal's homecoming wasn't going to be easy. For once again Eric was not thinking of how to solve this problem and take care of Crystal, but how to place blame on Tori and I.

Every now and then, my eyes would join the rhythmic motion of my windshield wipers as they mechanically swept away the rain that inhibited my view. Never the less, they refused to wipe out the horrible thoughts of court that kept forcing its way into my being, mocking me. "Why do you possibly think that you'll get the children? You live with a woman doing God only knows what, and you expect a Judge to find that to be a stable living environment?"

But even though my thoughts seemed to turn against me, my Spirit was peaceful and I knew that God was close to me. "However, as the scripture says, 'What no one ever saw or heard, what no one ever thought could happen, is the very thing God prepared for those who love him.' But it was to us that God made known his secret by means of his Spirit. The Spirit searches everything, even the hidden depths of God's purposes. It is only a person's own spirit within him that knows all about him; in the same way, only God's Spirit knows all about God. We have not received this world's spirit; instead, we have received the Spirit sent by God, so that we may know all that God has given us." 1 Corinthians 2:9-12. As I quietly reflected on these scriptures, I wondered how many people would come to understand the wisdom and knowledge of God. Everyday as I lived the life of a lesbian in hiding, I grew as a Christian fully convinced that the hate that Tori and I and so many others were experiencing, was a small part of God's plan for changing me into the person that could be

248

more like God. This world as we know it, is filled with hate and injustice with no one winning completely. But through the hate that we experience, God molds us into people who care and love, because we understand what it is like to suffer just as the Lord Jesus suffered on the cross. For when I am weak, God is strong and His power can bring me through to the point of faith that helps me to be like Him.

The thunderous clap of lightning illuminated the courtroom perhaps motioning to us from afar that we were simply pawns in a chess game being moved to and fro in a complex war of good and evil. Dobbs shifted slightly in his chair, almost as if beckoning to Eric's new attorney, Harry, to dare to confront the issue, which this court motion was really all about. I had found it amusing when court had to be postponed for a month because Barbara, Eric's attorney, who had defended him up until this time, had 'conflicting interests', as she was also the attorney for the SRS in Winfield. Therefore in a sigh, of a great deal of relief, she had to let Eric's case go.

It became apparent through conversations that Dobbs had with Harry before court was to start, that Eric had been unhappy with Barbara for some time and had sought his advice in numerous occasions in the recent past. Harry had only one thing on his mind, to grandstand the court and emphasize in his opening remarks that I was a lesbian, a liar, and crazy!

When Dobbs had first heard him speak of how he intended to win, he in turn immediately called me and said, "Elizabeth, I don't think we can win this. This is going to be a war, and I'm not sure how to fight it." It was the first time that I had heard concern of doubt in Dobbs's voice, for in his years of practice he liked being the underdog and gaining total and absolute victory in his cases! Of course it scared me, but it was my kids that I was fighting for and I just felt within, that God was pushing me forward to yet another court and that I couldn't turn against his will. And I knew why, for God wanted the truth to be known, regardless of the outcome.

249

By the eve of court, Jeff had psyched himself up and me as well, that we could win this and that I was to meet with him 1 hour before court to discuss our strategy. As I waited by the large draping window on the third floor, the ominous sky peered down and sent shivers of nervousness throughout my body. Dobbs arrived promptly on time as usual and he practically shoved me into the conference room to wait while he tried to find Harry and the Judge so that he could 'feel' his way into their minds of how they were once again going to fight.

What seemed like hours had only been minutes, when Jeff burst back into the room. "In a low monotone voice, he asked me directly if I had ever told Eric or any of my family members that I was a lesbian?"

I was somewhat surprised that he asked this question and I quickly reiterated, "Of course not!"

"I think I know how to approach this. We'll stop them in their tracks when I ask, you, 'Are you a lesbian?' And you answer 'NO!' I know from listening to Harry talk that their whole case is based on you being a lesbian. But they have no viable proof! It's all we've got, Elizabeth. Just remember to not explain your answers, but to keep them short, sweet and sincere. Try not to act tense or vindictive towards the situation and let me be the lawyer!"

Together, we entered the courtroom, only to be greeted by scores of curious onlookers. And to my surprise, no sooner had the gavel sounded that court was in session, Dobbs arose from his seat and requested that the courtroom be cleared of all onlookers and witnesses. And to my great surprise, Harry didn't oppose the motion! The Judge's eyes practically popped right out and he sat silent for the longest time waiting for the objection and when it just didn't happen, he had no other alternative but to grant Dobbs's motion.

As the day progressed, Dobbs kept the character witnesses of Eric's from testifying by argumentatively stating, "why should we waste the court's time and money by listening to someone telling us how good a person Eric is?" And the court granted these motions. There were no

250

new testimonies given until we came to the fact of Rich's disappearing act and Crystal's 'coming out' about the alleged attack on her from her brothers. And of course, Harry reiterated that I indeed lived with Tori, whom he reminded the Judge, that he himself had stated that the children were to be no where around Tori. Dobbs barked out in an unusually resonant voice, "Tori and Elizabeth have a working relationship and that in this day and time and with our economy, that living in the same household benefited both of their incomes. Furthermore, since Tori has not hurt the children or damaged their relationship with their mother in anyway, that it was illegal to request that any certain person refrain from seeing any other certain person!"

At that, the Judge cleared his throat and declared a short recess! But, before dismissing for this short lunch break, the Judge issued Eric to have the children with him when he came back at 1:00. He further stated that it was imperative that he speak with them in his chambers to get at the bottom of the problems that had been stated with Crystal.

Walking out with Dobbs to his car, I knew that the Judge was wavering. If anything, court had provided proof through the SRS, that there were problems in Eric's home, for they stipulated that the boys were not to be left alone with Crystal. Not just this, but when Eric was on the stand he was explosive in his denial that there was nothing happening and that everything in his home was fine and that I was at fault. Would the Judge see through this and be wise enough to see how detrimental this denial could be to the healing and solving of this problem for Crystal?

In Jeremiah 9:4-6 it says, "Everyone must be on guard against his friend, and no one can trust his brother; for every brother is as deceitful as Jacob, and everyone slanders his friends. They all mislead their friends, and no one tells the truth; they have taught their tongues to lie and will not give up their sinning. They do one violent thing after another, and one deceitful act follows another."

How true this was today! Time and again I had come before this court asking that the best interest of my children be sought and every effort was met with a slammed door in my face. Gather the facts together and let's add it up and see who should be the best care taker for my children. Unfortunately, all the lies that people were determined to follow from the first time that someone made an issue of a person's sexual preference, ignited a fire that issued forth in a smoke filled haze of blindness that caused justice to be denied. If only people, could stop the hate, will we start to be able to bring justice back into the courtroom, not just for the homosexual, but for the children's sake.

Watching the silent minute hand of the clock tick so slowly by, only seemed to intensify the judgment, I felt had been cast upon me during each court session that I'd had. I felt like I was handing over my life on a meat platter where the Judge could choose to slice out my heart as the perennial appetizer or op to have it as the main course! Dear Heavenly Father, I just uplift my fears to you and I give you, Alex, Rich, and Crystal. You know that I love you and that I only want what is best for my kids. Please, keep them safe and help me to show them what is right regardless of what the outcome of court is again.

As our wait turned into an hour and a half, I began getting agitated listening to Dobbs render yet another tale to his liking. I'm not sure if anyone but the wooden chair that he'd carefully perched himself upon was listening. "What is taking them so long?" came harshly to my lips, but I knew better than to speak them aloud. For Dobbs's had assured me that the more time spent with the children reaffirming the truth would significantly pad our side for court in our favor.

Could he be right, my mind queried? Could the Judge really be listening to what Crystal had to say? Would she be bold enough to speak the truth? What about Rich and Alex would they confess that they were in the wrong? Dear God, please protect my babies!

By the time, the Judge's chamber doors opened, it had been over an hour and a half. Stiffly, the four of us

252

arose for court to be in session for the final time. The silence was broken as the Judge cleared his throat and began. "After much thought and after having spoken with the 3 minor children herein named, Rich, Alex, and Crystal. I am hereby declaring that joint custody is granted with Eric residential parent of Rich & Alex. The file on Crystal is long and complicated. Based upon what I have read and from the visit with Crystal, I do not feel compelled to make a decision until an in depth investigation can take place. Therefore I order that Crystal immediately become a ward of the State and is released into the custody of the Social Rehabilitation Services until such time as their recommendation from a formal investigation into the alleged sexual abuse can be given to the court. This case will be handed over to the County Prosecutor. That Elizabeth make $100.00 child support payments, payable to the court beginning immediately. That Eric and Elizabeth are to meet halfway between Winfield and Bay City under the original visitation agreement that I have set forth before them.

"What did that mean about Crystal, Dobbs?" I asked as I touched his arm. "It means, Elizabeth, that I think you'll get her or possibly Crystal will be taken out of the home while the investigation is under way. I don't know. We just have to wait and see."

CHAPTER TWENTY-TWO

The next six weeks were filled with turbulent turmoil as absolutely nothing happened with Crystal as a result of court. The prosecuting attorney had not issued an investigation and Dobbs was not able to do anything about it except wait it out. And to my utter amazement as soon as court was over, I received a notice in the mail from the SRS investigation stipulating that I was not to have any visitation with Crystal until the alleged sexual misconduct case was resolved, yet she continued to remain in Eric's house under the same conditions as before. Summer vacation was already next to over and it had been over a month and a half since Crystal had been at my home. Night after night, I had uplifted Crystal in prayer and even though I knew God was listening, I just felt like he was leading me down the path to scurry things along and so one morning, I simply picked up the phone and called the Judge.

Not that it's illegal to do this, but most attorneys including Dobbs would caution that it could cause the Judge to side with the other parent and rule in their favor, especially if you tick them off by something that you say! I'd also heard through the lawyer grapevine that it was practically impossible to get past a Judge's secretary and actually speak directly to him. Yet lo and behold, not only did I get to speak to the Judge, but he answered the phone himself!

When I had stated my reason for calling, he said that he'd find out why nothing had happened and he would call me back personally by the end of the day. Not only this, but he had no idea that Crystal was being kept from seeing me and with a great deal of anger resonating from his voice, he flatly stated that he intended to get to the bottom of this. Gleefully, I called Dobbs. When he heard the outcome of my call, "Well, miracles do happen don't they?" spurted out his mouth.

I didn't hear back from the Judge that day, but within 48 hours Dobbs called me back and relayed a phone conversation he had with him that resulted in the release of Crystal to come to my home for visitation again. That same day, I received a letter from the office of the county attorney that was a declaration simply stating 'that Crystal had been placed as a ward of the state in light of an investigation ordered by the court towards alleged misconduct concerning her two brothers, Rich & Alex.' Finally, Crystal would be protected and justice would prevail.

Wrong! Wrong! Wrong! How could I have thought that anyone in Winfield would take these accusations seriously? Yes, the police talked to the boys. Yes, the boys admitted pulling Crystal's panties down once. The police talked to Eric, who denied that any of these alleged incidence had occurred and that if he even suspicioned that his boys were being ornery, he would have immediately put a stop to it! NO, I was never questioned. NO, Dr. Robert Allen was never questioned nor was his letter to the court admitted as evidence. Yes, Crystal was interviewed by a complete stranger, a man at yet another mental health clinic, who videotaped their sessions. The only way I found this out was by making another phone call to the Judge and in return he gave me the phone number of the clinic. Calling the number, I contacted the man in charge of the interview and immediately I was met with an uncaring and finger pointing right at me, man! He admitted that there was a problem with the children being left alone and that he recommended that this not happen any longer. He also stated that Rich had too much control in his father's house and that this needed to stop. He also admitted that there were problems with Crystal, but not to the point of taking her out of the house and so he recommended that she stay at her dad's. Then when I pressed him over what Crystal had to say about what was happening in the house over the sexual misconduct of her brothers, he suddenly turned it into Tori being responsible for fabricating the whole incident and coaching Crystal on what to say! His words sent a numbing effect through my entire body especially when he ended the conversation with he would just see if the court was going to prosecute Tori for her part in this case!

When Crystal came to my house, I asked her about the interview and she stated quite frankly that she had blamed it all on Tori and that she wouldn't tell anybody the truth because if she did, 'then her brothers would go to jail or have to live in a foster home!' Anyway it was better at home now and the boys were not allowed to be left alone with her anymore! The last thing in the world that I wanted was for my sons to be taken away from their family! Yet because of Eric's unwillingness to handle the problems with Alex and his hatred for Tori's and my relationship, he allowed the children to get out of control. In his effort to convict me for being gay, he was destroying the children's complete belief system in God and teaching them to lie, hate and do evil to anyone who got in their way. No wonder God inspired these scriptures, Proverbs 6:16-19, "There are seven things that the Lord hates and cannot tolerate: A proud look, a lying tongue, hands that kill innocent people, a mind that thinks up wicked plans, feet that hurry off to do evil, a witness who tells one lie after another, and a man who stirs up trouble among friends." As I reflect on these scriptures, my mind that was once closed to the workings of God, opened to the judgment that God places on men when they are unwilling to follow His commands in the Bible. For as Psalm 15, stipulates "Lord, who may enter your Temple? Who may worship on Zion, your sacred hill? A person who obeys God in everything and always does what is right, whose words are true and sincere, and who does not slander others. He does no wrong to his friends nor spreads rumors about his neighbors. He despises those whom God rejects, but honors those who obey the Lord. He always does what he promises, no matter how much it may cost. He makes loans without charging interest and cannot be bribed to testify against the innocent. Whoever does these things will always be secure." These words are the exact opposite from what was stated in Proverbs 6. Why? When we do not hold on to the truths and commandments of God in the smallest way, we set ourselves up to be blind to the difference between what is right and wrong. When the Judge in my court case decided to slander me because of my being gay, he sentenced himself to blindness that resulted in injustice for not only me, but especially for Crystal, Alex, and Rich. Homosexuals were not only planned by God, but loved by God. Genesis 1:31, "God looked at everything he had made, and he was very pleased. Evening passed and morning came- that was the sixth day."

God never chose for the homosexual man to be persecuted and hated, but rather he was an intricate plan in the making of the world. In order to achieve a balance, God made people different. What better way to solve over crowding in the world, than to create a race of people who could not multiply. Why is something so simple to understand so hard for people to believe? Because a veil has fallen upon the face of men for their lack of clearly following the scriptures as God intended for them to be followed. People choose to hate one another and to tell lies about one another and do everything that God explained clearly in the scriptures, was exactly what He hated. This is why God sent His son, so that Jesus would be the light that would open their eyes to what sin is and what it is not, through the gift of the Holy Spirit. Jesus states strongly in Matthew 13:13-14a, "The reason I use parables in talking to them is that they look, but do not see, and they listen, but do not hear or understand. So the prophecy of Isaiah applies to them: Isaiah 6:9-10, "So he told me to go and give the people this message 'No matter how much you listen, you will not understand. No matter how much you look, you will not know what is happening.' Then he said to me, 'Make the minds of these people dull, their ears deaf, and their eyes blind, so that they cannot see or hear or understand. If they did, they might turn to me and be healed.'" This is the very condition of our world today, why else would there be so much persecution between people today? We hate what we do not understand! We don't understand because there is so much confusion over the interpretation of the scriptures from men who interpret them with hate instead of love. Sodom and Gomorrah is an example of evil people interpreting the scriptures falsely for in 2 Peter 2:6, we find God's true reason behind their destruction. "God condemned the cities of Sodom and Gomorrah, destroying them with fire, and made them an example of what will happen to the godless." God never intended for a whole race of people to be condemned, but for idol worship to be stopped! Ezekiel 16:48-50, "As surely as I am the living God, the Sovereign Lord says, 'your sister Sodom and her villages never did the evil that you and your villages have done. She and her daughters were proud because they had plenty to eat and lived in peace and quiet, but they did not take care of the poor and the underprivileged. They were proud and stubborn and did the things that I hate, so I destroyed them, as you well know.'" Again God tells us that it was their sin of not caring about people in need that brought about Sodom's destruction. Matt. 12:23-24, "And as for you, Capernaum! Did you want to lift yourself up to heaven? You will be thrown down to hell! If the miracles which were performed in you had been performed in Sodom, it would still be in existence today! You can be sure that on the Judgment Day, God will show more mercy to Sodom than to you!" Jesus said these words, because the people had not turned away from their sins, even after He had performed most of His miracles before them. What was their sin? It was lack of belief in God and refusal to give up the idol worship they clung to so tightly. It had nothing to do with being a homosexual.

When you don't follow the teachings handed down by God, you become blind and no matter how much a person tells you the difference between right and wrong, you will not understand enough to follow it. That is why time and again when I went to court my children and I received no justice. Justice comes from doing what God commands us to do. God commands us to follow Matt. 22:37-40, "Love the Lord your God with all your heart, with all your soul, and with all your mind. This is the greatest and the most important commandment. The second most important commandment is like it 'Love your neighbor as you love yourself.' The whole Law of Moses and the teachings of the prophets depend on these two commandments." If we disregard either of these commands, we become blind to justice in the world for we react with hate instead of love. So be careful that when you read a story in the Bible over what is taking place at that moment in time, that you do not throw out an entire race of people just because they wanted to rape two Angels in the forms of men, when they were men. What if the Angels had come in the form of women and the men of Sodom had wanted to rape a woman instead of a man, does that mean we should condemn all heterosexuals? It's clear to me, that it had nothing to do with sexual preference at all, but it was an act of violence against the visitors. Keeping this in mind the scriptures pertaining to Sodom and Gomorrah in the above passages are the real reasons behind their destruction by God. Their sins of not following God's teachings of love and caring for others, brought about their destruction!

The one thing that I have never doubted in the past or now, was God's love for me and His caring grace on the road of my life. But it was hard to understand how to handle all of the hurdles that had been placed so precariously before me. How could I protect my family from the hate that was hurting all of us? "In his life on earth Jesus made his prayers and requests with loud cries and tears to God, who could save him from death. Because he was humble and devoted, God heard him." Hebrews 5:7.

Tori, Brad and I found ourselves busy packing up our belongings to move once again. Our duplex was wonderful, but our needs had blossomed. Tori and I had prayed intensely for our business to multiply, so that not only could we still continue to pay all of the bills, but

259

also increase the cost of living, that a larger home would imply. God had not only met that need, but He blessed us with the chance to have a lease/option plan on a beautiful 4 bedroom Tudor style home in the newer part of Bay City.

Our new home was exquisite! But Tori had apprehension all over face and extreme sadness in her eyes, whenever we entered the house with yet another load of boxes. "What's wrong?" I asked as I took her in my arms.

"This reminds me so much of the lovely home we had in Winfield. I'm scared that it'll be taken away from us too! It's just too good to be true!" she quietly replied. My heart skipped a beat as her words sunk in. I didn't have any answers for her questions, because I was afraid too.

Not only were we afraid of keeping what we had, but we now had to figure out how we should present ourselves to our neighbors. Should we tell them we were living together (but only as friends and business partners) or should we act like I only resided here in the daytime? Silently Tori and I handled this by not saying anything at all. We were careful not to let our 'hair down' and quietly we enjoyed our life and love for each other behind the closed doors and curtained windows of our home.

Soon it became apparent that every move that we made was watched from behind the sheers in our neighbor's windows and promptly made known to the rest of our neighborhood and even the landlord. Their curiosity was only aroused more deeply when every other weekend my children were here. I could just feel the questions they wanted to ask when they yelled across the street, "Hi!" and I responded simply with a quiet gesture by the wave of my hand. I was afraid to say anything for fear of what Tori might or might not have already said to one of them.

Tori was a people person. And she quickly became a friend to all of our surround neighbors and welcomed their children with open arms into our home. But she questioned repeatedly to me when we lay talking in bed at

260

night, "I wonder why some of the kids ring our doorbell for Brad to play, but they can only play outside or in their own home? What's wrong with our home?" she said.

How could I not burst her bubble, yet comfort her at the same time? I thought. "You know, Tori, it's unusual for a single woman of your age to be able to afford such a nice home and drive a nice car and pronounce that your son goes to a private school and takes karate lessons without a man providing as well. Don't you think they wonder what's going on over here? Don't you also think they wonder what kind of relationship that we have? I mean I try to stay out of the way, but occasionally they see me drive the van or walk to the mailbox or holler for Brad to come in for supper? I'm just surprised that some of them haven't questioned you about me yet!" I calmly responded hoping that my words wouldn't upset Tori.

"I know. I guess I hoped that one day soon, we would be accepted as if we were a heterosexual married couple. Facing reality is just harder than I thought it would be! I always hoped that if we just got away from the people in Winfield and Alan and Eric, that we would be able to just blend into the scenery."

"Tori, stop it right now." I demanded. "We need to give all of these concerns and fears to God in prayer and get a good night's sleep." I firmly spoke. And with that I turned off the leaded Tiffany lamp by our bed and began. "Our Father..."

"We love because God first loved us. If someone says he loves God, but hates his brother, he is a liar. For he cannot love God, whom he has not seen, if he does not love his brother, whom he has seen. The command that Christ has given us is this: whoever loves God must love his brother also." 1 John 4:19-21. For God is a God of love and only satan works in hate. If for no other reason than this, understand that satan does not work in love, but in hate. Is there any scripture in the Bible that says that satan caused a person to love? No! Without God's immeasurable love, patience, and mercy, Tori and I would not still be together with God's Holy Spirit burning brighter than the North Star within our hearts. Through everything that's happened, most of it heartbreaking, the one thing that is still unshakeable is our love for God and the knowledge that nothing, especially people, can break us apart. Matthew 19:6, "So they are no longer two, but one. Man must not separate, then, what God has joined together."

CHAPTER TWENTY-THREE

Of the ten years Tori and I have been together, I feel compelled to give a short summary of what has taken place over the past three years that I have not written about in this book. I never regained custody of my children. The children were left alone together within a year, disregarding the findings of the court and I can do nothing to stop this. Within the first year, Rich decided that he no longer wanted to come on a regular basis and he, with his father's encouragement, refused on several occasions to come. I in turn contacted my attorney over this problem, and unfortunately before all was said and done, Rich and Alex were given permission through the court to only come to my house if they wanted too; but Crystal was still supposed to come. To further the insult against me, the child support was increased and in addition, I was totally responsible for all of the children's clothes.

Rich is now a Sophomore in college and does well in school, I see him during holidays and one day visits during the summer. He is studying to be a minister and is soon to be married to his childhood sweet heart. Alex is a Senior, who up until he went to high school, fought with his dad to come to my house regardless of the renewed court order, has shone brightly in athletics. But just like his brother, it has become easier to not fight his dad and he comes occasionally. Crystal is a Sophomore and a wonderful student in school and music, but the pressure of my commitment to Tori has been overwhelming to her moral teachings and she is having a difficult time loving me regardless of what her church teaches. She has chosen to fill her weekends with school and church activities so that she doesn't have to come to my home very often. I see her on holiday's and every couple of months.

Currently Brad has not seen or heard from his dad in six and a half years. For the sake of his custody remaining with his mother and with me, in the almost 9 years since Tori and I have lived in Bay City, Brad has never breathed a word of my living with him and his mother, to his grandparents. He is now being home schooled by his mother, for he was found to be very gifted. He is currently 14 years of age and at the Sophomore level in school.

After almost 6 years had passed since the purchase of the double-wide, that was repossessed from my running with my kids at Winfield, Tori and I were found guilty of falsifying my income taxes. Our attorney was able to lessen the penalty that was handed over by HUD to be prosecuted by the state attorney, and we were given a diversion with a one year probation and $17,000.00 fine. The fine was determined from the amount that the double-wide was undersold at auction. Once again God gave us victory and in one year we were able to pay off the total $17,000.00.

We have lived in the same house since our third and final move in Bay City. Once again, society through the false interpetation of the Bible, has made holding on to our house very hard. In order to keep living in our home, Tori was forced to enter into an agreement with our landlord to continue to pay rent along with $5,000 being paid every 6 months for the next 4 years. We have currently paid $35,000 of this requirement and with the Lord's amazing help, we have now secured a loan for the remainder of the money in Tori's name. This may be difficult for you to understand, why we could be coerced into doing this, but not only had we to keep up the front of Mark for the continued custody of Brad, but in order for our business to continue its upward momentum, we needed to stay put. Our family also needed a stable living environment and from having a bigger house, the increased space gave us all breathing room so both of our families could calm down from all of our court turmoils. And as anyone who has ever had a home knows, it gives you the

264

power to live without the interference of others. For a gay person this is essential to maintain because of the persecution that we face daily.

Tori and I still keep up the front of Mark, and I still hide any time her parents are around. Even in as large a city as Bay City, I am careful not to go outside too much so as to draw attention to myself in front of our neighbors or to be seen by Tori's parents if they should decide to give a surprise visit. My parents and siblings generally have nothing to do with me and I see them only when I go back to one of my children's events at school or during the holidays.

Tori and I live a very lonely life with no friends. The women that we became friends with when we first moved to Bay City moved away and separated company. Their love for each other was not strong enough to keep them together with the persecutions that society puts on homosexuals today.

1 Kings 3:9, "So give me the wisdom I need to rule your people with justice and to know the difference between good and evil. Otherwise, how would I ever be able to rule this great people of yours." Through all the troubles and tribulations that Tori and I have faced together, we now know exactly how wonderful it is to walk with Solomon in great wisdom. God has abundantly filled us with the knowledge of good and evil and the tremendous blessings of understanding His truth and His ways. We know that He is with us and although the path of being a homosexual is very rough, He gives us the courage to continue on and find renewed strength in Him on a daily basis.

I hope that this book will help you to understand the Scriptures pertaining to homosexuals, in a different light. And I pray with all my heart that with this knowledge you will welcome your children, family and friends back into your loving arms. For truly, God loves and cares for all His people. "And His Love Shone Down" is just the beginning to helping people over come the burden of lies and deceit by walking straight

265

forward with eyes and ears wide open into the loving arms of the Almighty God!